COMMON GROUND

Common Ground

EIGHTEENTH-CENTURY ENGLISH
SATIRIC FICTION AND THE POOR

JUDITH FRANK

STANFORD UNIVERSITY PRESS

Stanford, California

1997

Stanford University Press
Stanford, California

© 1997 by the Board of Trustees of the
Leland Stanford Junior University

Printed in the United States of America

CIP data are at the end of the book

For my grandparents,
Howard and Sophie Allen

Acknowledgments

I had two cancer diagnoses during the writing of this book. The friends and colleagues I thank here, therefore, helped me survive more than the usual fear attendant upon writing a book. At Amherst College, President Emeritus Peter Pouncey, former Dean of the Faculty Ronald Rosbottom, and the Department of English were adamant that I not have to worry about my career, lightening my load both materially and emotionally. I thank them for their classy interventions.

Fredric Bogel, Laura Brown, and Harry Shaw helped me get this project under way, and Jill Campbell's energetic and generous comments on the manuscript helped me finish. Margaret Hunt, whom I think of as my own personal eighteenth-century English historian, has been an invaluable resource to me in the years since I came to Amherst. Sharon Willis and the Susan B. Anthony Center at the University of Rochester took me under their administrative wing during my leave year.

Several parts of this book have been previously published. A version of Part I of Chapter 1 appeared as "The Comic Novel and The Poor: Fielding's Preface to *Joseph Andrews*," in *Eighteenth-Century Studies* 27:2 (Winter 1993/94). A version of Part II of Chapter 1 appeared as "Literacy, Desire, and the Novel: From *Shamela* to *Joseph Andrews*," in *The Yale Journal of Criticism* 6:2 (Fall 1993). Chapter 2 appeared in slightly different form as " 'A Man Who Laughs Is Never Dangerous': Character and Class in Sterne's *A Sentimental Journey*," in *ELH* 55:1 (Spring 1989). I am grateful for permission to reprint these sections.

For a variety of kinds of intellectual contribution and for sweetening the quality of my life, I thank Amanda Anderson, Michèle Barale, Phillip Barrish, Paula, Uri, Maya, and Tamar David, Ned DeLaCour, Tony Frank, Lisa Henderson, Laurie Herzog, Suvir Kaul, Rebecca Leopold, Catherine Newman, Jeff Nunokawa, Sam Otter, Mary Renda, Eve Kosofsky Sedgwick, Elizabeth Young, and Melissa Zeiger. Karen Sánchez-Eppler's brilliant commentary on parts of the manuscript helped me get past more than one painful stalemate. Andrew Parker read several drafts of the manuscript, and during its composition quietly helped me through periodic crises of confidence, reminding me at critical moments that the problem might be in the novel itself. I thank Cindy Patton for the intellectual energy that always jump-starts my mind, and for being an exemplary sponsor. Amy Kaplan teaches me how to live gracefully under the strain of unbearable contradictions. Getting to know Tamar Mayer coincided with an exciting creative surge in the last stages of this project, and knowing how she feels about coincidences, I gratefully acknowledge a causal connection. Tahl Mayer gave me the Lego helicopter that sits atop my printer, evoking flight. The radiant cats who have lived with me—Mookie, wherever he may be; Digger, whose morning bath atop my diskdrive I still miss every day; and John, who endures with wit and wisdom—helped me more than almost anyone else to write this book. And Elizabeth Garland has been egging me on and distracting me with equal persuasiveness since her wonderful return into my life.

Finally, I thank my mother, Marjorie Frank, for her love, her faith in me, and the example of her extraordinary resourcefulness. Her survival has made all the difference.

This book is dedicated, with loving gratitude for their manifold forms of support, to my grandparents, Howard and Sophie Allen.

J.F.

Contents

COMMON GROUND

Introduction

GENTLE AND POOR

ON COMMON GROUND

In a 1711 number of *The Spectator*, Mr. Spectator goes out riding with his friend, the benevolent Tory gentleman Sir Roger de Coverley, and they come upon a troop of gypsies. Sir Roger's first instinct is to turn the justice of the peace "upon such a Band of lawless Vagrants," but worrying that the gypsies might retaliate by poaching, he decides against it. He gives Mr. Spectator an account of the "Mischiefs they do in the Country, in stealing People's Goods and spoiling their Servants," as well as stealing stray linen, hogs, geese, and hens. The problem is, Sir Roger explains, that his servants are seduced by them:

> I have an honest Dairy-Maid who crosses their Hands with a Piece of Silver every Summer; and never fails being promised the handsomest young Fellow in the Parish for her Pains. Your Friend the Butler has been Fool enough to be seduced by them; and though he is sure to lose a Knife, a Fork, or a Spoon every Time his Fortune is told him, generally shuts himself up in the Pantry with an old Gypsie for above Half an Hour once in a Twelve-month.[1]

No sooner, though, does Sir Roger tell this story than he goes on to do precisely the same thing as his servants: getting his fortune told and his pocket picked at the same time. An older gypsy woman reads Sir Roger's palm, saying:

I

> That he had a Widow in his Line of Life: Upon which the Knight
> cryed, Go, go you are an idle Baggage; and at the same Time smiled
> upon me. The Gypsie finding he was not displeased in his Heart, told
> him, after a further Enquiry into his Hand, that his True-love was con-
> stant, and that she should dream of him to Night. My old Friend cryed
> pish, and bid her go on. The Gypsie told him that he was a Batchelour,
> but would not be so long; and that he was dearer to some Body than he
> thought: The Knight still repeated, She was an idle Baggage, and bid
> her go on. Ah Master, says the Gypsie, that roguish Lear of yours makes
> a pretty Woman's Heart ake; you ha'n't that Simper about the Mouth
> for nothing—The uncouth Gibberish with which all this was uttered,
> like the Darkness of an Oracle, made us the more attentive to it.

His claims that the gypsy is an "idle Baggage" alternating with en-
couragement to continue, Sir Roger displays a coy ambivalence toward plebeian utterance, an ambivalence expressed by Mr. Spectator
in the uncertainty over whether she can be understood—whether
her speech is gibberish or hyper-true. They ride away, Sir Roger in
high spirits, when the romance of palmistry is promptly deflated:
"in the Height of his good Humour, meeting a common Beggar
upon the Road who was no Conjuror, as he went to relieve him, he
found his Pocket was pickt: That being a Kind of Palmistry at which
this Race of Vermin are very dexterous."[2]

A reader even casually acquainted with eighteenth-century representations of the poor will be familiar with some of the elements
here: gentlemen approaching poor people to hear a story, romanti-
cally inclined servant girls, the landlord weighing the benefits and
costs of exerting his authority upon those he governs, the comic
and telling gibberish of lower-class utterance. The scene performs
the demarcation most characteristically made among the poor in the
early modern period, distinguishing between those who are respectable and laboring and those who are idle and profligate, those
who respect private property and those who poach and steal. It also
performs another, more facetious division, among the idle themselves, when it distinguishes between the oracular and the "common
Beggar . . . who was no Conjuror." This last split, I would suggest,
expresses something like the dual character of the poor in the eighteenth-century satiric novel. If the poor are a burden and a moral re-

sponsibility—threats to private property, recipients of charity, and objects of the Poor Laws—they are also conjurers, shaping the consciousness and the literary forms of the dominant culture.

This book reads four eighteenth-century satiric novels "from below," exploring the ways in which the eighteenth-century poor shape them both thematically and formally. Work on both the satire and the fiction of this period has tended to focus on the transition from patrician culture to a culture dominated by the logic of the market, or what Michael McKeon has described as the tension between aristocratic and progressive ideology.[3] In this work, the story of the rise of capitalism is usually one of the middle class struggling to define itself in opposition to the aristocracy, and the poor function as a figure or allegory for the emergent middle class.[4] And indeed, progressive fictions vigorously and polemically used the poor as such an allegory; as Bruce Robbins argues about the representation of servants, for example, "By the eighteenth century, the bourgeoisie had composed the subversive bits and pieces of hundreds of traditional servitors into such heroic portraits of its own servitude as Defoe's Moll and Richardson's Pamela, Lesage's Gil Blas and Beaumarchais' Figaro."[5] My readings of the satiric novel also deal with the social and cultural upheavals attendant upon the development of a capitalist economy, but rather than collapsing the social group called "the poor" into another social group, they focus on the very process by which dominant culture invests in and identifies with it. And I turn to the conservative rather than to the progressive novel because for conservative novelists, that process of investment and identification is more complex and troubled—and therefore, I believe, more telling about the ways the poor shape dominant culture.

I am influenced by two of the most important recent books about the effect of the lower classes on dominant culture: Robbins's *The Servant's Hand* and Peter Stallybrass and Allon White's *The Politics and Poetics of Transgression*.[6] Like theirs, my readings are driven by the insistence that the presence of the poor exerts a formative pressure upon the consciousness and the literary expression of the dominant classes. Fielding's *Shamela* represents a paradigmatic attack upon bourgeois writing, for example, but it also uses lower-class

characters to do so, and as such also constitutes an anxious meditation upon the dangers of lower-class literacy; his Preface to *Joseph
Andrews* attempts to recuperate the novel for genteel readers by giving it a distinguished classical lineage, but it is also about the necessity of nourishing written comic forms—those potentially inaccessible to a popular audience—with the enlivening sustenance of the
popular. Similarly, while *Humphry Clinker* has most often been read
as a conservative attack on the corruptions of commercial culture, it
performs that attack by attempting to manage and work through the
dislocations of the poor during the second wave of parliamentary
enclosure.

When Sir Roger becomes a dupe of the gypsy woman, we
might say that the joke here is simply that he is no more savvy than
his servants. But I would tend to stress the potentially motivated nature of his act, reading it as an act of imitation. In an earlier *Spectator*
paper, Sir Roger's high quality as a master is evidenced by his opposition to perquisites: "He has ever been of Opinion, that giving his
cast Cloaths to be worn by Valets has a very ill Effect upon little
Minds, and creates a Silly Sense of Equality between the Parties, in
Persons affected only with outward things."[7] The sentiment that servants are prone to imitating their betters is characteristic of the time
and indeed, one of its major comic topoi.[8] But that claim obscures—
strategically, perhaps—a process I return to throughout this study,
which is the imitation of the poor by gentlemen, an imitation ritualized in such social practices as the masquerade.[9] For even as he pur-
ports to tell us how mystified they are for listening to the gibberish of
gypsies, Sir Roger mimics his servants. And it is at the moment
of mimicry that a scene of desire and futurity opens itself to him.
The gypsy's prophecy is bogus and self-serving, to be sure, but as far as
Sir Roger is concerned, not only are the inner secrets of the Widow
revealed to him, but so is his own alluring and irresistible nature.

Indeed, this book suggests that in the eighteenth-century satiric
novel, the characters of gentlemen and gentlewomen are represented as formed through acts of imitation of and identification
with the poor. *The Politics and Poetics of Transgression*, which explores
the way cultural spaces are formed "within interrelating and dependent hierarchies of high and low," is a seminal book about the de-

pendence of dominant groups upon subordinate ones for identity formation.[10] Reading moments from early modern and modern English literature in which bourgeois consciousness constructs itself through contact with the low, Stallybrass and White describe this process as follows: "The low-Other is despised and denied at the level of political organization and social being whilst it is instrumentally constitutive of the shared imaginary repertoires of the dominant culture."[11]

The novels I read here all concern—in varying degrees of explicitness—the ways the poor were despised and denied on the political and social level over the course of the century: the curtailing of popular festivity, the shift from a paternalist to a contractual model of service, the social dislocations attendant upon enclosure, the reorganization of labor practices. And in the novels' representation of gentle consciousness the gentry mimic and identify with the weak, their imaginary repertoires formed out of such identification. In the first half of this book, I suggest that when gentlemen imitate the poor they shore themselves up subjectively and ideologically; that is, a sense of personhood or identity emerges in the process of constituting class authority. This occurs on the level of genre with Fielding: the Preface to *Joseph Andrews* enacts the social marginalization of popular forms at the same time that Fielding incorporates them into his new high-cultural form in order both to vivify it and to keep it ethical. It occurs on the level of character and characterization with Sterne; in *A Sentimental Journey* the impecunious gentleman imitates the poor with an arch passivity in order to ward them off and triumphantly differentiate himself from them. But in the second half, in my discussions of *Humphry Clinker* and Burney's *Cecilia*, I argue that the incorporation of the poor into gentle consciousness reflects a deep malaise, a mental/ideological state that I call melancholia. In these novels, when gentlemen and gentlewomen characters symbolically enact the disenfranchisement of a poor population increasingly threatened by the reorganization of property and labor practices, that act causes something closer to paralysis.

For the Whig writer of this *Spectator* paper, Sir Roger's romantic susceptibility to the gypsy's prophecy is laughable; gullibility here is the illusion that the poor could have anything to say about your subjectivity. And indeed, as a product of a Whiggish commercial outlook, it differs from the texts I read here in its treatment of the relation between gentleman and poor in several ways. Most importantly, while in Sir Roger's experience the future gets revealed (or pretended to be revealed), what gets revealed when gentlemen encounter the poor in the novels under consideration here is social trauma occurring in the present or past. When Sterne's Yorick has an anxiety attack upon hearing a caged starling lament its imprisonment, for example, he is trying to manage the rupture of service relationships that has made the affect of servants seem unreadable and threatening to gentlemen. When Humphry Clinker sees a ghost, his susceptibility to the occult does not lie in a vision of his future (which will entail his recognition as a gentleman's son), but rather in seeing a past that uprooted the poor from the land and sent them into the homes of the elite as wage-laborers. Even when these novels can pull off the insouciance of *The Spectator*, achieving something like its tolerant amusement over the shenanigans of the poor, there is always in the background a shadow of something lost. Indeed, reading these novels, one might regard gentle consciousness as the melancholic underside of the bourgeois juggernaut.

It is, of course, the progressive novels of this period—especially those of Defoe and Richardson—that most vividly create the sense of characters' inner lives; indeed, the novels I read here are more likely to be anxious about the very idea of an inner life. Recently, critics have attempted to interpret eighteenth-century comic fiction's focus on the external as a purposeful and compelling strategy, rather than regarding it as a sign of novelistic underdevelopment. Elizabeth Kraft, for example, has argued that these novels "are skeptical about the centrality of private identity and overtly aware of the advantages of having an arena of impersonality in which there is access to social communication based on external codes of behavior rather than on true identity or worth"; they express, she suggests, the tension in their age's conception of consciousness, between a constant and immortal essence and a mutable, sense-determined one.[12] As John Mullan and Claudia L. Johnson, among others, have shown, the sentimental literature of this period expresses a powerful strain of resistance to feeling. Even as the philosophical, novelistic, and medical literature of sensibility celebrated intense and delicate feeling, Mullan suggests, this literature worried the problem of how a language of personal feeling could possibly explain social relations, and often represented the outer limit of delicate feeling as nervous disorder.[13] Regarded by contemporaries as the province of scholars and writers—"constituted in various ways, out of an opposition to a 'world' of masculine desire, commercial endeavour, and material ambition"[14]—sensibility embodies a considerable cultural ambivalence not only about feeling, but about leisure as well. Indeed, I will argue in the next section that during this period the gentle were peculiarly susceptible to identifications with the poor, because theirs too was a status group defined in relation to labor—specifically, lack of labor—and the idea and practice of labor underwent radical change over the course of the century. Chapter 4, on *Cecilia*, deals most explicitly with the connections between labor and emotion, claiming that the creation and apportionment of gentlewomanly affect must be read as a facet of the reorganization of labor practices—and concomitant attempts to reconceptualize labor and charity—in the late part of the century.

In this study, then, I make a twofold claim about the creation and representation of gentle character: that it forms itself out of ambivalence about affect, and that that ambivalence is bound up in the changing social experiences of the poor.[15] In *Joseph Andrews*, for example, Fielding's construction of the character of Fanny Goodwill, peppered with many witticisms about his hesitancy to describe her, is shaped by anxiety about the kinds of urges literary images might elicit in a growing lower-class readership. In *A Sentimental Journey*, gentle character is constructed by fixing and rendering visible the threateningly unstable character of servants; for Sterne, a writer who notoriously celebrates, even luxuriates in affect, worries in this novel about the authenticity of affect in the face of its susceptibility to being forged by servants. Much of *Humphry Clinker* and *Cecilia* are taken up by characters excoriating other characters for an excess of feeling; in these novels gentle characters are defined as dispossessed, as though they internalize as part of their beings the social dispossession of the poor. It is because character is formed out of ambivalence toward affect that the second half of this book takes the category of melancholia as central. As I will elaborate later, melancholia may be regarded as above all an attempt to arrest affect, affect generated by loss. Indeed, in the novels I read here, the resistance to feeling or interiority documented by such critics as Kraft and Mullan does not, as Kraft suggests, originate in an ambivalence over the idea of "individual" identity itself. Rather, it comes from the novels' attempts to ward off the potentially devastating effects of social changes formative of the poor and of the gentry alike.

In its claim, then, that affect as we know it is formed in the interrelation of social groups as they react to social and economic upheaval, this book centers upon the conjunction of economic change, novelistic technique, and the constitution of affects. Further, as I show in the final section of this introduction, satire—which during this period is falling into disrepute under the pressure of contemporary attempts to redefine comedy—may be regarded as a generic form that performs the arresting of affect, refusing to idealize or cover over the devastating social effects of economic "progress," but at the same time unable to see and to say what has been lost. The satiric element in these novels is that moment where anxiety about the gentry's relation to the poor—and hence its very self-definition—is most richly performed and ritualized.

Nearly twenty years have passed since E. P. Thompson argued the importance of the historian/critic's "turning over the bland concepts of the ruling authorities and looking at their undersides," asserting further that "If we do not do this we are in danger of becoming prisoners of the assumptions and self-image of the rulers. . . . "[16] And while it may seem slightly outdated to evoke Thompson as a guiding spirit of this study, it seems to me that not the most sophisticated historical methodology or the most exquisitely calibrated qualifications of his strong claims can make that assertion any less relevant or urgent. Indeed, I completed this book during a period in which Thompson's words never seemed more necessary: a period of a Republican majority in Congress, when welfare reform was the top agenda item, and the poor were figured with a renewed virulence as a drain upon the economy and a moral threat to the nation.[17] My readings, which turn a different kind of ear toward these four novels in order to hear them "from below," aim to defamiliarize them, to demonstrate that the poor had a shaping effect on eighteenth-century English culture and sensibility beyond the enclosures established for them by both the cultural artifacts themselves and the history of their criticism. It is on common ground, I claim—those spaces where their lives meet those of the gentry in a traumatic and enlivening intersection—that the poor conjure these novels into something compellingly strange.

I. Poor and Gentle

In 1751 Fielding described the poor as those who "have no Estate of their own to support them, without Industry; nor any Profession or Trade, by which, with Industry, they may be capable of gaining a comfortable Subsistence."[18] Indeed, in this study I mean by "the poor" that wide variety of people who had no property of their own, and who were covered by the Poor Laws: this included not only infants and the aged and infirm, but agricultural workers, manual workers, smaller manufacturers, and small craftsmen as well—all those likely to become chargeable to their parishes as a result of such vicissitudes as old age, illness, marital abandonment, poor harvests, enclosures, and trade slumps.[19] In a definition such as this, "the poor" comprised the lion's share of the English population of the eighteenth century—by most estimates, about 75 percent of the population. If that definition seems so wide as to be potentially imprecise, it is worth noting that the problem of "the poor" has historically been not only one of how to discipline or care for them, but more fundamentally, how to define them (an act that, as Paul Slack has shown, is always imbricated in creating them). In particular, during the course of the early modern period there existed a tension between the definition of "the poor" as the indigent, and the definition of "the poor" in the more inclusive sense of the lower classes, or laborers. Slack argues that between 1530 and 1600, there was a "hardening of an existing discriminatory distinction, culminating in two powerful images of impotent and idle, virtuous and vicious poor." Beginning about 1590, however, and especially after 1640, there occurred what he calls "the discovery of the labouring poor."[20] Although, he suggests, the actual term "labouring poor" was generally not used before the eighteenth century, there arose around this time the perception that many destitute people were part of the mainstream of society rather than a small marginal and pathological group. After 1640, moreover, the poor began to be regarded as "not a threat, as they had been for a century, but an opportunity: a resource which only needed proper handling to be profitable."[21] Another perceptual shift, however, began to occur around the middle of the eighteenth century. As Gertrude Himmelfarb has shown, much of the history of poor law from the mid-eighteenth to the late-nineteenth century may be regarded as an attempt at definition and demarcation that sought to undo, or at least to complicate, the association of "the poor" with laborers. Culminating in the 1834 Poor Law, it comprised, among other things, an effort to contest and pry apart the phrase "labouring poor," severing the idea of labor from the idea of poverty, or what became known as pauperism.[22]

Recent historians, using such methods as demographics, have tended to contest the Marxists' account of the devastation wrought upon the poor as a result of the development of capitalism, arguing either that the poor were not made poorer during this period or that if they were, it was not merely because of the development of capitalism, but also because of enormous population growth and fluctuations in harvest output.[23] However controversial the measurement of quality of life, however, or the asssessment of the various influences upon it, it is clear that the impetus of economic expansion uprooted many people from traditional types of community and labor, and as such had a vital impact upon the nature of social relations during this period.[24] The government passed laws to facilitate the hiring of cheap labor: the Statute of Apprentices was whittled away to open up industrial employment to a wider population, for example, and the Act of Settlement of 1662 was relaxed in 1697 to permit the poor greater mobility.[25] The engrossing of small farms and enclosing of common fields to make larger and more profitable units, which I discuss in Chapter 3, turned people off the land, sometimes more quickly than they could be absorbed in commerce, manufacturing, or service, and sent them to the cities.[26] The Poor Laws reached a crisis toward the end of the century, according to Dorothy Marshall, partly because in the towns to which workers flocked the very concept of a parish—the basic unit of administration since Elizabethan times—was gradually becoming anachronistic.[27]

Thompson has written that "We can read eighteenth-century social history as a succession of confrontations between an innovative market economy and the customary moral economy of the plebs."[28] Many of the traditional forms and conventions of plebeian life were policed and curtailed as it was infused by the logic of the market. For much of the century laboring people knit together a sustenance from a wide range of employments and tried to attain a degree of domestic self-sufficiency.[29] Increasingly, however, those customary rights that had enabled them to avoid relying entirely upon wage labor—common and grazing lands, and the perquisites from the various trades, such as free fuel, vails, sweepings, and timber chips—were curtailed by a legal system operating on behalf of the interests of capital. Robert Malcomson argues that this constriction of remuneration to wages alone constituted a challenge to plebeian peoples' belief that "as 'free-born Englishmen,' they enjoyed certain fundamental liberties that could not be taken from them," liberties that included customary rights and perquisites, some degree of control over the conditions of their employment, and independence from wage labor. This concept of freedom was increasingly contested and undermined by a "newer, narrower and increasingly powerfully backed definition of their rights that considered only their 'freedom' to sell their labour, a kind of property, on the open market for whatever price they could get."[30]

The curtailing of customary rights and the creation of a mobile force of unprotected labor generated that series of tensions that constituted eighteenth-century England's version of class conflict. Thompson argues that as paternalist protection of the laborer broke down, so did paternalist *control* over the life of the laborer. The loss of non-monetary usages or perquisites, the enlargement of that class of workers independent of a subject relationship to the gentry—those who had "escaped from the social controls of the manorial village and were not yet subject to the discipline of factory labor"—and the fact that industrial growth generated a variety of by-employments—these are the factors Thompson points to as weakening the old forms of social discipline.[31] The unprecedented breakthrough that occurred in consumerism as well as in production also contributed to the erosion of old forms of social signification. In his celebratory account of the consumer revolution of the eighteenth century, Neil McKendrick writes,

> These characteristics—the closely stratified nature of English society, the striving for vertical social mobility, the emulative spending bred by social emulation . . . —combined with the widespread ability to spend (offered by novel levels of prosperity) to produce an unprecedented propensity to consume: unprecedented in the depth to which it penetrated the lower reaches of society.[32]

The potential leveling tendencies generated by emulative spending caused anxiety among the ruling classes; there is a huge body of literature at mid-century condemning the idleness and luxury of laboring people,[33] and Fielding's *Enquiry into the Causes of the Late Increase of Robbers*, which I discuss in Chapter 1, is a canonical expression of the attack on the poor for imitating the rich. This anxiety makes its way into literary culture through the figure of the mimicking servant, a figure I explore in the Preface to *Joseph Andrews*, which, I suggest, tries to contain cross-class imitation from below while justifying it from above, and in *A Sentimental Journey*, which worries about the subversive capacity of servants to parody sentimental affect.

The threat of class leveling also accounts for something that characterizes this period's relation to the poor: that in the eighteenth century the poor are not that different from you and me. If the poor are represented as the dispossessed sons of gentlemen, as in *Joseph Andrews* and *Humphry Clinker*, and the gentleman is represented as a poor person, as in *A Sentimental Journey*, that is partly because, as Robbins has argued (via Raymond Williams and Lawrence Stone), this is a period of a narrowing of the definition of the family, from the blood relations plus the servants, to a group of blood relations alone: the romance convention of the discovery of highborn parents expresses, Robbins suggests, the way in which "eighteenth-century servants were in fact newly displaced children, and might truly claim to have had and lost an illustrious parentage."[34] But it is also because a rather literal blurring between gentleman and poor is still possible during this time. Perceptions of the poor, not unlike perceptions of homosexuals, tend to vacillate over time—and to be held in a tension during any particular time—between the normative and the pathological, or what Eve Kosofsky Sedgwick would call universalizing and minoritizing discourses.[35] Although he is not the first to do so, Henry Mayhew, in the middle of the next century, marks a momentous and notorious shift in this regard, figuring poverty as constitutive of the very identity of the pauper, now divorced from the laborer. In Mayhew poverty (like homosexuality in Foucault) is no longer a series of practices, but rather an essential identity—indeed, an actual separate race: Mayhew claims that vagrants, beggars, and thieves constitute "wandering hordes" with completely different physiognomies and languages from "the more civilized portion of the community."[36] What characterizes the period under discussion in this study, I believe, is that while writers with different class interests demonstrate a variety of ways of thinking about the poor (we shall see momentarily how Defoe, for example, held universalizing and minoritizing views in a lively ironic tension), the idea that the poor are apt to mingle scandalously and indiscriminately with their betters is much more common than the idea that they constitute a different race.

During this period the category of "the gentry" was no less complex or contested than the category of "the poor." McKeon argues that there is a categorical confusion endemic to current scholarly attempts to define who the gentry were, one that mirrors a confusion of the period itself. He describes the debate between R. H. Tawney, for whom the bourgeoisie and the rural enterpreneurs are in the same class because they employ the same methods of production, and J. H. Hexter, for whom the gentry and the bourgeoisie are separate because the character of their property is different, as a debate between a "class" orientation and a "status" orientation toward defining the gentry; and he argues that "the gentry controversy became polarized in terms of this distinction" because "it is precisely during this period that the traditional, qualitative criteria of honorific status were being definitively infiltrated by the quantitative criteria of socioeconomic class."[37] John Barrell, too, has shown how eighteenth-century gentlemen reached a kind of definitional crisis as they attempted to explain and justify their cultural authority. He argues that as a result of the mercantile and imperial expansion of the eighteenth century, literature became concerned with representing the increasing diversity of occupation in England; and that the literature and philosophy of the period worried about how to find a disinterested position from which to apprehend unity in the social structure from all these diverse pieces. The landed gentleman was thought to be best suited for such a disinterested perspective, for two reasons: "his permanent stake in the stability of the nation, and his freedom from engaging in any specific profession, trade, or occupation which might occlude his view of society as a whole."[38] But alongside this belief there was considerable and increasing difficulty defining just who gentlemen were. Barrell describes the various attempts, by Steele, Mandeville, and Defoe, to detach the idea of the gentleman from that of the freeholder; and he argues that this occurs because "to own land was no longer a convincing guarantee that one's interests were identical with the permanent interests of the state, because the ownership of land was inevitably and increasingly involved in an economy of credit, where values and virtues were unstable, and where a man was estimated not by an 'objective' standard, but in terms of an opinion of his credit worthiness which was liable to fluctuate whatever the source of his income."[39] The infusion of status categories by quantitative criteria calls definitions of the gentry into question as much as it does definitions of the poor.

According to McKeon, it was primogeniture that institutionalized status inconsistency in the gentry[40]; and it was the figure of the younger son that carried all the volatility of that inconsistency. Lawrence Stone and Jeanne Fawtier Stone suggest that unlike in other countries in Europe, the English landed elite was remarkable for the downward mobility of most of its male children. "Generation after generation, younger sons were left to trickle downwards through the social system, with only some education, some money, and influential patronage to give them a head start in life":

> His fortune in the main had to be of his own making, and his only status was that of a gentleman, although a gentleman with connections. His early experience would have habituated him to handling differences of status and made him particularly aware of them. He was a man whose potential for success depended either on exploiting his family ties by making himself indispensable to more fortunate relatives and connections, or on his making his way by his own exertions, either by marriage to an heiress, or in a trade or profession (in all of which his status might be a help, or occasionally a hindrance).[41]

And because they did not inherit courtesy titles and therefore were not protected against arrest by creditors, "there was therefore almost no bottom to the pit of indigence into which a younger son of an English peer could fall."[42]

If the gentry had a complex relation to the middle classes, then, those gentlemen who had to labor also occupied a tricky space in relation to the poor, who were by definition linked to labor; younger-son status had built into it the threat of such sons falling out of their status group and becoming just like the indigent. For progressive writers, on the other hand, it held out the promise of their most brightly exemplifying their status group, through qualities acquired by hard work and diligence. For an upstart writer like Defoe, who worked hard at redefining the category of the gentleman—aiming, he claimed, to "set up a new Class truly qualify'd to inherit the Title"[43]—the younger son was the paradigmatic gentleman. Defoe's profuse, lively, and often savage *The Compleat English Gentleman* attacked the state of the English heir, arguing that without a proper education these gentlemen "wallow[ed] in sensuality, sloth, and indolence . . . " (p. 8).[44] Defoe's tract is a massive assault on the idea of gentility residing in the blood; there is, for example, a long passage about how the traditional farming out of gentle babies to commoners to be breast-fed means that gentle blood is routinely contaminated as heirs "drink in the blood of a slave or a drudge, the blood of a clown and a boor . . . " (p. 74). Over and over Defoe threatens to collapse the distinction between gentle and mechanick, only to disavow that effort and to claim that on the contrary, he is trying to separate them even more radically (pp. 18–20, 31). And he figures the younger son, who has been of necessity educated to a profession, as the paragon of gentlemanliness. In an acrimonious debate between an heir and his younger brother, the ignorant and untaught elder brother states that he does not think younger brothers should be called gentlemen, while the younger brother argues the superiority of younger brothers, who are polished by a liberal education (pp. 44–58). Defoe sums up the moral by saying:

> our gentlemen have inumerable examples at their very door of the advantages of learning . . . they may see the demonstracion of it even in their own familyes, where the bright and the dull, the blind and the clear, the man of sence and learning and the blockhead, is as often to be disscern'd as the heir and the cadet are seen together, where one is untaught and good for nothing because he is to have the estate, and the other is polish'd and educated because he is to make his fortune; the last is to be prepar'd to liv by his witts, and the other is to have no wits or, at best, no learning, because he can liv without them, as if education like an apprentice-ship was for no body but they that were to trade with it and make a trade of it. (p. 68)[45]

Heirs may not need educations for the purposes of work, Defoe concedes, but interestingly, when he argues the need for cultivating heirs, he uses a rhetoric of labor. Arguing that the "natural capascityes" of gentlemen are not, contrary to current opinion, the same as learning, he writes,

> It is apparent that treasure of wit and parts is given from Heaven to be cultivated and improv'd; and as God set Adam to till the ground after the fall, and told him, if he did not do it, ay, and labour and sweat at it, too, he should have no bread, and it should bring forth nothing but briars and thorns to him without tillage and cultivation: so it is in his brains and understanding to this day, if he will kno' he must learn. . . . [W]hat ever brightness of parts, what ever genius, wit, and capacity the man is naturally furnish'd with, it is requir'd that those jewells should be polished, that learning be apply'd to them . . . (pp. 110–11).

The passage relents a little in the image of the jewel being polished, figuring, at that point, the capacities of the elder son as precious material to be worked on. But before that it yokes the figure of the heir with Adam, the paradigmatic figure of labor, in a series of insistent intensifying clauses ("if he did not do it, *ay, and* labour and sweat at it, too, he should have no bread, *and* it should bring forth nothing but briars and thorns to him . . . " [emphases mine]). Not only does Defoe imagine the younger son as rendered "polish'd and educated because he is to make his fortune," but he also surrounds the cultured heir with tropes of labor, suggesting a certain chafing against the very definition of a gentleman as a man with an income sufficient to keep him in leisure.

As Defoe's assault on the category of the gentleman suggests, the ideological force of the labor/idleness problematic resonates for gentlemen as well as for the poor. And indeed, in the conservative novels I read here—written by the daughter of a poor gentleman scholar and by male writers who were either younger sons or the children of younger sons[46]—representations of the laboring or idle poor are always likely to set off tremors in representations of the non-laboring gentleman. In *A Sentimental Journey*, for example, Yorick's shabby genteel idleness makes him, much to his dismay, indistinguishable from the shabby beggar. Once Humphry Clinker is revealed to be Bramble's son, Smollett's novel is at a loss about what to do with him; the romance convention that reveals him to be a gentleman's son seems insufficient to solve the problem that, as *Humphry Clinker* represents it, labor is almost always lethal, bound up in mortal loss. Indeed, at late century labor becomes a particularly volatile category, as it begins to be commodified and reorganized on large scales and a body of literature arises to explain what the experience of work is like, why it is that men work, and how labor may best be extracted from them.[47] A certain strand of political economy expresses doubt and anxiety about labor's corrosive effects; most famous is Adam Smith's suspicion that the division of labor might make industrial workers stupid and ignorant. On the other hand, labor begins to be pried apart from the definition of the poor at this time partly in order to naturalize it; when in the next century paupers are defined as a separate race, the force of that definition is to place them outside the pale of normative laboring humanity. According to Himmelfarb, Burke was one of the first to argue strenuously for the separation of the terms "labouring people" and "poor." In "Letters on a Regicide Peace" (1797) he writes,

> We have heard many plans for the relief of the "*Labouring Poor.*" This
> puling jargon is not as innocent as it is foolish. . . . Hitherto the name
> of Poor (in the sense in which it is used to excite compassion) has not
> been used for those who can, but for those who cannot labour—for
> the sick and infirm; for orphan infancy; for languishing and decrepit
> age; but when we affect to pity as poor, those who must labour or the
> world cannot exist, we are trifling with the condition of mankind. It is
> the common doom of man that he must eat his bread by the sweat of
> his brow, that is, by the sweat of his body, or the sweat of his mind. . . .
> I do not call a healthy young man, chearful in his mind, and vigorous
> in his arms, I cannot call such a man, *poor*; I cannot pity my kind as
> a kind, merely because they are men. This affected pity, only tends
> to dissatisfy them with their condition, and to teach them to seek re-
> sources where no resources are to be found, in something else than
> their own industry, and frugality, and sobriety.[48]

Burke's prose, with its contempt for efforts to arouse his pity, and its lumping together of those who earn a living "by the sweat of his body, or the sweat of his mind," suggests that the ideological force of the distinction between "laborer" and "poor" is to refashion labor into a condition so universal it cannot be pitied—into "the common doom of man."

As this process of ideological redefinition occurs, the category of the gentleman becomes vulnerable to its universalizing impulses. Those gentlemen who must either work or be poor are indistinguishable from the mass of the poor; and at the same time the idleness that defines the heir itself becomes denaturalized. If, as Barrell suggests, writers like Steele, Defoe, and Mandeville are ambivalent about the gentleman's relation to work—because on the one hand "any degree of participation on his part in the affairs of society must . . . oblige him to descend from the elevated viewpoint his status and leisure define for him" while on the other "if he does nothing, he can learn nothing"[49]—by the end of the century the universalizing logic of the commodification of labor makes this tension acute and gives it a strong moral charge. Like Smollett's novel, Burney's *Cecilia* represents labor as a terrible thing, as "the life of a savage." But when, overwhelmed with debt from dissipated living, the fashionable gentleman Harrel blows his brains out, he blames his ruin on his own idleness. He writes in his suicide note: "Had I a son, I would bequeath him a plough; I should then leave him happier than my parents left me. . . . Idleness has been my destruction; the want of something to do led me into all evil."[50]

II. 'Satire' Versus 'Comedy'

That I call these novels "satiric," when I could just as plausibly define them as "comic" (as Kraft does of the very same novels in *Character and Consciousness in Eighteenth-Century Comic Fiction*), requires that we turn our attention to yet another category in flux during this period. Under the impetus of sentimental ideology, which regarded man as benevolent and good-natured, and which offered a vision of God as "*the God of love, of hope, of peace, of all consolation,* cheerfully smiling in favour on us,"[51] there was during the eighteenth century an effort to redefine laughter, and to demarcate the boundaries of appropriate laughter. Stuart Tave, whose *The Amiable Humorist* is the authoritative work on the history of comedy in this period, has shown that a large body of literature on laughter and the comic—by such writers as Lord Shaftesbury, Francis Hutcheson, Anthony Collins, Lord Kames, Fielding, and Addison and Steele—attempted to counter Hobbes's influential definition of laughter as "sudden glory," a moment of pleasurable apprehension of one's superiority over another, and to offer in its stead a theory of sympathetic laughter. In the process of redefining laughter, the category of satire was also refined and redefined. As early as the seventeenth century there was an attempt to make satiric forms less profane, an effort neatly encapsulated in the debate over the term's etymological origins; the false but suggestive Greek *satyra*—lecherous and satyrlike—gave way to the derivation from the Roman *satura lanx*, a well-filled platter.[52] And while the attempt to distinguish satire from mere bad nature is virtually transhistorical, the early to middle part of the eighteenth century saw, Tave suggests, a "ceaseless laboring of that distinction, the frequent appearance of that careful and rather nervous phrase, 'true satire,' the compelling necessity of explaining exhaustively one's own good nature."[53]

Many writers after Addison, however, no longer accepted that distinction; as Ronald Paulson points out, to them, "satire *was* an ill-natured attack on a particular enemy of the satirist."[54] Thus defining the best mode of comic writing came to entail privileging what was called humor over wit, and prying apart the categories of comedy and satire. If in Restoration theory of comedy it was a commonplace that the function of comedy is to expose and ridicule fools and knaves, by the mid-nineteenth century it was believed that the best comic works offered amiable and benevolent characters whose foibles were to be regarded as lovable rather than despicable.[55] Paulson puts this categorically: "Almost all theories of comedy before the eighteenth century equate comedy and satire, and most theories since then rigorously distinguish . . . ridicule (satiric laughter) from the risible or ludicrous (comic laughter)."[56]

Sir Roger de Coverley is generally regarded as a primary figure in the transition from satire to comedy, a precursor to such benevolent and whimsical comic characters as Parson Adams and Uncle Toby. Describing the shift in the portrayal of Sir Roger, Paulson writes: "Here easy to see and early in the century is a character who begins as a humor-character in the old sense, representing politically objectionable principles, and who soon becomes the author's 'favourite,' loved rather than ridiculed for his follies."[57] It is usually his Toryism that is considered the politically objectionable part of Sir Roger that the writers of *The Spectator* came to represent indulgently. But I would argue that making Sir Roger fit for comic rather than satiric representation entailed resolving a more serious problem of character and politics than his party allegiance: his indiscretions with the poor. For in *Spectator* No. 2 there is the suggestion that he "has frequently offended in Point of Chastity with Beggars and Gypsies"—a suggestion which is, however, "look'd upon by his Friends rather as a Matter of Raillery than Truth"[58]; and Nos. 410

and 544 concern Will Honeycomb's story about Sir Roger's gallant behavior to a prostitute, a story that needs to be explained and repudiated.

There is an uncertainty, both in *The Spectator* and in the criticism, about the magnitude of these indiscretions. Sir Roger's kinsman Captain Sentry writes in after his death to say that many of *The Spectator*'s readers may have misunderstood the passage in No. 410 "wherein Sir Roger is reported to have enquired into the private Character of the young Woman at the Tavern." Gently but firmly clarifying, he writes, "I know you mentioned that Circumstance as an Instance of the Simplicity and Innocence of his Mind, which made him imagine it a very easy thing to reclaim one of those Criminals, and not as an Inclination to be guilty with her."[59] Even more interesting is Tave's own defense of Sir Roger in this regard. When he describes that incident as "a slip of the pen," it is unclear whether he is ventriloquizing the voice of Mr. Spectator or making his own claim; moreover, he dismisses the allusion to Sir Roger's sexual indiscretions with beggars and gypsies in a footnote, arguing that it was made before his character was really developed, and calling it "a jesting, untrue suggestion," as though Sir Roger is a real character whom Tave knows.[60] But as marginal as Sir Roger's indiscretions may seem, and as casually and discreetly as they may be swept under the carpet, they in fact had a symbolic resonance grave enough to require drastic authorial intervention. The tradition (fostered, as Tave describes it, by Eustace Budgell, John Campbell, and Theophilus Cibber, to name a few contemporary commentators) is that "this blunder [with the prostitute], harmless as it seems, made Addison resolve to kill him off lest someone else should murder him."[61] And interestingly, in the act of killing him off, *The Spectator* creates an ambiguity over how Sir Roger died, an ambiguity that recapitulates the uncertainty about his behavior to the poor. One of Sir Andrew Freeport's correspondents informs him that "the old Man caught a Cold at the County Sessions, as he was very warmly promoting an Address of his own penning, in which he succeeded according to his Wishes." A letter to Mr. Spectator from Sir Roger's butler, however, reports the following circumstances of his death:

> I am affraid he caught his Death the last County Sessions, where he
> would go to see Justice done to a poor Widow Woman and her Fa-
> therless Children that had been wronged by a Neighbouring Gentle-
> man; for you know, Sir, my good Master was always the poor Man's
> Friend.[62]

Addison not only creates a double version of Sir Roger's death—
one suggesting a self-serving act, and the other a self-sacrificing
one—but also creates, in this passage, one gentleman who oppresses
the poor, and one who is "always the poor Man's Friend." In doing
so he externalizes in two antithetical figures the split and uncertain
nature of Sir Roger's character regarding the poor, and has the moral
part decisively oppose the immoral.[63] It is telling that the object
of Sir Roger's protection is a "Widow Woman and her Fatherless
Children." It is as though only an aggressive paternalism can alleviate
the casual but lethal crime of excessive closeness to the poor—the
transgression that needs to be redressed before the gentleman can
become an object of sympathetic laughter. Sir Roger dies, in other
words, of the rigors of making his character fit for comic rather
than satiric representation. And this drama suggests that satire is the
genre in which the gentleman gets too close to the poor, in an act
uncertainly figured as one of desire, misapprehension, exploitation,
salvation.

It is, perhaps, counterintuitive to think of satire as the genre that
would *not* require Sir Roger's death as compensation for his transgressive mingling with the poor, since satire is so severely hierarchical, so predicated upon the creation and maintenance of distinct
categories. Indeed, in distinguishing it from satire, theorists of benevolent humor represented it as the more democratic of the gen-
res, a genre more tolerant and accommodating of difference and individuality. In a canonical comment on English character and humor during the reign of George II, Hazlitt wrote:

> But in the period of our history in question, a security of person and
> property, and a freedom of opinion had been established, which made
> every man feel of some consequence to himself, and appear an object
> of some curiosity to his neighbours: our manners became more do-
> mesticated; there was a general spirit of sturdiness and independence,
> which made the English character more truly English than perhaps at

any other period—that is, more tenacious of its own opinions and purposes. The whole surface of society appeared cut out into square enclosures and sharp angles, which extended to the dresses of the time, their gravel-walks, and clipped hedges. Each individual had a certain ground-plot of his own to cultivate his particular humours in, and let them shoot out at pleasure; and a most plentiful crop they have produced accordingly. The reign of George II was, in a word, the age of *hobby-horses.* . . . "[64]

Hazlitt's emphasis on "freedom of opinion" and "a general spirit of sturdiness and independence" is typical of writing on English humor during the period he describes, with its assertion of a free and democratic culture. But notice too the concomitant sharp delineation of spaces: the "security of person and property," the "cutting out" of "the whole surface of society" into "square enclosures and sharp angles, which extended to the dresses of the time, their gravel-walks, and clipped hedges." One might expect that such imagery would evoke little boxes made of ticky-tacky, a monotonous sameness of character. For Hazlitt, however, enclosure *creates* individuality, just as it creates an abundance of crops; it is because property is enclosed and "secure" that there can be variety in character. The "independence" and "freedom" thought to create English "humor" are, in this passage, predicated upon the sharp separation of those with property and those without—indeed, even the dispossession of the poor, if we understand enclosure to have entailed the curtailing of certain kinds of customary rights to land use.

It is also important to note that the category of English humor was created during a time at which there was an assault on popular festivity, and an attempt to separate the spheres of popular and bourgeois culture. Stallybrass and White argue that the creation of the bourgeois public sphere entailed separating middle-class audiences from their enjoyment of popular culture, and that gentlemen, who traditionally enjoyed the popular pursuits of the country, were central objects of derision and pressure in this regard. As Malcomson writes,

During the first half of the eighteenth century in particular, many gentlemen were not entirely disengaged from the culture of the common people. They frequently occupied something of a half-way house between the robust, unpolished culture of provincial England and the cosmopolitan, sophisticated culture which was based in London.[65]

Stallybrass and White gloss Malcomson by maintaining that the "booby squires" attacked by late-seventeeth-century comedy were "viewed with contempt by the town in part because they had not yet dissociated 'classical' from popular culture: they actively lived *both* and it is precisely this hybridization, this 'both/and' which is here under massive pressure."[66] That the category of benevolent comedy was created at this time suggests the necessity for a genre fit to enable and accommodate such a separation. The de-hybridizing logic of this specific historical notion of comedy inevitably came into tension with the classical notion. The comic always carries with it its neoclassical origins as a genre that represents the low: it is the low-within-the-classical. But interestingly, Tave claims that in most eighteenth-century accounts of laughter, "Aristotle . . . was given a short paragraph at the beginning and gently dismissed," because, Tave believes, "The Aristotelian founding of laughter on the contemplation of something ugly or defective seemed to hang too close to Hobbes."[67] Revising his explanation to account for the class element of this evocation and dismissal of Aristotle, one could argue that during this period even the classical account of comedy as a genre representing the low was too hybrid, and needed to be quietly effaced.

Fielding, I believe, was more sensitive than most to the ambiguities of the category of benevolent humor. In its creation of the genre of the comic novel, I argue in Chapter 1, his Preface to *Joseph Andrews* argues as vigorously as any eighteenth-century text for the separation of popular and bourgeois culture. But it is also ambivalent about this separation. Satire is not a prominent category in the Preface, whose central definitional effort is to distinguish between the categories of the burlesque (popular culture, in which the low imitate the high) and the comic (written culture, in which rank and manners have a natural correspondence). The spectre of egregiously cruel satire does, however, appear—tellingly, in the scenario of people laughing at "Ugliness, Infirmity, or Poverty" or at "a wretched Family shivering with Cold and languishing with Hunger."[68] As he attempts to clear out a space for the "comic" that would be free of the contaminating elements of popular culture, the category of cruel and false satire appears in Fielding's text to mark the potential oppressiveness of that very effort. Creating diabolical figures who laugh at poverty is the Preface's way of recognizing that inventing the comic entails a separation of popular and elite public spheres, which is an act of both symbolic and material violence to the poor.

In contesting the democratic claims of English humor, I do not mean to romanticize satire, which is clearly a conservative and hierarchical genre, nor to suggest that satire itself was not involved in policing the boundaries between gentlemen and the poor.[69] If Sir Roger were represented satirically rather than comically, those boundaries would still be policed: in satiric representation he would be excoriated for his behavior to the poor, ridiculed as either an exploitative hypocrite or as a man with low and uncontrollable sexual urges. The difference between that stance and comic representation is that the latter attempts to efface or explain away his transgressive proximity to the poor so that we may laugh indulgently at him, regarding him as well-intentioned and benevolent. Indeed, the comic may be regarded as the genre that polices the boundaries between the propertied and the poor while insisting upon and celebrating its democratic nature. A certain, anthropology-influenced tradition of theory of satire, which reads satire as a ritual act, provides a useful framework for thinking about this dynamic. Michael Seidel, for example, reads satire through Girard's account, in *Violence and the Sacred*, of how civilizations build themselves by getting over, and getting accustomed to, founding crimes. For Girard, Seidel writes, "what was once unthinkable becomes, after a fashion, legal": "the historical and human record of temporal continuity is the accommodation of uneasy memories in the codifying of regressive tendencies so that communal rituals of sacrifice and scapegoatism displace the barbarism of founding acts."[70] Satire, however, attempts to halt this process, refusing to consent to the collective fiction that the unthinkable is in fact legal. Seidel writes, "The satiric representation or fiction refuses to entertain notions of the accommodating, idealizing lie; that is, it refuses to break into normative form."[71] I am historicizing this insight by suggesting that the creation of the early-to-mid-eighteenth-century version of the comic, which entailed its decisive move away from satire, required an "accommodating, idealizing lie." It was predicated upon the denial of the murderous intensity of its impulse to police the boundaries between gentlemen and the poor. This brave new world of comedy—which is also the world of enclosure, the curtailing of popular festivity, the commodification of labor—requires the cover-up of what might be called the founding crime of Sir Roger's murder; it requires the idealizing lie that he died in the exercise of benevolence.

It is to insist on the fact and the anxious-making power of the proximity between gentlemen and the poor during this period—and to foreground, rather than effacing, the force of the culture's desire to police the boundaries between them—that I call these novels "satiric." I also use that generic term to mark the novels' conservatism. For, as Seidel points out, satire's refusal of the normative lie is a kind of arresting of history's progress: "So there is in the satiric act a kind of perverse neutralization of historical progression, a stop without the guarantee of a new start."[72] In the second half of this book, describing the process that halts historical progression, I link the halting properties of satire to those of the mental state psychoanalysis calls melancholia. I have been drawn to this category because *Humphry Clinker* and *Cecilia* are strikingly organized around ambivalence over the appropriateness of strong emotion, in particular the proper degree of grief for the loss of a loved one. In these novels there is always the felt danger that that grief will be excessive, paralyzing, ridiculous, or, in Burney's novel, solipsistic and abnegating of the social. According to psychoanalytic accounts, melancholia is a blockage or refusal of mourning of a lost object that originates in an ambivalent relation to that object, or the inability to see what one has lost in the object.[73] These novels are fundamentally about losses in the realm of the social—losses connected to social injuries perpetrated on the poor, and a concomitant injury to the self-image of gentlemen. And what I call the melancholia of *Humphry Clinker* and *Cecilia* derives from their inability to see clearly what has been lost as the poor become transformed by the forces of enclosure and the division and commodification of labor. I read satiric moments in these novels—moments that forcefully, indeed obnoxiously, disrupt the journeys around which the novels' plots are organized—as heightened and stylized expressions of the novels' ambivalence over seeing what the culture has lost.

I take my methodological cues from Fredric Jameson's description of narrative form as "an ideological act in its own right, with the function of inventing imaginary or formal 'solutions' to unresolvable social contradictions."[74] It is insofar as ideology is a collective fantasy or wish-fulfillment that psychoanalytic concepts may be useful to describe it. I am describing in these readings what I think of as cultural attitudes, collective mental states (or what Stallybrass and White call "shared imaginary repertoires") of the dominant culture. In using psychoanalytical concepts, I do not mean to suggest a kind of transhistorical consciousness: it would be quite unwise and ahistorical to assume that melancholia existed in the same way in the eighteenth-century English psyche as it did, say, in Freud's patients. In this study psychoanalysis functions not as a master narrative, but rather as an interpretive method; for the language of psychoanalysis is, to my mind, the richest and most fluid way to describe consciousness—especially the displacements, projections, and identifications through which subjectivities are formed through contact with one another. My intention is to demonstrate how psychic and aesthetic practices emerge in dynamic interrelation with economic ones, and—if not, perhaps, to enclose and cultivate the common ground between gentle and poor, to gather from it the interpretive fuel to illuminate the impact of the socially marginal on some of English culture's most valued aesthetic forms.

৵৺৶

As I suggested earlier, Chapter 1 displaces those accounts of Fielding's Preface to *Joseph Andrews* and *Shamela* that read them as high-cultural responses to emergent bourgeois fictions, by concentrating primarily on the lower-class figures and characters that constitute the vehicle for such a critique. I open with readings of these texts to illustrate how concerns about lower-class literacy helped shape one of the central defining moments of the early novel. The Preface, I suggest, worries Fielding's shift from popular—that is, the-atrical—entertainment to literary representation, repudiating the realm of popular culture at the same time that it ambivalently reflects on the potential immorality of comic writing and the benevolent as-pects of the burlesque. *Shamela* represents lower-class literacy as ag-gravatedly eroticized and utopian; and the transition from Fielding's parody of *Pamela* to *Joseph Andrews* may be read as an attempt to defuse this intense desire for upward mobility, thereby warding off the possibility of the lower class's access to fictions of upward mobil-ity. Chapter 2, a reading of *A Sentimental Journey*, explores the ways in which an impecunious gentleman creates and negotiates his dif-ference from those in the lower classes. Focusing on character and the act of characterization, I demonstrate how Sterne's novel imag-ines scenarios in which the potentially subversive utterance of the lower classes is stabilized by a more or less severe corporal discipline. At the same time, by voluntarily and self-consciously inhabiting the position of the lower classes, the gentleman paradoxically wards off a similar fixing of his own utterance and character. It is this act, I sug-gest, that constitutes him as a gentleman. In *Humphry Clinker*, I argue in Chapter 3, gentlemen also take on attributes of the poor, particu-larly their relation and resistance to dispossession in the wake of the second wave of parliamentary enclosures in England. Here, how-ever, rather than empowering the gentleman, that identification is the result of a radical disavowal—the magical way the gentleman preserves himself from having to acknowledge the social dislocations attendant upon the agricultural revolution.

Chapter 4 centers on the historical moment at which women take over the act of charity. It reads Burney's *Cecilia* as a meditation upon, and a critique of, the creation of the domestic woman, the gentlewoman who was, in Nancy Armstrong's argument, defined by subjectivity alone. This chapter attempts to shift the emphasis from the way in which the domestic woman was created in opposition to an aristocratic model, in order to emphasize another crucial— and perhaps more immediate—influence on the formation of her subjectivity: the crucible of the relation between leisured women and the poor, a relation mediated by charity. Like that in *Humphry Clinker*, the current of melancholia that runs through *Cecilia*—as well as its related affect, shame—emerges, I will argue, out of the reorganization of labor practices in the late part of the eighteenth century. Not only do leisured women take on the burden of bearing the emotions attendant upon the reorganization of labor; the emotions themselves, I suggest, are imagined through the very tropes used to describe labor in this period.

As in *Humphry Clinker*, Burney's novel worries about the excessive nature of grief, its major synecdoche for female affectivity. It is charity that functions as the social act authorizing and moderating the expression of emotion. But while charity promises to be a social cure for the excessively personal behaviors of grief and shame, it also *creates* a new and damaging surplus of emotion. While in *A Sentimental Journey* the gentleman constitutes himself as such in the act of charity, in *Cecilia* the task offered to women as the very expression of feminine propriety ends up being deeply damaging to female reputation, making the gentlewoman virtually disintegrate. The creation of the domestic woman must be read in relation to the explosive interaction between leisured women and the poor, then, at a moment when such interaction was both encouraged and unviable. Moreover, *Cecilia*'s commitment to the practice of satire, I argue, derives from the way satire is imagined to have the power to stave off both the creation of the domestic woman and the process of the reorganization of labor that such creation entails.

Finally, the conclusion focuses upon what is perhaps eighteenth-century England's most extraordinary novel about labor, Burney's *The Wanderer*, arguing that it portrays a post-French-revolutionary English culture in which the imperative to labor is so powerfully universal it almost entirely overwhelms gentle identity. Moreover, at the same time that it creates an overwhelming, even sublime vision of human labor, Burney's novel represents satire as impotent and antiquated—no longer capable, in the novel's imaginary, of warding off the social and economic processes it has been marshaled to combat.

CHAPTER I

'What You Seek Is Nowhere'

THE COMIC NOVEL
AND LOWER-CLASS LITERACY

Like the transition from traditional open-field to capitalist agriculture (which I will discuss in detail in Chapter 3), or the transition from a paternalistic to a contractual model of labor and service, the rise of literacy in England is one of those historical processes whose length and ubiquitousness challenge our claims to a rigorous historical specificity. What the plentiful figures on literacy in the premodern period show us is that it was always already, seemingly transhistorically, on the rise. These figures bear out what we easily intuit: that literacy was class and gender based, the upper classes and men becoming literate first; that those in the city were more apt to be able to read and write than those in the country; and that servants, with their emulation of their masters' ways, and their roles as cultural intermediaries between the upper and lower classes, were a particular source of irritation to those who feared that reading and writing would create desires for upward mobility. It seems safe to say that in early-eighteenth-century England some servants, and some women, and some apprentices could read.[1]

But if it is risky to argue that the period of *Pamela* and *Joseph Andrews* was a critical point in the actual numerical increase of lower-class literacy, it should nevertheless be clear enough from the alarm that surrounded the reception of *Pamela* that the rise of the novel

gave this problem a particular urgency. As the novel started to become a mass-cultural form, no one text clamored as much as Fielding's *Shamela* about its power to shape subjectivities and to act as an
agent for cultural change. Shifting, therefore, the focus of the criticism that has dwelt upon Fielding's attack on Richardson and the
challenge to middle-class aesthetic values it entailed, this chapter
reads Fielding's Preface to *Joseph Andrews*, and a certain trajectory
from *Shamela* to *Joseph Andrews*, in light of the pressures exerted upon
them by ambivalence over lower-class literacy. While such ambivalence is not surprising from a writer who both made his living by the
spread of literacy and had a strong interest in the preservation of class
hierarchy, its power to shape the deep formal and ideological struc-
tures of these texts is greater than one might expect. For it influences
the way the Preface to *Joseph Andrews* imagines the ethics of the
comic novel, and it shapes *Joseph Andrews*'s particular kind of realism,
its way of thinking sexuality, and its creation of the heroine who is to
serve as an alternative to Pamela, Fanny Goodwill.

I. *From Aural / Visual to Written: The Preface to 'Joseph Andrews'*

> Surely he hath a very ill-framed Mind, who can look on Ugliness,
> Infirmity, or Poverty, as ridiculous in themselves: nor do I believe
> any Man living who meets a dirty Fellow riding through the
> Streets in a Cart, is struck with an Idea of the Ridiculous from it;
> but if he should see the same Figure descend from his Coach and
> Six, or bolt from his Chair with his Hat under his Arm, he would
> then begin to laugh, and with justice.[2]

The little criticism that exists about Fielding's Preface to *Joseph
Andrews* has generally understood its significance to lie in Fielding's
differentiation of his new comic form, the "comic Epic-Poem in
Prose," from such previous narrative forms as the romance and his
own parodic *Shamela*, as well as in his placement of it within the classical literary canon.[3] But as my opening quotation from it suggests,
Fielding is at least as concerned about the reception of this new
form, and the Preface may also be read as a kind of ethics of representation of the poor. When Fielding raises the specter of inappro-

priate or immoral laughter, he does so in relation to the spectacle of poverty, warning that the "Ridiculous" works properly, "with justice," only when it serves as a moral commentary on the spectacle of the poor imitating the rich. Indeed, as I suggested in the previous chapter, Fielding was highly sensitive to the social ambiguities of the idea of the ridiculous—the "comic" part of "the comic Epic-Poem in Prose." It is a category so ambivalent in the Preface that it requires a considerable labor of definition and justification.

Accordingly, this chapter seeks to dislocate the account of Fielding's Preface that sees it as most concerned with constituting a high-cultural response to romance. Rather, I argue that it is more crucially concerned with another generic shift with important historical implications: Fielding's shift from popular—that is, theatrical—entertainment to literary representation. Such a dislocation allows us to shift the focus from the predominantly middle-class readers of the romance to the problematically non- and semi-literate spectators of early eighteenth-century burlesque theater. While we might like to think of the canonical Fielding as a renegade satirist capable of singlehandedly motivating legislation of the theater, there were in fact larger social and historical issues involved in the Licensing Act that turned him to the novel: the London theater of the 1730s provoked legislation because it was a turbulent social space. The shift Fielding announces in the Preface, from an aural/visual to a literary mode of artistic production, may be read, I argue, as a manifestation in the realm of the aesthetic of the larger social processes that attempted to exclude the lower classes from forms of collective festivity. Moreover, his displacement of the "Burlesque" from the voices of his lower-class characters to the voice of the gentleman author may be read as an attempt to symbolically ward off the possibility that a "dirty Fellow" might ride in a "Coach and Six": that the poor might imitate their betters.

But Fielding's act of high canon formation is not unambivalent about the ways in which it regulates and repudiates the popular. By examining moments of anxiety in this text—moments in which Fielding raises the possibility that we could find spectacles of misery and poverty comic—I will argue that this account of generic transi-

tion is accompanied by an anxious reflection on the potential immorality of written representation, and a concomitant meditation
on the types of pleasure to be gained from comic writing. My argument alternates between analyzing the logic of the Preface's figures
within the text itself, and attempting to elaborate these figures' social and historical meanings. I will turn to the issue of what *Joseph
Andrews* actually performs in the second part of this chapter.

Fielding labors to define the burlesque at the moment when he
wants most seriously to dissociate himself from it in order to describe his new kind of writing, "which," he says grandly, "I do not
remember to have seen hitherto attempted in our Language" (*JA*, p.
3). He employs classical generic categories in order to bestow upon
his new fiction the prestige of a classical genre. This act of catego-
rization operates through the establishment of a series of binary oppositions—tragedy vs. comedy, high vs. low, sublime vs. ridiculous;
once those oppositions are set up, and Fielding restores the missing
term *Margites* as the binary opposite to the term *Iliad*, he can invent
the category of the comic epic, which will henceforth have a respectable lineage. In other words, the primary function of the elab-
oration of Aristotelian distinctions in the Preface is the conferral of
high-cultural status upon the comic epic-poem in prose. This new
form contrasts with the works of uncertain lineage he has written
before; Fielding agrees with Lord Shaftesbury, who asserts of "the
Burlesque" that " 'there is no such Thing to be found in the Writings of the Antients' " (*JA*, p. 5).

The Aristotelian categories have another job as well, however:
the comic epic-poem in prose, Fielding argues, differs from the epic
in the same way that comedy differs from tragedy in Aristotle—it
introduces "Persons of inferiour Rank, and consequently of inferiour Manners" (*JA*, p. 4). The Aristotelian lineage of Fielding's
new form, then, also legitimizes its attention to the poor. While this
is certainly not the first time in Western literature that comedy has
been said to represent the lower classes, it is a particularly vexed instance; as I will show, the Preface is crucially about how problematic
this conjunction is.

Fielding does not merely attempt to establish the comic epic's familial relation to the classical epic; he also sets up a non-canonical category in opposition to it, which he calls the "Burlesque." When he evokes the burlesque it is to call it "mere Burlesque," deprecating the type of writing he had done in his plays and in *Shamela*. Here is Fielding's attempt to differentiate "Parodies or burlesque Imitations" from "the Comic," which he also calls "the Ridiculous" (I will use the two terms interchangeably):

> Indeed, no two Species of Writing can differ more widely than the Comic and the Burlesque: for as the latter is ever the Exhibition of what is monstrous and unnatural, and where our Delight, if we examine it, arises from the surprizing Absurdity, as in appropriating the Manners of the highest to the lowest, or *è converso*; so in the former, we should ever confine ourselves strictly to Nature from the just Imitation of which, will flow all the Pleasure we can this way convey to a sensible Reader. . . . (*JA*, p. 4)

In a manifesto whose fundamental activity is the careful establishment of differences, the comic and the burlesque represent for Fielding the very epitome of difference. Functioning as what Peter Stallybrass and Allon White call the "low-Other,"[4] the category of the burlesque is invoked as a "monstrous" and "unnatural" foil against which the comic is constituted as natural and proper. The burlesque low-Other, Fielding claims, has a specific class content; it may be defined as an "exhibition" of cross-class imitation—most particularly, the low imitating the high—that arouses delight. Imitation across classes, Fielding suggests in this definition, is inherently "monstrous and unnatural." The comic, on the other hand, offers us "Persons of inferiour Rank, and consequently of inferiour Manners" (*JA*, p. 4): in a form "confin[ed] . . . strictly to Nature," rank and manners have a natural correspondence.

Significantly, Fielding illustrates the distinction between the two modes through an analogy to painting ("Comic History-Painter" vs. "Caricatura"). Arguing that while the comic history-painter copies nature, caricatura exhibits "Monsters, not Men," Fielding writes,

> Now what *Caricatura* is in Painting, Burlesque is in Writing; and in the same manner the Comic Writer and Painter correlate to each other.

And here I shall observe, that as in the former, the Painter seems to have the Advantage; so it is in the latter infinitely on the side of the Writer: for the *Monstrous* is much easier to paint than describe, and the *Ridiculous* to describe than paint. (*JA*, p. 6)

If the burlesque is performed to its best advantage visually, the ridiculous takes place in the realm of the "described," or written. The two terms, then, suggest not only opposing *levels* of culture (high and low), but also a difference of levels that articulates itself through a contrast in artistic media. One of the burdens of this passage is the argument that we should regard "the Ingenious *Hogarth*" as a "comic history-painter" rather than a practitioner of "caricatura"—as, analogously to Fielding, a comic rather than a burlesque artist. Ronald Paulson, however, has regarded the distinction between Fielding and Hogarth as paradigmatic of the different epistemological worlds of elite and popular culture in the eighteenth century. In an analysis of Hogarth's *Industry and Idleness*, Paulson writes, "These visual subculture images set up a substitute code, [in E. P. Thompson's phrase] 'an unwritten popular code'. . . . They also show that there is one way of reading or viewing for the educated audience of Fielding's *Enquiry* [*into the Causes of the Late Increase of Robbers*] and another for the essentially visual/aural culture of the uneducated 'inferior part of mankind.' "[5] He adds that *Industry and Idleness*

> leads us to conclude that Hogarth associates the visual language of images with the subculture; the language of words—at least of written, inscribed words like those of the Ten Commandments—with the dominant or master's culture.[6]

So while Fielding's Preface distinguishes between various *literary* forms, the comic novel and the romance, I would argue that its evocation of Hogarth and elaborate attention to the visual suggest that it is also crucially concerned with evoking the difference between aural/visual and literary modes of representation, and with announcing Fielding's move from the former to the latter.

When Fielding alludes to the burlesque, he alludes to a written form: "Writings of the Burlesque kind." But the burlesque in fact came down to Fielding in two forms, the written and the non-

written. It was an important genre in the chapbooks that circulated
among the semiliterate and literate of the working classes.[7] At the
same time, in the Restoration and early eighteenth century burlesque was also a theatrical form, in which the neoclassical and the
heroic were uttered by the low: for example, Thomas Duffett's burlesque of Elkanah Settle's *The Empress of Morocco* (1673) transformed
Settle's heroes into "corn-cutters, draymen and a 'scinder-Wench,'"
while in his burlesque of *The Tempest* (1674), an orange-woman,
rather than an actress, played Ariel.[8] Fielding's own plays remain a
primary example of the burlesque in its theatrical instantiation. I am
not claiming that the burlesque was inherently a popular form:
it was clearly directed to an educated audience, one competent in
the conventions of the heroic drama. Its nonliterary status, however, like that of farces, pantomimes, and those other theatrical
forms derisively known as "entertainments," made it accessible to a
wider audience. Indeed, Albert J. Rivero has suggested that there
was in the theater of Fielding's time a tension between the compet-
ing claims of reading and the spectacle. "Audiences nurtured on
French pantomimes, harlequinades, and Italian operas," he writes of
the milieu in which Fielding wrote, "could not be expected to relish
the meaning and wit of regular comedy. The town demanded spectacle, 'acting' rather than 'reading' plays."[9] Rivero argues that when
Fielding's plays thematized the act of reading, his aim was "to teach
his audience to read dramatic action as though it were a difficult
book. . . . "[10]

In the major strategy of theatrical burlesque, heroic dialogue
was uttered by low characters: Fielding's new literary form, however, employs a quite different strategy:

> In the Diction I think, Burlesque itself may be sometimes admitted; of
> which many Instances will occur in this Work, as in the Descriptions
> of the Battles, and some other Places, not necessary to be pointed out
> to the Classical Reader; for whose Entertainment those Parodies or
> Burlesque Imitations are chiefly calculated.
>
> But tho' we have sometimes admitted this in our Diction, we have
> carefully excluded it from our Sentiments and Characters: for there it
> is never properly introduced, unless in Writings of the Burlesque
> kind, which this is not intended to be. (*JA*, p. 4)

This passage argues that the burlesque will only be "sometimes admitted," designed for the pleasure of a "classical reader." And most important, Fielding announces its containment in the voice that manages description: in the name of propriety, it is "carefully excluded" from the voices of the characters "of inferiour Rank," and hitherto limited to that of the gentleman author. One might call this burlesque in only one direction: while the gentleman author imitates the manners of the lowest, the lowest are prevented from imitating those of the highest.

The regulation of the burlesque in the comic epic occurs in the interest of a more abstract and deferred pleasure than the burlesque, "a more rational and useful Pleasure," Fielding writes (*JA*, p. 6). While the burlesque generates "exquisite Mirth and Laughter" (*JA*, p. 5), in the ridiculous "we should ever confine ourselves strictly to Nature from the just Imitation of which, will flow all the Pleasure we can this way convey to a sensible Reader" (*JA*, p. 4). One feels the censorship leveled on the practitioner of the comic, whose project takes place under the rubric of strict confinement. So restrained is this form of pleasure that only a "sensible" reader feels it; the comic does not "so strongly affect and agitate the Muscles" as the burlesque (*JA*, p. 6). Indeed, the extreme caution of the formulation "all the Pleasure we can this way convey to a sensible Reader," opens up a world of other ways of conveying pleasure and other kinds of readers who are feeling pleasure. The dignifying of the comic— a mode of representing those of inferior rank and manners—into a classical literary genre intended for a cultural elite entails an abstraction from the cruder and more bodily pleasures of the burlesque.

Such an abstraction from bodily pleasures was an important part of the creation and consolidation of the bourgeois public sphere in the late seventeenth and early eighteenth centuries, which, according to Stallybrass and White, entailed a "general transformation of the sites of discourse," a transformation that "marked out a number of changes in the interrelationship of place, body and discourse during the period." Focusing on the Restoration theater, for example, they claim that the hybridization of classical and popular culture lived by many gentlemen of the period was under attack, and describe the theatre as a site of the disciplining and refinement of the public body. And in the early part of the eighteenth century, "self-exclusion from the sites of popular festivity . . . was a major symbolic project for the emergent professional classes."[11] Fielding, whose social and cultural allegiances were extremely complex, vividly embodies this hybridization of classical and popular culture. For years, until his theatrical activity was curtailed by the Licensing Act, he successfully straddled the realms of high and low culture. He did so, moreover, in a turbulently mixed social space. Studies of eighteenth-century playhouse audiences pay little attention to the attendance of the lower classes, concentrating chiefly upon the transition from elite to bourgeois audiences reflected in the emergence of bourgeois sentimental drama. We do know, however, that if the audience was "dominated by the affluent," in the upper gallery sat apprentices and footmen, who paid little or nothing for admission.[12] Joseph Andrews' becoming "a little too forward in Riots at the Play-Houses and Assemblies" (*JA*, p. 27), and the near-riot of the "Gentlemen" in the "Footman's Gallery" in *Tom Jones*,[13] hint at a class whose riotous behavior, both inside and outside the confines of the theater, came to be considered a major social problem during the period. The refining of this noisy and mixed body entailed a kind of phenomenological shift, from "a dispersed, heterodox, noisy participation in the *event* of theatre" to the "silent specular intensity" of reading.[14] Fielding's move from the burlesque theater to neo-classical literature, then, is a move from low to high that is simultaneously a transition in modes of experiencing culture: from the collectivity watching the stage to the more culturally prestigious activity of the individual reading.

The construction of the bourgeois public sphere in the late seventeenth and early eighteenth centuries entailed not only the gentleman's self-exclusion from sites of popular recreation; this was also a time when the ruling classes were intervening in and curtailing the recreations of the poor themselves. Robert Malcomson has documented the fact that to the ruling classes "recreation was commonly seen as an impediment, a threat of substantial proportions, to steady and productive labour. . . ."[15] Along with the fairs whose gradual demise Stallybrass and White have documented, the theater seems to have been a primary target for the regulation of poor and working people. According to Vincent J. Liesenfeld, Sir John Barnard's 1735 introduction of a bill to Parliament to limit the number of playhouses reflected the growing hostility of the bourgeoisie to existing theaters (especially the one in Goodman's Fields), which they believed caused moral decay in the London neighborhoods that housed them. Not only did new theaters, it was claimed, bring "higher rents, liquor, and prostitution into their neighborhoods"; but "the mischief of the drama threatened trade as much as body or soul. . . . "[16] When Barnard spoke in the House of Commons for his new bill, he complained of "the Mischief done to the City of London by the Play-Houses, in corrupting the Youth, encouraging Vice and Debauchery, and being prejudicial to Trade and Industry." According to Liesenfeld, "it was this threat to industry more than any other single factor that provoked attacks on the theaters in 1735."[17] He also argues that the series of playhouse riots by footmen that occurred in February 1737 should be read in the context of a series of civil disorders in 1736–37 that seemed to seriously threaten the stability of the government; in the spring of 1737, the Parliament whose last piece of business was the passing of the Licensing Act addressed the problem of "the general spirit of insurrection it believed pervaded the nation."[18] During this period plays often interacted in a volatile way with an already restless class of people, making the social space of the theater dangerous enough to require governmental regulation.

In the Preface, then, both Fielding's shift from the aural/visual to the literary, and his displacement of the burlesque from the voices of his lower-class characters to the voice of the gentleman author for the enjoyment of the "classical Reader," may be read as manifestations in the realm of the aesthetic of the larger social process that attempted to exclude the lower classes from theatrical entertainment. In *Shamela*, Fielding had already illustrated the social chaos that ensues when the burlesque is not limited to the "Diction," but also appears in the "Sentiments and Characters." And read alongside the Preface, Fielding's other, darker treatise of cross-class imitation— the *Enquiry into the Causes of the Late Increase of Robbers*—makes explicit the regulatory character of his aesthetic program.[19] In this treatise, cross-class imitation is regarded as a social catastrophe:

> In free Countries, at least, it is a Branch of Liberty claimed by the People to be as wicked and as profligate as their Superiors. Thus while the Nobleman will emulate the Grandeur of a Prince; and the Gentleman will aspire to the proper State of the Nobleman; the Tradesman steps from behind his Counter into the vacant Place of the Gentleman. Nor doth the Confusion end here: It reaches the very Dregs of the People, who aspiring still to a Degree beyond that which belongs to them, and not being able by the Fruits of honest Labour to support the State which they affect, they disdain the Wages to which their Industry would intitle them; and abandoning themselves to Idleness, the more simple and poor-spirited betake themselves to a State of Starving and Beggary, while those of more Art and Courage become Thieves, Sharpers, and Robbers.[20]

In this passage "emulation" carries a strong political charge, implying "aspiration" upward. If the emulating poor are rather harmless objects of ridicule in the Preface, here Fielding savages their bolder brothers who, for example, gain admission into public places "upon no other Pretence or Merit than that of a laced Coat" in order to hustle credulous heirs (*Enquiry*, p. 93).[21] Fielding's interesting claim that if the poor cannot achieve the status of, say, the tradesman, they would just as soon starve underscores what is for him the power of the urge to imitate over even basic biological needs.

It is the significatory instability of all classes of people in this period that generates what might be regarded as a pervasive epistemological malaise in Fielding's work. As he writes in "An Essay on the Knowledge of the Characters of Men,"

> Thus while the crafty and designing Part of Mankind, consulting only their own separate Advantage, endeavor to maintain one constant Imposition on others, the whole World becomes a vast Masquerade, where the greatest Part appear disguised under false Vizors and Habits; a very few only shewing their own Faces, who become, by so doing, the Astonishment and Ridicule of all the rest.[22]

Fielding's use of the figure of the masquerade to describe a universal opacity of motive and character evokes the sartorial burlesque that vizors and habits were meant to perform. Describing the cross-class dressing that went on in both directions at the masquerade, Terry

Castle writes, "the provocative travesties of rank and occupation intimated a potentially disarming fluidity in the realm of social circumstance, as critics of the masquerade . . . were obsessively to point out."[23] This social fluidity came from the new energies of commercialism, which rendered older status categories unstable.[24] Indeed, England's transformation into a commercial society and the power of money to level distinctions between the various ranks were the social ills around which the Opposition organized its platform, complaining of a general moral degeneracy in the nation that originated in Walpole's court.

In the Preface to the *Enquiry*, giving a brief history of "the Commonality" from feudal times to his own, Fielding claims that "the Introduction of Trade"

> hath . . . given a new Face to the whole Nation, hath in a great measure subverted the former State of Affairs, and hath almost totally changed the Manners, Customs, and Habits of the People, more especially of the lower Sort. (*Enquiry*, pp. 69–70)

The image of the nation's "new face" recalls the "false Vizors and Habits" worn by people in the "Essay on the Knowledge of the Characters of Men," and the assertion there that only "a very few . . . [shew] their own Faces." The social emulation engendered by the spread of trade generates a transformation of the lower classes into their own diametrical opposite: "the Narrowness of their Fortune is changed into Wealth; the Simplicity of their Manners into Craft; their Frugality into Luxury; their Humility into Pride, and their Subjection into Equality" (*Enquiry*, p. 70). And among them, robbers are the most impudent of imitators:

> There is at this Time a great Gang of Rogues, whose Number falls little short of a Hundred, who are incorporated in one Body, have Officers and a Treasury; and have reduced Theft and Robbery into a regular System. There are of this Society of Men who appear in all Disguises, and mix in most Companies. (*Enquiry*, p. 76)

The affectation of these rogues makes them organize into societies that burlesque government, and allows them access to all parts of society.

Fielding is attacking an explosion of cross-class imitation in English society brought on by the spread of trade—an imitation that directly threatens the property-owning classes: he wonders that "a Nation so jealous of her Liberties . . . should tamely and quietly support the Invasion of her Properties by a few of the lowest and vilest among us" (*Enquiry*, p. 76). And the *Enquiry*'s solution to the problem of the peripatetic, robbing, and emulous poor is their discipline into a classifiable and productive work force.[25] Along with such measures as severer laws against vagrancy, the limitation of wages and the reform of workhouses, this transformation entails, most salient to the Preface, the exclusion of the poor from public places, or "Temples of Idleness" (*Enquiry*, p. 82).

Fielding is speaking, then, for the property-owning classes who regarded cross-class imitation on the part of the poor as a disastrous social problem, and who regarded the diversions of the people as threats to morality and industry. He in fact holds two contradictory positions: if the cross-class imitation of the poor in social reality generates anxiety, we have seen that the burlesque, the *representation* of such imitation, generates too much *pleasure*—the intense bodily pleasure that, like the diversions of the people that need to be "limited and restrained," needs to be smoothed into the "more rational and useful Pleasure" of the comic. Fielding's new art form not only arises simultaneously with the exclusion of the poor from traditional and collective sites of entertainment; by containing cross-class imitation it also effects a similar discipline in the realm of the aesthetic.

This discipline is mostly symbolic; the Preface might be regarded as a cultural fantasy that one could appropriate the fun and energy of the burlesque while at the same time controlling the class aspirations that it entails. But when we take into account the shift from the aural/visual to the literary announced by the Preface, the discipline it enacts appears slightly more material. Not only would this shift have caused a quieting of the mode of reception of Fielding's work; it would also probably have changed the constitution of his actual audience. For we might assume that a proportion of the apprentices and servants who attended his theatrical works were unable to read, and that those who could would have had some diffi-

culty getting access to the novel as a form of diversion. Richard
Altick argues that until the first cheap reprint series of standard authors in the 1770s, books could only be purchased by the relatively
wealthy; and J. Paul Hunter suggests that while "the young and am-
bitious—the ones most likely to have found the means to learn to
read," passed books around, getting access to books required effort.[26]
When I call this shift disciplinary, I do not mean to suggest that it
had much impact on the lives of those servants and apprentices in
Fielding's audience. I mean simply that Fielding's new art form is
meant to weed out certain kinds of audience as well as certain kinds
of reception.

At the same time, though, the Preface feels anxious about its
disciplinary effects. While it explicitly uses as a precedent the Aristotelian link between comedy and "Persons of inferiour Rank," it
labors uneasily to define the circumstances under which it could be
morally acceptable for a middle-class and classical audience to find
the poor an object of laughter. I want to return here to the Preface's
claim that the burlesque and the comic represent the very epitome
of difference. One does not have to look very hard to discover that
the category of the burlesque is in fact constitutive of the comic.
Using "the Ridiculous" as a synonym for "the Comic," Fielding
writes, "The only source of the true Ridiculous (as it appears to me)
is Affectation." While this reified character trait is clearly regarded as
a human universal, Fielding's primary examples of affectation concern the specific social phenomenon of poor people imitating the
rich:

> Surely he hath a very ill-framed Mind, who can look on Ugliness, In-
> firmity, or Poverty, as ridiculous in themselves: nor do I believe any
> Man living who meets a dirty Fellow riding through the Streets in a
> Cart, is struck with an Idea of the Ridiculous from it; but if he should
> see the same Figure descend from his Coach and Six, or bolt from his
> Chair with his Hat under his Arm, he would then begin to laugh, and
> with justice. In the same manner, were we to enter a poor House, and
> behold a wretched Family shivering with Cold and languishing with
> Hunger, it would not incline us to Laughter, (at least we must have
> very diabolical Natures, if it would:) but should we discover there a
> Grate, instead of Coals, adorned with Flowers, empty Plate or China

> Dishes on the Side-board, or any other Affectation of Riches and
> Finery either on their Persons or in their Furniture; we might then in-
> deed be excused, for ridiculing so fantastical an Appearance. (*JA*, p. 9)

The poor render themselves ridiculous in this passage by appropri-
ating, burlesque-like, the manners of the highest. Elsewhere, in the
"Essay on the Knowledge of the Characters of Men," Fielding describes affectation, the source of the ridiculous, as an actual burlesque actor:

> [A]s Affectation always over-acts her Part, it fares with her as with a
> Farcical Actor on the Stage, whose monstrous over-done Grimaces
> are sure to catch the Applause of an insensible Audience; while the
> truest and finest Strokes of Nature, represented by a judicious and just
> Actor, pass unobserved and disregarded.[27]

Characterized by excess and monstrosity, and contrasted to that kind
of representation, which like the comic, confines itself to a "just"
imitation of nature, affectation appears here to be synonymous with
the burlesque.

   So while the Preface explicitly states its agenda as an imperative
to transcend the burlesque by producing its opposite, Fielding's
theory in fact blurs the distinction between the two, and the binary
opposition collapses. In this way it follows what Stallybrass and
White describe as a recurrent pattern in the representation of low-
Others: "what is *socially* peripheral is . . . frequently *symbolically* central. . . . The low-Other is despised and denied at the level of political organization and social being whilst it is instrumentally constitutive of the shared imaginary repertoires of the dominant culture."[28]
If the recreation of the lower classes is repudiated in the Preface,
Fielding's category of the comic nevertheless requires the burlesque
symbolically. While the ridiculous is celebrated as a more rational
and abstract kind of pleasure than the burlesque, Fielding's aesthetic
tract does not easily relinquish the latter category. Indeed, the burlesque is referred to with nostalgia, as Fielding casts a fond backward
eye on the mode that "contributes more to exquisite Mirth and
Laughter than any other," that "purge[s] away Spleen, Melancholy
and ill Affections," and that fills audiences with "Good-Humour
and Benevolence" (p. 5). When we consider how freighted good-

humour and benevolence are as moral qualities in Fielding's writing, qualities that lead to charity and good works, we can appreciate the utopian possibilities of the burlesque.

Meanwhile, although it is explicitly characterized as rational and useful, the category of the ridiculous in fact carries within it contradiction and ambivalence. Fielding claims that the moral ambiguity of this category stems from some writers' misunderstanding of the generic term Ridiculous:

> Nor will some Explanation of this Word be thought impertinent by the Reader, if he considers how wonderfully it hath been mistaken, even by Writers who have profess'd it: for to what but such a Mistake, can we attribute the many Attempts to ridicule the blackest Villanies; and what is yet worse, the most dreadful Calamities? (*JA*, p. 7)

Arguing, oddly, that sadism could result from a generic or semantic error, Fielding chastises the author who, laboring under such misapprehension, writes "*the Comedy of Nero, with the merry Incident of ripping up his Mother's Belly*" or who attempts "to expose the Miseries of Poverty and Distress to Ridicule" (*JA*, p. 7). Similarly, in the discussion of affectation I have just quoted, he alludes to people who might have "very diabolical Natures" and be inclined to laughter at "Ugliness, Infirmity, or Poverty" or at "a wretched Family shivering with Cold and languishing with Hunger" (*JA*, p. 9). These fiendish figures, whose lurid presence interrupts the measured prose of the Preface, are the index of the text's anxiety about the potentially inherent immorality of comic literary representations of the poor.[29]

I have cited Fielding's claim that "The only source of the true Ridiculous . . . is affectation," and argued that like the burlesque, affectation refers to cross-class imitation. Indeed, it is through the mediating term of *affectation* that the burlesque enters the realm of the ridiculous. We may regard *affectation* as the name for that which gives the ridiculous moral sanction: when affectation is added to a pathetic spectacle it makes laughter justifiable: "But should we discover there . . . any . . . Affectation of Riches and Finery either on their Persons or in their Furniture, we might then indeed be excused, for ridiculing so fantastical an Appearance" (*JA*, p. 9).[30] Like the joke in Freud, affectation "*will evade restrictions and open sources of pleasure that have become inaccessible.*"[31] Rather than regarding it as an intrinsic characteristic of the ridiculous, as Fielding polemically argues, we may regard affectation, which is none other than the burlesque moment, or the moment of cross-class imitation, as that part of the ridiculous designed to mitigate its own potential excesses. The restriction evaded by the admixture of affectation is taking pleasure in reading about the poor, as if literary comic representation were inherently a tendentious act. For the Preface to *Joseph Andrews* suggests that it *is*—that as a social practice, the work of novel-making entails both the appropriation of the poor and the containment of their mimetic voices.

II. Literacy and Desire: From 'Shamela' to 'Joseph Andrews'

I want now to turn to the actual work Fielding does in maintaining the novel as a high-cultural realm, by examining the fate of lower-class literacy in the transition from *Shamela* to *Joseph Andrews*. Early readings of *Shamela* focused upon the ways in which Fielding uses the servant community in the Booby household as an allegory for Walpole's administration and coterie, whom the Opposition attacked as uncultured, mercenary, and corrupt,[32] and more generally, upon what Michael McKeon calls "the culturally fraught effrontery of the rise of the undeserving," represented in such diverse figures as Pamela, Colley Cibber, and Conyers Middleton.[33] These readings argue that *Shamela* derides not only the politics, but also the language and literature of the emergent bourgeoisie. But by concentrating upon the ideological struggles over culture and literary representation waged by two different sections of the ruling class—the emergent bourgeoisie and the landed gentry—criticism of *Shamela* has often sidestepped the fact that in Fielding's parody servants not only function as an allegory of the middle classes, but also stand in for the lower classes, of which they occupied the highest position. As Robbins has argued, it is through servants that the English novel has tended to represent the vast variety of working people and poor.[34]

In their capacity as what J. Jean Hecht has called "cultural intermediaries," between the elite and the lower classes, as well as between the country and the city, servants in the eighteenth century were an often volatile marker of class instability. Their mobility between classes of people and their access to their masters' and mistresses' lives enabled them to spread throughout the social system everything from clothes to speech, moral values, and political ideas.[35] Moreover, along with women and apprentices, servants stood at the boundary of the literacy/non-literacy divide, and as such were a particular source of anxiety to the eighteenth-century ruling class, which was acutely aware of the ideology-forming powers of the printed word. This section argues, then, that if *Shamela* is about bad bourgeois writing, it is also about the lower class's very access to writing. In *Shamela* lower-class literacy is aggravatedly eroticized and utopian, and it is an important project of the novel to defuse this obsession, to "decathect" literacy.

A theatrical work of Fielding's, *The Grub-Street Opera*, prepares us for the problem of servant literacy later aggravated in *Shamela*. At the end of Fielding's play, the servants, who, like those of the Booby household, almost obligatorily represent Walpole and his supporters, quit the service of the Apshinkens, singing comic songs of sharing and community. Robin, the Walpole figure, sings of the dissolution of class hierarchy and private property:

> I once as your butler did cheat you,
> For myself I will set up now;
> If you come to my house I will treat you
> With a pig of your own sow.

And in a scenario reminiscent of *Pamela*, Master Owen Apshinken, the son of a gentleman, marries Molly, the daughter of his father's tenant, who celebrates the power of love to transcend class hierarchy:

> If I too high aspire,
> 'Tis love that plumes my wings,
> Love makes a clown a squire,
> Would make a squire a king.[36]

The servants in *The Grub-Street Opera* may represent Walpole's administration, and the tone of the ending may be qualified by irony, but the servants' power to level class distinctions and to imagine alternative communities is clearly celebrated.

And significantly, Fielding's play has a kind of letters fetish. Throughout the play the servants are haunted by "letters" and "writing": William says of Robin, "Sure letters run strangely in his head!" while Robin exclaims, "Surprising! Sure some little writing devil lurks in the house."[37] It is that little writing devil, and the misunderstandings it occasions, that set in motion the plot culminating in a utopian transcendence of class hierarchy.

If in the theatrical work upward mobility may still be represented as comic and utopian, in Fielding's literary burlesque the servants' aspirations take on a more sinister tone, a tone apparently sinister enough for Hugh Amory, with an attitude characteristic of much criticism of *Shamela*, to read it as "a lurid tale of carnal freedom, spiritual corruption, and the subversion of all human society."[38] Accordingly, the first act of *Shamela* is to defuse the scandal of Pamela's literacy. According to McKeon, so far does Pamela inhabit the liminal status of cultural mediator that she is, in his witty metaphor, "'beached' at the top of the hierarchy of domestic service"; the prefatory letters to *Pamela* have to account for her "polite Education," explaining it as a result of her living in an "elegant Family."[39] In *Shamela*, Pamela's upper-class pretensions and capabilities are "corrected" in a visually immediate way. The first thing we know about Shamela, when she asks her mother to "commodate [her] with a ludgin,"[40] is that she cannot spell. Fielding marks her as a servant through the traditional orthographical markers of semiliteracy, although he drops this quickly, confining his representation of her class status to spicy epithets and saucy snaps of the fingers. What is happening is a fairly crude domestication of Pamela's dangerous capability, though the text slightly disguises the crudity of this operation by implicitly suggesting that Shamela is in fact *smarter* than Pamela—by presenting her as the ideological construct now known as the smart cookie.

If Fielding takes away Pamela's polite education when he renders her Shamela, one figure in the text takes over Pamela's role of cultural intermediary: Parson Williams. His tone at once intimate and pedantic, Williams functions as Shamela's mentor, giving her his version of "good books," lecturing her about religious matters, and, most famously, teaching her to "write in the present tense" (S, p. 313). Shamela echoes what Squire B says about Pamela's writing—"I . . . am quite overcome with your charming manner of Writing"[41]— when she says of one of Williams' letters, "You find, Mamma, what a charming way he hath of writing" (S, p. 318). In *Shamela*, then, what we might call the scandal of Pamela's literacy—her amazing facility with standard English—is transferred onto a clergyman, who takes over Pamela's role of cultural intermediary, and whose literacy goes hand in hand with class resentment; Williams contemptuously says of the squire, for example, "let such wretches know, they cannot hate, detest, and despise us, half so much as we do them" (S, p. 318). Indeed, one might go so far as to argue that the energetic attack on the clergy in *Shamela*, manifested most vividly by Parson Williams' disproportionately large role, is an effect of this displacement.

While Parson Williams is a poacher, a rake, and, in the words of Parson Oliver, "a busy fellow, intermeddling with the private affairs of his patron" (S, p. 338), he also represents an ideal of masculine sexuality. Despite his cynicism and worldliness, he is the love match of Fielding's Material Girl, the husband who is, in his own words, "the object of your love, and to satisfy your desire" (S, p. 334). Significantly, it is his very learning that Shamela finds sexually exciting. She writes of one of his letters, "It is, I think the finest I ever received from that charming man, and full of a great deal of learning," and adds rapturously, "*O! What a brave thing it is to be a scholard, and to be able to talk Latin!*" (S, p. 317). Walter J. Ong writes that "the older idea of the grammarian as a totally learned man . . . is curiously enshrined today in our word 'glamor,' a Scottish by-form of 'grammar,' meaning originally vast learning, deep or mysterious lore, and thus the power to enchant or cast a spell and hence to 'charm' us."[42] Williams' learning is linked to his sexual glamour in the same way that Booby's vulgarity is linked to his sexual incompetence. Shamela punningly joins the two terms by the word "qualifications" when she says "*O what regard men who marry widows should have to the qualifications of their former husbands!*" (S, p. 330). Similarly, describing one of

Booby's attempts on Shamela, Mrs. Jervis expresses a delicate disdain
for the lack of cultivation he exhibits:

> As soon as my master saw her, he immediately threw his arms round
> her neck, and smothered her with kisses (for indeed he hath but very
> little to say for himself to a woman). He swore that Pamela was an ugly
> slut (pardon, dear Madam, the coarseness of the expression) compared
> to such divine excellence. (S, p. 313)

Booby's having "very little to say for himself" combines two kinds
of incompetence, his unprepossessing sexual technique mirroring
his linguistic vulgarity.

Even though *Shamela* is explicitly a polemic against upward mobility, then, in Parson Williams upward mobility, through the acquisition of cultural capital, is eroticized. And if he constitutes one direction into which the powerful overdetermined literacy of Pamela
is diffused, in *Joseph Andrews* his own learning is further diffused. One
of the novel's main projects is to detach literacy from the eroticism it
produces in *Shamela*, or to decathect literacy. Some minor parallels
between them suggest that in some ways Williams functions as a trial
run for Joseph Andrews. Booby complains that Williams' family was
"raised from the dunghill" by his family (S, p. 333), and in the mock-
lineage given Joseph, the narrator supposes "for Argument's sake"
that he "sprung up, according to the modern Phrase, out of a
Dunghill" (*JA*, p. 21). Williams' "pure round cherry cheeks" recall
Joseph's ruddy cheeks: "his Beard was only rough on his Chin and
upper Lip; but his Cheeks, in which his Blood glowed, were over-
spread with a thick Down" (*JA*, p. 38). Moreoever, Shamela's exclamation "O! what a devilish thing it is, for a woman to be obliged to
go to bed to a spindle shanked young squire she doth not like, when
there is a jolly parson in the same house she is fond of!" (S, p. 333)
may be compared to the narrator's contrast of Joseph to "the spindle-
shanked Beaus and Petit Maîtres of the Age" in *Joseph Andrews* (*JA*,
p. 194). The erotic appeal given Williams in his merry countenance
and thick legs will appear in Joseph, who, unlike Williams, has very
modest educational attainments.

Joseph is represented as having a talent for reading and writing,

but when Parson Adams asks him "if he did not extremely regret the
want of a liberal Education," he replies,

> "he hoped he had profited somewhat better from the Books he had
> read, than to lament his Condition in this World. That for his part, he
> was perfectly content with the State to which he was called, that
> he should endeavor to improve his Talent, which was all required of
> him, but not repine at his own Lot, nor envy those of his Betters."
> (*JA*, pp. 24–25)

Joseph's docile lack of desire for upward mobility is manifested in
his reading of such "good Books" as the Bible and *Whole Duty of
Man*, books which contrast with the "good books" Williams encourages Shamela to read, such as Whitefield's sermons (*S*, pp. 311,
327). Moreover, one of the novel's first acts is to deny Joseph "In-
struction in *Latin* . . . by which means he might be qualified for a
higher Station than that of a Footman" (*JA*, p. 26). The degree of
literacy that Joseph has, then, is immediately domesticated; imagining Latin as the engine of social mobility, the novel concertedly refuses him that mode of literacy that would enable a rise in station.

If Joseph is the character into which Parson Williams' erotic appeal gets translated in *Joseph Andrews*, Parson Adams, "an excellent
Scholar . . . a perfect Master of the *Greek* and *Latin* languages" (*JA*,
p. 22), takes on Williams' classical education. And one of Adams' major formal functions in the novel is to defer the erotic union of
Joseph and Fanny, a deferral that makes possible the final establishment of correct identities and class positions.

> They . . . had conceived a very early liking for each other, which had
> grown to such a degree of Affection, that Mr. *Adams* had with much
> ado prevented them from marrying; and persuaded them to wait, 'till a
> few Years Service and Thrift had a little improved their Experience,
> and enabled them to live comfortably together. (*JA*, p. 48)

The guileless Fanny is uncharacteristically coy about mentioning
Joseph when she first meets Adams: " 'La! Mr. *Adams*,' said she, 'what
is Mr. *Joseph* to me? I am sure I never had any thing to say to him,
but as one Fellow-Servant might to another' " (*JA*, p. 144). When,
after the lovers' long-deferred reunion, Joseph impulsively asks the

parson to marry them, "*Adams* rebuked him for his Request," because the banns have not yet been published (*JA,* p. 160). Significantly, that reunion occurs under the sign of the destruction of writing: Fanny faints when she recognizes Joseph's voice from another room, at which point "*Adams* jumped up, flung his *Aeschylus* into the Fire, and fell a roaring to the People of the House for Help" (*JA,* p. 154). Indeed, learned writing is divorced from eroticism in *Joseph Andrews* to the extent that it becomes its very antithesis. In a trope as natural and familiar to us (and the eighteenth century) as the absent-minded professor, the esoteric pursuits of the hapless scholar are represented as comically irrelevant to real-life matters of love and reunion. There is a sense in which writing is destroyed because the novel wants to privilege the immediacy of the erotic over it. I want to suggest, though, the ideological nature of this natural-seeming figure, by emphasizing that the divorce between literacy and eroticism occurs as a solution to a union between them—in Pamela first, then in Parson Williams—perceived as a threat to the stability of class hierarchy. That is, the celebration of the erotic reunion between the two servants has as its precondition their disqualification from literacy.

And indeed, the same kind of splitting between literacy and eroticism occurs, even more radically, in the female characters. In *Joseph Andrews* Shamela is split into two figures: Slipslop, who "professe[s] great regard for . . . Learning" and is "a mighty Affecter of hard Words" (*JA,* pp. 25–26), and the new heroine, "poor Fanny," who takes on the problematic of "modest beauty,"[43] and of whom the very first description says the following:

> poor *Fanny* could neither write nor read, nor could she be prevailed upon to transmit the Delicacies of her tender and chaste Passion, by the Hands of an Amanuensis. (*JA,* p. 49)

The text insists that Fanny be not only unable to read and write, but unable to profit from writing in any way. It explains Fanny's radical disqualification from literacy as an effect of her feminine modesty: she cannot "be prevailed upon to transmit the Delicacies of her tender and chaste Passion, by the Hands of an Amanuensis." Writing, in other words, corrupts and renders unchaste female sexual desire: that is why Fanny's "Passion," as though it were her body being handled, would go by—or perhaps through—the amanuensis's *hands* rather than *hand*, in the sense of handwriting. While in the case of the male characters literacy is linked to sexual prowess, in the female characters written representation compromises and contaminates chaste sexuality. As Parson Oliver says of Shamela's authorship of *Pamela*,

> though we do not imagine her the author of the narrative itself, yet we must suppose the instructions were given by her, as well as the reward, to the composer. Who that is . . . I shall leave you to guess from that *Ciceronian* eloquence, with which the work abounds; and that excellent knack of making every character amiable, which he lays his hands on. (*S*, p. 307)

Here the text simultaneously refuses Shamela the ability to write and suggests that she is corrupt because of her association with writing; moreover, it figures the writing of the amanuensis as the eager laying on of hands.

In contrast to Fanny, in whom the absence of the letter is linked with chastity, we have Slipslop, Shamela's other double, in whom an avid semiliteracy is linked with a hideous corporality and tainted sexuality. Like Shamela, who has made a "slip with Parson Williams" and had a baby, Slipslop "made a small Slip in her Youth, [and] had continued a good Maid ever since." Now menopausal,

> She imagined, that by so long a Self-denial, she had not only made amends for the small Slip of her Youth above hinted at: but had likewise laid up a Quantity of Merit to excuse any future Failings. In a word, she resolved to give a loose to her amorous Inclinations, and pay off the Debt of Pleasure which she found she owed herself, as fast as possible (*JA*, p. 32).

Like Shamela, Slipslop espouses a quantitative approach to virtue: because the value of her virginity is commodified and therefore relative, she does not recognize the irreducibility of the "slip," which is why she can "continue[] a good Maid" even after ceasing to be a good maid. She is someone who in our own time would undoubt-

edly be characterized as having a "lifestyle." Slipslop has "some Respect for *Adams*; she professed great Regard for his Learning, and
would frequently dispute with him on Points of Theology" (*JA*,
p. 25). She is also the novel's most codified figure of cross-class imitation:

> The Lady . . . desired to know what she meant by that extraordinary
> degree of Freedom in which she thought proper to indulge her
> Tongue. "Freedom!" says *Slipslop*, "I don't know what you call Free-
> dom, Madam; Servants have Tongues as well as their Mistresses." "Yes,
> and saucy ones too," answered the Lady: "but I assure you I shall bear
> no such Impertinence." "Impertinence! I don't know that I am imper-
> tinent," says *Slipslop*. (*JA*, p. 43)

Slipslop echoes her mistress's words while inflecting them with in-
dignation, all the while disavowing any association with or knowledge of rebellion ("I don't know what you call Freedom, Madam").

In Fanny, then, the absence of writing is linked with chastity,
while the figure of Slipslop combines the letter with its concomitant
social rebelliousness and sexual promiscuity. These associations suggest that female sexual corruption inheres in the letter. Shamela and
Slipslop's "slip" is literacy itself; in *Shamela* writing is a kind of artificial ruse in the western-metaphysical sense described by Derrida. As
Shamela's mother says to Lucretia Jervis, "I received the favour of
your letter, and I find you have not forgot your usual poluteness,
which you learned when you was in keeping with a lord" (*S*, p. 316).
Her malapropism *poluteness* combines politeness—propriety of
writing style—with a pollution linked to the way she got it, by sexual access to the upper classes. One of the projects of *Shamela* and
Joseph Andrews is to defuse the powerful moral charge of the
Richardsonian concept of "virtue," which means female chastity;
Shamela's putative chastity is seen to be fake ("vartue"), while in
Joseph Andrews the very definition of virtue as chastity is ridiculed by
its being upheld by a man. I would suggest that if in Richardson
"virtue" expresses itself as chastity, in *Joseph Andrews* it expresses itself
as illiteracy. Lower-class illiteracy, that is, takes on the moral weight
of chastity.

In the female servants of *Joseph Andrews*, then, Fielding deca-

thects literacy by attaching it, in the case of Slipslop, to an ugly and
sexually compromised body, while making both Fanny's virtue and
her erotic appeal in some sense an effect of her illiteracy. But while
the novel dissociates literacy from eroticism, it does not dissociate it
from the body altogether; rather, it dissociates it from the erotic
body and attaches it to a grotesque one. Slipslop is the vestigial fragment of the burlesque in the novel. We recall that describing "burlesque painting," in the Preface to *Joseph Andrews*, Fielding describes
it as painting "a Man with a Nose, or any other Feature of a prepos-
terous Size, or to expose him in some absurd or monstrous Attitude" (*JA*, p. 7). Slipslop, with "her Nose . . . rather too large, and
her Eyes too little," her pimples, limp, and large breasts (*JA*, p. 32), is
a programmatic exemplification of the burlesque. Meanwhile, Parson Adams' corporality is such a major source of the carnivalesque
in the novel that Fielding feels a need to apologize in the Preface,
asking his readers to "excuse me, notwithstanding the low Adventures in which he is engaged" (*JA*, p. 11). At the end of the episode
in which the poet and the player kidnap Fanny, Adams is represented as having risen

> in such a violent Hurry, that he had on neither Breeches nor Stock-
> ings . . . He had on his torn Cassock, and his Great-Coat; so did a
> small Strip of white, or rather whitish Linen appear below that; to
> which we may add the several Colours which appeared on his Face,
> where a long Piss-burnt Beard, served to retain the Liquor of the
> Stone Pot, and that of a blacker hue which distilled from the Mop.
> (*JA*, p. 270)

An earlier carnivalesque episode in an inn results in Adams' receiving
a pan full of hog's blood in the face (*JA*, pp. 119–20). The pleasure
of these scenes comes from the congruence of the scholarly Adams
and blood and piss—or the juxtaposition of writing and the burlesque.

While the figure of Slipslop may suggest that corporality is a
way of representing *false* learning—that is, the deformation of her
body functions as a comically physical manifestation of the deformation of language—the figure of Adams suggests that in the logic
of Fielding's project a burlesque corporality goes along with learn-

ing in general. The most obvious commonsense effect of rendering literacy burlesque is to show the pressures of the low upon an ideal of classical learning: Slipslop's learning is "exposed" as vulgar and pretentious, while Adams' status as a butt of low jokes underscores the lowness of the world in which a classical ideal is struggling for authority. To say this is to remain within the realm of that Fielding criticism that reads him as satirizing modern bourgeois and Grub-Street aesthetic practices. But this pattern must also be read in the context of the novel's concerted disqualification of its lower-class characters from literacy. One might argue that the classical may have contact with the popular only on the condition that the lower classes not desire access to it; or, conversely, that the lower classes may be rendered illiterate by the novel only in conjunction with the compensatory gesture of making their potential object of desire look ludicrous and unworthy of attainment. My claim is that the figure of Adams—the scholar mired in the world's muck, whose quixotic character makes him both the moral center of the novel and the locus of a particular kind of realism—depends upon the construction of a desire cleansed of literacy, and a literacy cleansed of desire.

❦

In Fielding's well-known parody of Aaron Hill's fulsome prefatory material to the second edition of *Pamela*—a parody that barely had to alter the original—Parson Tickletext exclaims of Richardson's novel, "If I lay the book down it comes after me. . . . It hath witchcraft in every page of it" (S, p. 305). Calling the novel a "little, unpretending, mild Triumph of *Nature*," as opposed to "the false, empty *Pomp* of the Poets,"[44] Hill's preface endlessly reiterated *Pamela*'s lack of artifice. And so bewitching is the immediacy of Richardson's prose style to Tickletext that in an erotic haze, he confuses a character with a real person: "Oh! . . . methinks I see Pamela at this instant, with all the pride of ornament cast off" (S, p. 305).[45] The decathecting of literacy and desire in the transition from *Shamela* to *Joseph Andrews* occurs within a general framework in which reading subjects are figured as desiring subjects. This section elaborates that framework, arguing that Fanny, Fielding's rewriting of Shamela—his *non*-writing Shamela—stands at the center of *Joseph Andrews'* anxieties about its own representational practice. In a written work that seeks to divorce writing from eroticism, the figure of Fanny can elicit desire because she is illiterate (for if we were desiring a literate woman, we would experience the indignity of desiring Slipslop). Indeed, it is her very disqualification from being a *subject* of literacy that makes her delectable as an *object* of literacy. Under the pressure of that contradiction, the novel constantly worries over her status as a literary image.

While the novel actually describes her body at length, the figure of Fanny often evokes ambivalence about the image, as though the novel hesitated to write her. Mourning the loss of the piece of gold that is Fanny's token of love, for example, Joseph reminds himself, "*[B]ut surely*, Fanny, *I want nothing to remind me of thee. I have thy dear Image in my Heart, and no Villain can ever tear it thence*" (*JA*, p. 58). Like the Jewish God, Fanny—insofar as she is a "dear Image"—is an image to be sublimated and internalized rather than represented.[46] Indeed, at times the novel seems not to want her to be an image at all. One might read that curious problem of the beginning of the novel—the fact that the narrator insists that Joseph has no erotic attachment, only to introduce Fanny belatedly, explaining this contradiction with a facetious comment about the novel's opacity (*JA*, p. 48)—as a formal hitch symptomatic of the novel's hesitancy over writing Fanny. That extended deferral of the sight of her body is characteristic of the novel's treatment of Fanny, and so is a self-conscious rhetoric of hesitation. At the end of the novel, describing her undressing for the bridal bed, the narrator exclaims "How, Reader, shall I give thee an adequate Idea of this lovely young Creature!" (*JA*, p. 343). This rhetorical exclamation of her hyperbolic beauty, and its conventional claim about the incommensurability between the beauty of her body and the power of words to represent it adequately, may be reanimated in the context of the novel's more general hesitation to describe Fanny.

When Fanny finally does enter the novel, she does so in the dark, in a long scene that plays extensively on the anxieties and comic misunderstandings resulting from her and Adams' mutual lack of recognition. They eventually recognize one another not through sight, but by hearing each other's voices: "Sure I should know that Voice," Fanny says of Adams, and he replies, "There is something also in your Voice, which persuades me I have heard it before" (*JA*, p. 143). Not only is her voice emphasized by the novel, but as that reciprocal recognition suggests, Fanny tends to recognize others by their voices. The reunion scene with Joseph, for example, also occurs within the context of voice, Fanny recognizing him from the song he sings from another room:

> *Adams* had been ruminating all this Time on a Passage in *Aeschylus*, without attending in the least to the Voice, tho' one of the most melodious that ever was heard; when casting his Eyes on *Fanny*, he cried out, "Bless us, you look extremely pale." (*JA*, p. 154)

Jill Campbell has suggested that the novel associates Joseph "with the feminine realm of ghostly presence or voice"[47]; this passage urges us to read that stress on voice as a phonocentric repudiation of writing. Adams cannot hear the voice because he is, typically, ruminating on writing; Fanny's radical illiteracy, on the other hand, makes her particularly suited to be moved by voices.

The novel's hesitation to describe Fanny and its stress on her association with voice reach their densest interaction at the moment immediately before Fielding first describes Fanny, where he issues the following warning:

> [I]ndeed, Reader, if thou art of an amorous Hue, I advise thee to skip over the next Paragraph; which to render our History perfect, we are obliged to set down, humbly hoping, that we may escape the Fate of *Pygmalion*: for if it should happen to us or to thee to be struck with this Picture, we should be perhaps in as helpless a Condition as *Narcissus*; and might say to ourselves, *Quod petis est nusquam*. (*JA*, p. 152)

While, as I will show, the Pygmalion story is thematically the very opposite of the Narcissus story, Fielding's syntax sets them up as in fact the same myth, or at the very least, logical extensions of one another. He does this with the word "for": we hope we will escape the fate of Pygmalion, *for* that would make us as helpless as Narcissus. The passage's syntactic obscuring of the differences between the

two myths is part of its strategy: it tries to lead the reader impercep-
tibly out of the realm of Pygmalion and into that of Narcissus.

The myths Fielding playfully evokes are both crucially about
the desire elicited by representations. Ovid describes Pygmalion's
creation of Galatea in the same terms—"So does his art conceal his
art"[48]—as Aaron Hill describes Richardson's style. Like the prefatory material to *Pamela*, the Pygmalion story is a celebration of the
aliveness of the representation, and the satisfaction of the desire
elicited by it. But meanwhile Fielding's preface to his description of
Fanny has slid from the story of Pygmalion—the story of the rep-
resentation-becoming-the-thing-itself—to the story of Narcissus,
which is about the impossibility of union, the aggravated and irre-
ducible *image*-ness of the image. As Ovid says of Narcissus, "He
loves an unsubstantial hope and thinks that substance which is only
shadow."[49] This tricky slide from one myth to another also effects
the disappearance of the woman's body from the scene—a disappearance enacted not only in the shift from Pygmalion to Narcissus,
but also within the Narcissus story itself, which is predicated upon
Echo grieving so much her body disappears, leaving her all voice:

> Only her voice and her bones remain: then, only voice. . . . She hides
> in woods and is seen no more upon the mountain-sides; but all may
> hear her, for voice, and voice alone, still lives in her.[50]

One might claim that the passage's climactic shift out of English into
Latin is still another way it makes the figure of the woman vanish; for
as Ong points out, as a cultural institution Latin entailed a complex
masculinist ethos, and the entry of women into the schools in the
eighteenth and nineteenth centuries coincided with its decline.[51]

While we might, as Fielding certainly did, identify Richardson's writing style with the story of Pygmalion, in this passage the
representation of the female body occurs, paradoxically, within a
fantasy of its disappearance and its relegation to the ghostly realm of
voice. And when the narrator warns us that looking at Fanny we
may be prompted to say, like Narcissus, "*Quod petis est nusquam*"—
"What you seek is nowhere"—he is articulating a danger which we
may take to be in fact a wish: a wish that the erotic object be in fact

nowhere, an "unsubstantial hope, a shadow." Not only does *Joseph Andrews* will the lower-class woman to remain within the realm of the aural rather than the literary, but it wishes that the desire elicited by her image could be diffused by calling attention to its ontological status as pure representation. If reading is to generate desire—a phenomenon that much of the novel tries to negate—Fielding emphasizes that such desire cannot be realized, that its object is nowhere. While this is a general lesson about the novel, I would argue that it is most crucially aimed at the lower-class readers whose sexual desire is figured as indistinguishable from their desire for upward mobility.

But I do not want to read Fielding as concerned in any simple way with preserving class privilege at the expense of the poor. For the disciplinary gestures of *Joseph Andrews* come along with other kinds of gestures that we might call democratizing: not only bringing the classical into contact with the popular, but also imagining the upward mobility of the servant characters. McKeon has suggested that the novel qualifies its own egalitarian ending by making it a function of family romance, the restoration of lost familial relations: therefore, "what 'happens' at the end of *Joseph Andrews* (and *Tom Jones*) is less a social than an epistemological event; not upward mobility but . . . the acquisition of knowledge."[52] The potential social instability generated by a rise in station, then, is tempered by the revelation that Joseph was in fact *always already* gentle. I am suggesting a similar mitigation of the upward mobility fantasy in the novel's decathecting of literacy. By decathecting literacy in the transition from burlesque to novel, Fielding creates an egalitarian fantasy of social mobility while wishing that fantasy inaccessible to those perhaps most eager for it.

Such a double and contradictory move comes not without its affective costs; the intensity of Fielding's ambivalence over lower-class literacy pushes this most genial of novels into a kind of melancholy. The elegaic mode of Fielding's comic novels has been discussed most recently in Campbell's compelling article about *Joseph Andrews'* portrayal of gender, recognition, and mortal loss, " 'The Exact Picture of his Mother': Recognizing Joseph Andrews." Campbell argues that Joseph's implication in femininity—embattled chastity, for ex-

ample, and the "feminine realm of ghostly presence or voice"—links
him to what Fielding figures as an essentially feminine "hope for reunion rather than resignation to absence in a world characterized
not only by violence and death but by separations and mistakings."
For in *Joseph Andrews*, she writes,

> [A]n elegaic strain may represent not only mourning for the absence
> of the dead but some element of mourning for the absence of the liv-
> ing to each other—an absence otherwise accommodated as the com-
> edy of Adams's absentmindedness, for example, or of slap-stick confu-
> sions, an absence treated largely satirically rather than sentimentally.[53]

My argument slightly slants Campbell's claims about ghostly realm
of voice and its evocation of mortal loss, by reading it as the realm of
the aural, as implicated in literacy. That Fanny is not recognized because unseen by Adams, for example, may be read as a function of
the novel's reluctance to present her as an image to a desiring reader,
and its wish to keep her within the realm of voice. That Fanny and
Joseph must be continually separated, and Fanny continually endan-
gered, is partly an effect of a logic in which Adams, as the embodi-
ment of the letter, must keep them apart. Like the Preface's melancholy about leaving behind the aural/visual realm of the theater and
about regulating the burlesque in the novel, *Joseph Andrews'* melancholy may betray a certain ideological exertion: the effort it takes to
police the boundaries between literacy and desire.[54]

And yet, a utopian undercurrent persists in *Joseph Andrews*.
Adams' triumphant shout of "*Hic est quem quaeris, inventus est*,"—
"Here is the one whom you seek; he is found" (*JA*, p. 339)—re-
writes "What you seek is nowhere" in a masculine key, uniting Latin
and the reunion of Joseph and his father. Indeed, the utopian undercurrent persists in the slight hint of a promise that literacy will be re-
cathected. The figure who lends Adams the money to pay his inn
bill and who later reappears at Booby Hall, restoring identities, re-
uniting families, and enabling marriage to occur, is a pedlar. But
Fielding's providential agent gets Book IV off to a disastrous false
start, when he reveals information that threatens to prohibit the sexual union of Joseph and Fanny: the fact that they might be brother

and sister. One might defamiliarize this conventional swerve on the way to sexual union by suggesting that in this case, its prohibition occurs because the pedlar emanates the promise of reading, functions, as it were, as a magical token of literacy. For as Margaret Spufford has shown, among the goods sold by these paripatetic pedlars were books.[55] On the way to its resolution, then, the narrative takes a false step, by moving according to the old logic; but the pedlar may be said to recathect literacy by ultimately facilitating the marriage of Joseph and Fanny. He also saves Parson Adams' son Dicky from drowning—the son who will later regale a gathered audience with his Latin lesson:

> "And now, Child, What is the *English* of *Lego*?"—to which the Boy, after long puzzling, answered, he could not tell. "How," cries *Adams* in a Passion,—"What hath the Water washed away your Learning? Why, what is *Latin* for the *English* Verb *read*? Consider before you speak."— The Child considered some time, and then the Parson cried twice or thrice, "*Le*—, *Le*—." —Dick answered, "*Lego*."—"Very well;—and then, what is the *English*," says the Parson, "of the Verb *Lego*?"—"*To read*," cried *Dick*.—"Very well," said the Parson, "a good Boy, you can do well, if you will take pains. . . ." (*JA*, p. 314)

Dicky may be unpromising, or recalcitrant, but Fielding's text stutters and repeats the words—*lego, I read*—that will, perhaps, guarantee the eight-year-old a better life than service.

CHAPTER 2

'A Man Who Laughs Is Never Dangerous'

THE GENTLEMAN'S DISPOSITION
IN 'A SENTIMENTAL JOURNEY'

If the fixture of *Momus's* glass, in the human breast, according to the proposed emendation of that arch-critick, had taken place . . . nothing more would have been wanting, in order to have taken a man's character, but to have taken a chair and gone softly, as you would to a dioptrical bee-hive, and look'd in,—view'd the soul stark naked. . . . But this is an advantage not to be had by the biographer in this planet,—in the planet *Mercury* (belike) . . . the intense heat of the country . . . must, I think, long ago have vitrified the bodies of the inhabitants . . . so that . . . all the tenements of their souls, from top to bottom, may be nothing else . . . but one fine transparent body of clear glass (bating the umbilical knot). . . .

But this, as I said above, is not the case of the inhabitants of this earth;—our minds shine not through the body, but are wrapt up here in a dark covering of uncrystallized flesh and blood; so that if we would come to the specifick characters of them, we must go some other way to work.[1]

The purpose of this chapter is to explore those other ways the sentimental novelist goes to work unwrapping the body's dark covering and determining the specific characters of others, and how the gentle self is constituted in the process. Tristram Shandy's witty fantasy of vitrified bodies finds its counterpart in *A Sentimental Journey*, where Yorick, referring to French women, tells the Count de

B****, "I could wish . . . to spy the *nakedness* of their hearts, and through the different disguises of customs, climates, and religion, find out what is good in them, to fashion my own by. . . . "[2] Yorick's wish is a typically sexualized version of the sentimental traveler's project: the spying of the hearts of others in the service of bourgeois self-improvement and self-empowerment. About a year earlier, Smollett's *Travels Through France and Italy* signaled a fairly new phenomenon in mid-eighteenth-century England: the availability of the Grand Tour to the educated middle class. Smollett, of course, appears in *A Sentimental Journey* as "the learned SMELFUNGUS," the quintessential "splenetic" traveler, and part of the novel's project was the creation of an alternative traveling subject. According to Gardner D. Stout, Jr., Sterne's sentimental novel functioned as "part of [a] program of reform and is intended to demonstrate that delicacy and decorum, good manners and cosmopolitan tolerance are civilizing and humanizing virtues conducive to a benevolent disposition toward our fellow-men."[3] *A Sentimental Journey* apparently succeeded so well that Frank Felsenstein, Smollett's modern editor, complains: "More than any other factor, Sterne's clever, though hardly fair, portrait served to undo the reputation of the *Travels*."[4]

As Terry Eagleton and others have shown, sentimentalism, with its doctrine of innate and spontaneous humanitarian benevolence, was ideologically central to the construction of the bourgeois subject. According to Mary Poovey, as an economic strategy, "its paradigm of innate benevolence initially sanctioned the laissez-faire individualism that gradually transformed England from a paternalistic hierarchy to a modern class society."[5] As an ideology, sentimentalism created a bourgeois subject whose "feminized" character marked him as distinct from and morally superior to the aristocracy.[6] Robert Markeley has argued that the supposed innate benevolence of the bourgeois was deployed as a justification for usurping from the aristocracy the role of England's moral conscience:

> Sentimentality manifests the anxiety of a class-stratified society trying both to assert "traditional" values and to accommodate as "gentlemen" increasing numbers of economically—if not always politically—aggressive merchants, professionals, small landowners, and money-

men. . . . For many middle-class authors, sentimentality—the generosity of feeling—becomes their claim to a cultural power-sharing based on a liberal interpretation of "Breeding" that equates hereditary power with moral sensitivity.[7]

It is important to note that this "generosity of feeling" resides in the *body* of the bourgeois, most particularly in his blood; the signifier that marks the breeding of the aristocrat is redefined as a mark of innate and physiological responsiveness to suffering.

If sentimentalism functioned as an ideology by which the middle classes could compete with the aristocracy for moral and cultural authority, it was also a response to an historical crisis involving the growth of the poor population in the early part of the eighteenth century. According to Ann Jessie Van Sant, contemporaries felt the pressure of large numbers of distressed poor, and regarded their own time as the age of benevolence and charity. She reads the Poor Law and the public philanthropic institutions as two contrasting strategies to manage that threat: the former sought to make them invisible by getting rid of beggars, while the latter "particularized their objects, who could then be seen not in throngs, swarms, or hordes, but in groups small enough to be both manageable and capable of appealing to the sympathy of observers."[8] In this ideological trajectory sentimentalism is once again tied to the body—this time the body of the poor, which may or may not be legible. Writing on *The Man of Feeling*, Bridget Orr has argued that the sentimental novel provided a response to "the struggle to produce a coherent discourse which could account for the social cost of the agrarian revolution and industrialisation":

> The text attempts to construct a closed system in which anxiety and guilt can be transformed into a pleasurable (and fashionable) aesthetic experience, where the suffering caused by enclosure, urbanisation, imperial expansion and the marriage market can be represented as natural or accidental, and the victim produced as a pathetically grateful object who provides an unthreatening opportunity to confirm the benevolist's socio-economic dominance at the moment of announcing his ethical superiority. . . . A universal capacity for sympathy expressed in voluntarist action is shown to be capable of remedying the ills produced by *homo economicus*.[9]

The success of the sentimental transaction in relation to the poor depends upon such visual evidence as the wooden limb or the lined countenance; in *The Man of Feeling* Harley depends upon physiognomy to distinguish the deserving poor from people trying to defraud him of his money and sympathy. The signs, however, are not always stable, so Harley "falls victim to the ruses of artful Londoners of 'decent' appearance."[10]

In *A Sentimental Journey* the determination of character is represented as most difficult in regard to the lower classes, especially servants. And it is represented as crucial given that the unpropertied gentleman, Yorick, is that part of the middle classes that comes perilously close to being identical with the poor. In this chapter I will argue that one of the central concerns of sentimental ideology is the determination of character, and that this determination is crucial to the benevolist's negotiation of class difference, through which he creates himself as a gentleman. The fixing of character takes place through the testimony of the body; Sterne's novels imagine scenarios in which the potentially subversive utterance of the lower classes is stabilized by a more or less severe corporeal discipline. At the same time, by voluntarily and self-consciously inhabiting the position of the lower classes, Yorick wards off a similar fixing of his own character. Through self-parody, the apotropaic enactment of his own potential marginalization, he both withstands the oppression of the aristocracy, and becomes privy to the secrets of others' hearts. In other words, he constitutes himself as a gentleman.[11]

I. Sentiment and the Body on the Rack

Almost every reader of the sentimental novel has noticed that sensibility manifests itself through the body: through blushing, hand-holding, the beat of the pulse, the mute gesture. In many cases, the body is not an obfuscatory covering; rather, it is a physiology that guarantees the subject's transparency, making intentions and true character visible to others. This happens particularly in the case of women, whose bodies are utterly legible, and of the benevolist himself, who exemplifies the "feminine" qualities of pity and pathos.

When Yorick first encounters Madame de L****, for example, it is the relaxation of her facial muscles that reveals "the same unprotected look of distress which first won me to her interest"; and, in turn, "the pulsations of the arteries along my fingers pressing across hers, told her what was passing within me" (p. 97), namely, the pity that makes him want to embrace her. Later, Yorick feels the grisset's pulse after she treats him courteously:

> Any one may do a casual act of good nature, but a continuation of them shews it is a part of the temperature; and certainly, added I, if it is the same blood which comes from the heart, which descends to the extremes (touching her wrist) I am sure you must have one of the best pulses of any woman in the world (p. 164).

The beat of the grisset's pulse assures Yorick of the correlation between an act of good nature and the body temperature that signifies her true nature. And as he learns the essence of her character, the grisset learns his, through a kind of x-ray vision: "[S]he had a quick black eye, and shot through two such long and silken eye-lashes with such penetration, that she look'd into my very heart and reins" (pp. 168–69). At moments such as these, the novel is blithe with assurance about the legibility of the subject, which is enabled by the body's circulatory system.[12]

In Sterne there at times appears another version of the body as well, however: the imprisoned or tortured body, caught up in the Bastille or the Inquisition. The evocation of the imprisoned body signals a moment of affective excess in the text. For instance, in the chapter entitled "The Captive," Yorick, nervous that he will be imprisoned in the Bastille for lack of a passport, elaborately tortures himself by imagining a single captive languishing in jail. I want to analyze the figure of the captive and a related figure—the machine—in relation to the cluster of chapters in which they are embedded, those chapters that concern Yorick's panicked attempt to procure a French passport. Both of these figures, I will argue, signal an attempt to solve the dilemma of character, or the reliability of affect in determining character. I will begin with a detour through a passage in *Tristram Shandy*, where the body on the inquisitorial rack is evoked to prove something, described for the sake of an argument about conscience. In this passage we can discern the function of the tortured body in the logic of self-legibility.

The sermon by Parson Yorick that Corporal Trim finds in the Stevinus and reads aloud to Walter Shandy, Uncle Toby, and Dr. Slop is a meditation on the nature of conscience. That we may take it as a serious argument in the midst of *Tristram Shandy*'s banter is indicated by the fact that Dr. Slop, who vociferously approves of the Inquisition and other forms of Catholic "cruelty, murders, rapines, blood-shed" (*TS*, p. 160), falls asleep at the sermon's moral climax. Moreover, the sermon was actually preached by Sterne himself in 1750 at an annual assize.[13] This sermon, on the text from Hebrews 13:18, "For we trust we have a good Conscience," concerns self-knowability. In it Parson Yorick disproves the notion that a man can be certain "whether he has a good conscience or no" (*TS*, p. 145). Man is fundamentally self-opaque, "a bubble to himself" (*TS*, p. 153).[14] Although once the conscience was "placed on high as a judge within us, and intended by our maker as a just and equitable one too,—by an unhappy train of causes and impediments, [it] takes often such imperfect cognizance of what passes,—does its office so negligently,—sometimes so corruptly,—that it is not to be trusted alone." It is now a "once able monitor" (*TS*, p. 154). The metaphor of the judge suggests that Yorick's sermon is interested in self-knowledge not only in its epistemological sense, but also insofar as it enables self-policing. Indeed, the sermonist's examples of self-delusion mostly concern criminality; as befits its original purpose as an assize sermon, what initially seems to be an argument about man's relation to his self increasingly gives way to a meditation on the citizen's relation to the apparatuses of the law.

Since the conscience meant by God to be trusted alone has become a fallen judge, a man must, in judging the merit of his actions, consult something outside his conscience: this something is variously called "religion and morality," "the unchangeable obligations of justice and truth," and "what is written in the law of God" (*TS*, p. 154).[15] This law functions as a supplement[16] for the conscience that was "once able" but is now fallen and inadequate. But even the conscience "guided and informed" by God's law may not work; in fact, the invention of human law is predicated upon its failure. Human laws, Yorick argues, are not

> "a matter of original choice, but of pure necessity, brought in to fence against the mischievous effects of those consciences which are no law unto themselves; well intending, by the many provisions made,—that in all such corrupt and misguided cases, where principles and the checks of conscience will not make us upright,—to supply their force, and, by the terrors of gaols and halters, oblige us to it." (*TS*, p. 155)

"What is written in the law of God," then, itself requires supplementation: human laws that threaten the body. "The terrors of gaols and halters" are what in the final instance ensure self-knowledge, correcting the "misguided."

The law needs the recourse of punishment, "the terrors of gaols and halters," because even supplementary human laws may not suffice. These laws are figured as writing.[17] "'So if you would form a just judgment of what is of infinite importance to you not to be misled in,'" Yorick argues, "'Look,—What is written in the law of God?—How readest thou?'" (*TS*, p. 154). The conscience should determine "'not like an *Asiatick* Cadi, according to the ebbs and flows of his own passions,—but like a *British* judge . . . who makes no new law, but faithfully declares that law which he knows already written'" (*TS*, p. 164). Here the conscience is described in its most lawless and solipsistic state, while British law is celebrated for adhering to the letter. Yet at the same time the text registers a suspicion of the written law. Previous to the contrast between the British judge and the Oriental tyrant, and in another context, the sermonist gives the character of a man who is "crafty and designing in his nature":

> "View his whole life;—'tis nothing but a cunning contexture of dark arts and unequitable subterfuges, basely to defeat the true intent of all laws,—plain dealing and the safe enjoyment of our several properties. . . . When old age comes on, and repentance calls him to look back upon this black account, and state it over again with his conscience,—CONSCIENCE looks into the STATUTES at LARGE;—finds no express law broken by what he has done;—perceives no penalty or forfeiture of goods and chattels incurred;—sees no scourge waving over

his head, or prison opening his gates upon him:—What is there to af-
fright his conscience?—Conscience has got safely entrenched behind
the Letter of the Law; sits there invulnerable. . . ." (*TS*, p. 151)

Human laws have a textual sense (the Letter) and a spiritual sense
("the true intent" or the *spirit* of the law), and the two senses are at
odds with one another. It is difficult to formulate the precise problem posed by the Letter of the Law: whether the threat posed to the
law's intent comes somehow from the very textuality of the law, or
whether the problem is that the law is not *adequately* written, so that
what is required would be a greater number of "express" laws. In either case, however, because the scourge and the prison are not made
sufficiently visible to it, the conscience is not afraid.

Yorick's sermon, then, explicitly argues that the proliferation of
kinds of laws restores the legibility of the conscience if man will just
consult them.[18] According to the logic of the sermon, however, the
constant supplementation of both human and divine laws reveals
their failure to render the conscience self-knowing. Significantly,
the sermonist calls the spirit of the law that the self-knowing conscience is supposed to protect—"the true intent of all laws"—"plain
dealing and the safe enjoyment of our several properties." In a sermon about various kinds of laws, this is the only place where he says
what laws are for; what is finally at stake is the honesty of business
transactions and the protection of property. Douglas Hay argues that
in the early part of the century the number of capital statutes in
England grew dramatically, as such social developments as "the constant extension of inland and foreign trade from the late seventeenth
century, the exploitation of new mines, the wealth of London and
the spas and the growth of population" made offences against property more common. William Blackstone wrote, "there is nothing
which so generally strikes the imagination, and engages the affections of mankind, as the right of property," and his editor Christian
referred in 1793 to "that law of property, which nature herself has
written upon the hearts of all mankind."[19] Using the language of
sentiment, writers on the law in the eighteenth century naturalized
property by associating it with the body. For the eighteenth-century
bourgeoisie the issue of sentiment was crucially tied to the determi-

nation of character, and that determination in turn was regarded as vital to the protection and defense of private property.[20]

In Yorick's sermon, the discussion of man's monitoring of his *own* conscience eventually slides into a discussion of how a person can be sure *others* will be honest. Discussing his banker and physician, both of whom are atheists, Yorick explains that he can trust them because "'I'm persuaded that they cannot hurt me, without hurting themselves more.'" Without religion, however, should interest make it worth their while to injure him, "'I must lay at the mercy of HONOUR, or some such capricious principle.—Strait security for two of my most valuable blessings!—my property and my life'" (*TS*, p. 159).[21] In the concluding section of the sermon, where the argument reaches its application for the congregation, Yorick provides several precepts not for self-knowledge, but for protecting oneself against the corrupt consciences of others. The list begins cynically with "'Whenever a man talks loudly against religion,— always suspect that it is not his reason, but his passions which have got the better of his CREED,'" and concludes suspiciously with "'Trust that man in nothing, who has not a CONSCIENCE in every thing'" (*TS*, p. 164).

In Yorick's sermon, no law is able to realize the true intent of all laws: the protection of property. None works to allow one to see into the conscience of other people; the only relation about which one can be confident is tenuously based on interest. One particular figure in the text, however, recuperates and solves the problem of the mutual opacity of motives in human transactions: the figure of the Inquisition.

In the figure of the Inquisition, the sermon replays the problem of the inadequacy of British law in determining true character—in a French context, refiguring it as monstrous law. The Inquisition, the judiciary of Catholicism, carried a powerful affective charge at this time (indeed, through the Revolution), as Britain waged repeated war with France for imperial power and as anti-Catholicism centered around the fear of Jacobite rebellion remained virulent.[22] Sterne and his uncle Jacques Sterne, the Archbishop of York, participated in what Wilbur Cross calls "the fierce religious passions awak-

ened by the events of 1745, when every church . . . rang with de-
nunciations of Rome and all her ways."[23] France, the country where
A Sentimental Journey takes place, may be read as a signifier for anxiety over the brutality of the aristocracy and the protection of property: the moment Yorick sets foot upon French soil he begins to
worry about the *droits d'aubaine* and the potential confiscation of his
property by the French monarch. If France signifies manners, it also
means the gothic. As in the gothic novel, it is a site upon which various class anxieties are transposed and strategies of punishment and
surveillance are rehearsed.

The Inquisition appears in the sermon in order to illustrate the
consequences of "a religion not strictly governed by morality" (*TS*,
p. 160). The two features Yorick attacks in Catholicism are its extreme formalism (adherence to the letter) and its use of physical
punishment: these features, as we have seen, are in fact the two primary characteristics of the British law as he describes it. Yorick con-
demns Catholicism because while religion's function is to shore up
and amend the conscience, "Popery" encourages self-blindness; the
"few instrumental parts of religion" like attending church and performing the sacraments "cheat [a man's] conscience into a judgment
that, for this, he . . . has discharged truly his duty to God" (*TS*, p.
159). In other words, it is like the Letter of the Law that fortifies the
conscience of the crafty and designing man and allows him to neglect the law's spirit.[24]

Moreover, the Inquisition may be read as a case of "the terrors
of gaols and halters" that the conscience requires as a result of its
failure at self-policing. For Parson Yorick, the Inquisition is "a studied system of cruelty," and the trials of its prisoners "mock trial[s]."
It is the figure for anti-justice. Yet the figure is vexed; for one might
call the long description of inquisitorial punishment a mere amplifi-
cation of what is, more briefly and tactfully, suggested to be the effi-
cacy of British law: "the terrors of gaols and halters" and "the
scourge waving over his head." Indeed, one might argue that the Inquisition is an *exemplary* figure for the enforcement of the law; for
seizing upon the body, it renders the soul, which is otherwise deep
within the vision-distorting "bubble" of the human self, visible.

The primary figure of speech employed in the description of the prisoner on the rack (*TS*, pp. 161–63) is the imperative, and it is the command to see: " 'Behold this helpless victim,' " " 'observe the last movement of that horrid engine!,' " " 'consider the nature of the posture in which he now lies stretched,' " " 'behold the unhappy wretch led back to his cell!' " In torture, the body is rendered transparent: " 'Behold this helpless victim deliver'd up to his tormentors,—his body so wasted with sorrow and confinement, you will see every nerve and muscle as it suffers.' " This is a hyperbolics of seeing, a moment where the insistence of the affect leads to an impossibility: the sight of actual nerves and muscles. This overstatement prepares us for the next: the visibility of the soul as it comes out of the mouth. " ''Tis all nature can bear!—Good God! *See* how it keeps his weary soul hanging upon his trembling lips,—willing to take its leave,—but not suffered to depart!' " The muscles, nerves, and even the soul of the exemplary innocent are exposed by turning his body inside out.

The prisoner on the rack, then, is subjected to a torture whose primary purpose is to render it visible; once the body becomes permanently visible—in the passage from the sermon, hyperbolically seen—knowledge can be obtained about it.[25] Indeed, in Sterne the act of punishment is crucially linked to the act of determining character. Both the description of the captive in *A Sentimental Journey* and the passage on Momus' glass and the vitrified inhabitants of Mercury contain a series of images of light, drawing, and portraiture. In the *Shandy* passage and the suggestions for discovering character that follow, character is "drawn," "sketched," copied by pentagraph, drawn "*against the light*," refracted by rays of light (*TS*, pp. 84–85); in *A Sentimental Journey* Yorick looks "through the twilight . . . to take [the captive's] picture," darkens his light, goes on to "another part of the portrait," and has trouble sustaining "the picture of confinement which my fancy had drawn" (pp. 201–3). Like the sermon's description of the body on the rack, Yorick's fantasy culminates in the soul's becoming visible: "I saw the iron enter into his soul" (p. 203). His body arranged in a play of light and darkness, the prisoner is subjected to the discipline of visual art.

II. The Unreliable Affect of Servants

The figure of the body on the inquisitorial rack, then, signals a crisis of legibility, and then the overcoming of that crisis by corporeal punishment that renders visible what is frighteningly invisible: the soul. Interestingly, Smith's *The Theory of Moral Sentiments* opens with the body on the rack:

> As we have no immediate experience of what other men feel, we can form no idea of the manner in which they are affected, but by conceiving what we ourselves should feel in the like situation. Though our brother is upon the rack, as long as we ourselves are at our ease, our senses will never inform us of what he suffers. They never did, and never can, carry us beyond our own person, and it is by the imagination only that we can form any conception of what are his sensations. . . . [26]

David Marshall writes of this passage, "*The Theory of Moral Sentiments* begins by supposing a skeptical epistemology that assumes sympathy but insists that neither sight nor the other senses will suffice to communicate to us the feelings and experiences of another person."[27] The body on the rack is the figure for the potential halting or blockage of sympathy because of the radical subjectivity of sensation—and then the overcoming of that blockage through an act of the imagination. What is represented as a matter of sympathy in Smith is worked out as a matter of conscience in Sterne, but it is clear that both sentimental writers use the figure of the tortured body to confront a similar epistemological problem: the inability of subjects to see the hearts of others.[28]

As if to literalize Smith's hypothetical tortured man, in *Tristram Shandy* somebody's brother *is* on the rack: Trim's brother Tom has been caught in the Inquisition in Lisbon. As Trim reads the description of the tortured body aloud to Walter Shandy and Uncle Toby, he clearly labors under no blockage of sympathy, but cries out "in a most passionate exlamation," "'Oh! 'tis my brother.'" In a comic version of torture, Walter Shandy urges Trim to continue reading, until Trim begs to be allowed to stop and Walter concedes that "'tis cruelty to force him to go on with it . . . " (*TS*, pp. 161–63)—not, perhaps, "a studied system of cruelty," but cruelty just the same, and to the same effect. Trim's function as a comic parallel to the tortured man is also suggested earlier in the text, in the chapter preceding the sermon, where the narrator provides "a description of his attitude" while reading (*TS*, pp. 140–42). Lest the reader falsely suppose Trim to be standing "in an uneasy posture," Tristram Shandy "take[s] the picture of him," describing the precise arrangement of his body. Trim, arranged in a not uneasy "posture," matches the tortured man, who is in a much more painful one: "Consider the nature of the posture in which he now lies stretched—what exquisite tortures he endures by it!" Tristram Shandy attempts to "take the picture of him in at one view": in *A Sentimental Journey*, in his fantasy of the captive, Yorick "look[s] through the twilight of his grated door to take his picture" (p. 201). Although explicitly compared to a classical orator the angle of whose body hits precisely "the true persuasive angle of incidence," Trim's body is also more subtly associated with those of men caught up in a severer corporeal punishment. The subtle coercion the text exercises upon Trim's body is mitigated and rendered humorous by its taking place in the realm of aesthetics, and by its elevation of the servant to the status of a classical orator. It is, however, purposeful, guaranteeing a stable relation between Trim's words and his affect.

During his performance Trim's physiology makes visible and vivid his agitation. At one moment "Trim's face turned as pale as ashes," while a sentence later "the tears began to trickle down" and "his colour return[ed] into his face as red as blood" (*TS*, pp. 161–62). When the sermon is completed, Walter Shandy praises Trim for his performance:

> Thou hast read the sermon extremely well, *Trim*, quoth my father. . . . I should have read it ten times better, Sir, answered *Trim*, but that my heart was so full.—That was the very reason, *Trim*, replied my father, which has made thee read the sermon as well as thou hast done; and if the clergy of our church, continued my father, addressing himself to Dr. *Slop*, would take part in what they deliver, as deeply as this poor fellow has done,—as their compositions are fine . . . the eloquence of our pulpits . . . would be a model for the whole world." (*TS*, pp. 164–65)

Preceded by the elaborate description of the arrangement of his body into the mode approved by neoclassical aesthetics, Trim's performance provides for Walter Shandy a spectacle of complete moral authority.

Trim is recognizable as that product of discipline Foucault calls a "docile body." In Foucault's account the disciplining of the body is general, cutting across social class; and indeed, in *A Sentimental Journey* Yorick uses the same language of arrangement and posture as Tristram Shandy does in his description of Trim to describe how he will attempt to read the character of the Duc de Choiseul: "Fool! continued I—see Monsieur Le Duc's face first—observe what character is written in it; take notice in what posture he stands to hear you—mark the turns and expressions of his body and limbs . . . " (p. 207). The French aristocracy, then, also stands in expressive postures. In *A Sentimental Journey* it is servants, however, who require a more explicitly coercive discipline.[29] Sheldon Rothblatt has shown that in the eighteenth century, especially in London,

> what can be called the traditional master-servant relationship underwent striking change. London domestics of all ranks began to feel the effects of a dynamic, commercial society, in which they were in short supply relative to demand. They perceived opportunities for social mobility simply unknown in distant rural parishes. The result was a rupture in the values governing service relationships.[30]

Further, Eve Kosofsky Sedgwick has demonstrated how Yorick's "need to describe and justify, under the guise of celebrating, the particular shape of the bond between [himself and La Fleur]" is "a sign not of a stable, hereditary, traditional, paternalistic bond to a servant, but of an anxious and ideologically threatened one."[31] Indeed, the narrative is generated in the first place by a glance of "the most civil triumph in the world" from a servant asking Yorick "You have been in France?" (p. 65). As Sedgwick argues, "The prestige that has lent force to his misprision (his sneer?) seems to belong not to a particular personality but to a position. . . . "[32] Yorick's journey in search of human nature—his journey of self-constitution as a benevolist—is undertaken as a response to a challenge from a servant.

To further understand why Trim's body requires the discipline of arrangement into angles, it is relevant to quote Yorick's initial description of the servant *he* takes on in France, La Fleur. La Fleur, like many French characters in Sterne, is a lover and a dandy. He has one characteristic, however, that one would not necessarily expect from a coxcomb:

> I was hourly recompenced by the festivity of his temper. . . . I had a constant resource in his looks in all difficulties and distresses of my own—I was going to have added, of his too; but La Fleur was out of the reach of every thing; for whether 'twas hunger or thirst, or cold or nakedness, or watchings, or whatever stripes of ill luck La Fleur met with in our journeyings, there was no index in his physiognomy to point them out by—he was eternally the same. . . . (pp. 126–27)

The physiognomical univocality of La Fleur's face and his body's imperviousness to the most strenuous of physical hardships seems a gratuitous detail in the novel; it plays no part in what ensues, and is in fact apparently forgotten by Sterne, who remobilizes La Fleur's face later on. I would suggest that La Fleur's being "out of the reach of everything"—his body's recalcitrance to signify—is related to the corporeal discipline Trim undergoes, and has to do with the potentially subversive physical illegibility of servants. La Fleur's unchanging physiognomy and the corporeal discipline undergone by Trim suggest that one characteristic of servants is their ambiguous relation to affect.

Another recurring image in *A Sentimental Journey*—the machine—provides an analogous and more elaborate version of what we might call the dilemma of La Fleur's physiognomy. The caged starling who complains over and over, "I can't get out," is the most striking instance of this image. The starling appears in the cluster of chapters organized around Yorick's attempt to procure a passport. These chapters, which concern Yorick's legal right to be in France, foreground and make urgent the problems I have argued that France signifies—the threat of confiscation of property, the terror of gaols and halters, and the illegibility of others[33]—and they reach their affective climax in Yorick's fantasy of the imprisoned body.

Yorick encounters the starling just as he has managed to over-come his fear of imprisonment; its song has a powerful effect upon him:

> I vow, I never had my affections more tenderly awakened. . . . Me-chanical as the notes were, yet so in tune to nature were they chanted, that in one moment they overthrew all my systematic reasonings upon the Bastile. . . . (p. 198)

The mechanical notes of the starling cause Yorick to launch into apostrophes to slavery and liberty that are meant as a commentary upon the situation of the starling; but they may be read as a gloss upon the "overthrowing" of his reason as well. The mechanical or imitated emotion of the caged starling produces in Yorick an invol-untary pity that weakens and unnerves him. Several chapters later Yorick sits in the office of the Count de B**** reading *Much Ado About Nothing* to beguile the time. Since he gets through the first three acts one may assume he encounters the lines spoken by the bas-tard malcontent Don John: "I am trusted with a muzzle and enfran-chised with a clog; therefore I have decreed not to sing in my cage. If I had my mouth I would bite; if I had my liberty I would do my lik-ing. . . . "[34] Hovering outside the network of nobility, political power, and the marriage market, Don John figures his lack of birth and favor as a form of captivity. While I do not want to pressure the allusion too much, it is difficult to resist reading it as a suggestion of the potentially sinister nature of the starling, and as a vague threat of subversion on the part of the disenfranchised. In any case, the starling is treated sadistically in the text. It is purchased by La Fleur for a bot-tle of wine, then circulated from hand to hand, first by lords and then "into the lower house, and . . . the hands of as many commoners," having "little store set by him." Finally, it is aggressively aestheticized:

> from that time to this, I have borne this poor starling as the crest to my arms. . . . And let the heralds officers twist his neck about if they dare. (pp. 204–5)

Yorick's account of the starling concludes with a fantasy of its mur-der that seems comically like a wish.

Significantly, the starling is taught to imitate emotional utterance by one of the British disenfranchised, the groom to "the Honourable Mr. ****" (p. 204). Yorick figures servants as captives: "the sons and daughters of service part with liberty," he says piously, "but not with Nature in their contracts; they are flesh and blood, and have their little vanities and wishes in the midst of the house of bondage" (p. 247). The starling is most obviously supposed to work as an analogy to Yorick, but it works as a figure for the sons and daughters of service as well. Taught to imitate emotion by a servant, the starling signifies the potentially subversive instability of pathetic utterance. While in Yorick's fantasy servants remain "flesh and blood," the starling represents the possibility of a human lament that would be somehow inhuman, a pathetic utterance on the part of the lower class that would upset the distinction between affect and the imitation of affect, pathos and parody.[35]

It seems no accident, therefore, that Yorick's fantasy of the captive follows directly upon the heels of his encounter with the starling. "The bird in his cage pursued me into my room," he says; "I sat down close to my table, and leaning my head upon my hand, I begun to figure to myself the miseries of confinement" (p. 201). Like the description of the prisoner on the rack in the *Shandy* sermon, the fantasy of the captive comes to stabilize the subversive indeterminacy between pathetic utterance and parody—an indeterminacy which threatens to produce in the benevolist an involuntary sympathy. Culminating in the visibility of the captive's soul ("I saw the iron enter into his soul"), Yorick's fantasy renders a body transparent through discipline.

III. Discipline and the Novel

I have already argued that, linked by images of light and portraiture to the passage on drawing character in *Tristram Shandy*, the fantasy of the captive (pp. 201–3) makes clear the links between corporeal punishment and the determination of character. Those particular images foreground the work of artistic representation, suggesting that such representation is itself a form of corporeal discipline.³⁶ "I gave full scope to my imagination," Yorick says; and the language of the fantasy emphasizes his imagination's agency in the captive's actual imprisonment. "I took a single captive, and having first shut him up in his dungeon, I then look'd through the twilight of his grated door to take his picture." At times the prisoner is merely "beheld" by Yorick, but later, Yorick says "As I darkened the little light he had, he lifted up a hopeless eye towards the door, then cast it down. . . . " The fantasy of surveillance produces a "character" about whom knowledge is generated: "pale and feverish," the captive has been in solitary confinement for thirty years, has children, hopes for his imminent release, and possesses a visible soul. The work of characterization performed by the sentimental novelist takes place through a fantasy of punishment.

Linking the acts of surveillance, discipline, and characterization, then, *A Sentimental Journey* suggests that the sentimental novel is itself a form of social control. That it regards itself as a social intervention should not be surprising since many of these novels are so frankly didactic. What seems interesting here, however, is the way *A Sentimental Journey* figures this intervention as a discipline—as the punishment of a body (or, as I will argue momentarily, the discipline of the mind) in the service of rendering the self transparent. The fragment concerning the effect of Euripides' *Andromeda* on the profligate citizens of Abdera functions as an exemplary scenario of the benign effects of a disciplinary pathetic literature.

The Abdera fragment is taken from the chapter on "Love-Melancholy" in Burton's *The Anatomy of Melancholy*, and is supposed to illustrate the social and moral power of love; Yorick has just told us that when he is in love he feels generous, while when he is not, he finds his heart "locked up" (p. 129). The story concerns the profligate town of Abdera in Thrace, whose citizens, after seeing a performance of Euripides' *Andromeda*, cannot stop repeating a "pathetic address":

> Every man almost spoke pure iambics the next day, and talk'd of nothing but Perseus his pathetic address—"O Cupid! prince of God and

men"—in every street of Abdera, in every house—"O Cupid! Cupid!"—in every mouth, like the natural notes of some sweet melody which drops from it whether it will or no—nothing but "Cupid! Cupid! prince of God and men"—The fire caught—and the whole city, like the heart of one man, open'd itself to Love. (pp. 130–31)

The involuntary repetition of iambic "notes" may be compared to the "notes" mechanically uttered by the caged starling. The profligate Abderites produce mechanical pathetic utterance—utterance at once involuntary and regulated by meter. Their imaginations have been "operated" upon by gentle disciplinary "strokes": "nothing operated more upon their imaginations," Yorick says, "than the tender strokes of nature which the poet had wrought up . . . " (p. 131). Unlike the mechanical repetition of the starling, this repetition has positive effects:

> Friendship and Virtue met together, and kiss'd each other in the street—the golden age return'd, and hung o'er the town of Abdera—every Abderite took his oaten pipe, and every Abderitish woman left her purple web, and chastly sat her down and listen'd to the song— (p. 131).

One might expect that the Abderites would be aroused by rapture, but instead they are disciplined, and the social order restored.[37]

The Abdera fragment is situated after the four short "Montriul" chapters in which La Fleur, the toast of the Montriul poor, is introduced, and directly before the novel's major scene of alms-giving, a scene that concerns Yorick's constitution of himself as a public figure. "[A]s this was the first publick act of my charity in France," Yorick says, "I took the more notice of it" (p. 132). In this scene (pp. 132–34) Yorick gives money to a variety of "sons and daughters of poverty" who present themselves to him in ceremonial poses of supplication and gratitude—the highly stylized pathetic tableaux characteristic of sentimental literature. In addition, the poor utter phrases of obedience to higher authorities: "*Vive le Roi!*" "*pour l'amour de Dieu*," "*mon cher et tres charitable Monsieur*," and, most gratifying to Yorick, "*my Lord Anglois*." Meanwhile, Yorick coyly vacillates about how much money he has. He begins: "For my own part,

there is no man gives so little as I do; for few that I know have so little to give. . . . " At the end of the scene, after giving away his last
sous, Yorick is confronted by "a *pauvre honteux*, who had no one to
ask a sous for him, and who, I believed, would have perish'd, ere he
could have ask'd one for himself. . . . ":

> God God! said I—and I have not one single sous left to give him—But
> you have a thousand! cried all the powers of nature, stirring within
> me—so I gave him—no matter what—I am ashamed to say *how much*,
> now—and was ashamed to think, how little, then: so if the reader can
> form any conjecture of my disposition, as these two fixed points are
> given him, he may judge within a livre or two what was the precise
> sum.

Yorick teases the reader about his precise economic status, figuring
the psychomachia of alms-giving not so much as a matter of generosity or parsimony, as a matter of whether he is rich or poor. The
Abdera fragment serves as an enabling transition from the introduction of an unreliable servant to the gentleman's constitution of himself as both a benefactor to the poor, and as a character who is himself unknown and multivalent. Like the fantasy of the captive, the
scenario of disciplinary pathetic literature functions as a symbolic
domestication of the lower classes in the service of the benevolist's
self-empowerment. And that self-empowerment works partly by
Yorick's vacillation about his own class status—a vacillation, as I will
show, that generates the novel's self-parodic tone.

IV. Discipline and Satire

I have argued that *A Sentimental Journey* represents the act of
characterization as a form of discipline and surveillance, and that the
novel contains scenarios of pathetic literature that have disciplinary
effects. When the idea of the sentimental novel itself is actually thematized, however, the novel does not appear as a locus of value. For
example, when the *fille de chambre* of Madame R**** purchases *Les
Egarements du Coeur & de l'Esprit*, Yorick regards the act as a sexual
indecorum, indeed, as a sexual invitation. Commencing a flirtation,

he asks, "And what have you to do, my dear . . . with *The Wanderings of the Heart*, who scarce know yet you have one?" (p. 188). In this scene the sentimental novel has potentially mischievous effects. Indeed, the sentimental novel is systematically represented as a degraded object throughout *A Sentimental Journey*. Michael Seidel argues, for example, that the (by now highly overdetermined) starling "mimics the kind of authority and circulating powers *A Sentimental Journey* possesses as a celebrated novel. It seems that the captive is an English bird and would gain fame in the way novels do—by circulating around London in all houses and among all classes."[38] The force of Sterne's joke about the circulation of the starling lies actually in its *lack* of authority; the quickness with which it is passed from hand to hand and demoted in class suggests the transitoriness of its interest and value. In the figure of the starling the novel is figured as a faddish commodity circulated by anonymous consumers. A similar figuration of the sentimental novel occurs in the fragment Yorick finds on a sheet of waste paper under a currant leaf holding a pat of butter. This fragment, which contains a story so pathetic "it will touch the heart of cruelty herself with pity—"(p. 255), may be read as another figure for Sterne's own fragmentary sentimental text; its fate is to be wrapped around a bouquet of flowers La Fleur gives to a woman.

A Sentimental Journey, then, disavows its own authority and self-consciously rehearses its own marginalization. By producing figures for the marginalized sentimental novel, Sterne dissociates his own project from the apparatus of social control, displacing the implied disciplinary capacity of literature onto other kinds of narrative. Consequently, his novel seems free from motives of power. By representing itself as objectified and circulated among commoners and servants, the novel suggests the inefficacy of its own moral project. But we know that this self-parodic gesture is defensive because the novel fantasizes a literature that *does* have disciplinary power.

Yorick's fantasy of Aeneas and Dido, a set piece inserted in the scene where he awaits the verdict on his passport in the Count de B****'s office (pp. 224–26), is another instance of the disciplinary capacity of literature. Like the fantasy of the captive and the Abdera

fragment, the Aeneid fantasy comes to solve a problem of indeterminacy of character—an indeterminacy, in this case, of the character of the aristocrat:

> I could not conceive why the Count de B**** had gone so abruptly
> out of the room, any more than I could conceive why he had put the
> Shakespear into his pocket—

Like the Abdera fragment, the fantasy of Aeneas and Dido functions
as a symbolic transition between an anxiety about class status and its
resolution. Directly after the fantasy Yorick is given his passport,
which guarantees him the freedom to be mobile in France and to
continue "spying the nakedness of . . . hearts." This time, however,
the language of discipline is less apparent, because the discipline is
directed toward himself.

Unlike other scenarios of sympathy in the novel, the Aeneid
fantasy is highly controlled. Yorick sets it up by apostrophizing the
mind's capacity for self-surrender: "Sweet pliability of man's spirit,
that can at once surrender itself to illusions, which cheat expectation and sorrow of their weary moments!" This is clearly a different
kind of emotion from that involuntary or "mechanical" sympathy
evoked by the starling. Yorick recounts his vision of Aeneas meeting
Dido in the underworld:

> I force myself, like Eneas, into them—I see him meet the pensive
> shade of his forsaken Dido—and wish to recognize it—I see the in-
> jured spirit wave her head, and turn off silent from the author of her
> miseries and dishonours—I lose the feelings for myself in hers—and
> in those affections which were wont to make me mourn for her when
> I was at school.

While Yorick begins by identifying with the powerful Aeneas, he
slides into identification with Dido, the pathetic victim. This identification with a figure of woe helps Yorick overcome his fear of
monarchy: "I was never able to conquer any one single bad sensation
in my heart so decisively, as by beating up as fast as I could for some
kindly and gentle sensation, to fight it upon its own ground."
Through the distancing medium of literature, Yorick regains his
composure in an act of successful identification: "I lose the feelings

for myself in hers—and in those affections which were wont to make me mourn for her when I was at school." He also constitutes himself by appealing to an idealized past self—to the British school-boy learning to participate in the privileged cultural tradition of classical learning.[39] While the Abdera fragment leads to the consti-tution of the multivalent benevolist, the Aeneid fragment functions as a symbolic passage from fear of imprisonment to a guarantee of freedom. I will conclude with an examination of the political signif-icance of the passport, and its role in vouchsafing for Yorick a secure status as a gentleman.

Mistaking the benevolist's search for the secrets of character as the search for state secrets, the French police pay Yorick a call be-cause they take him for a literal spy. Yorick views the activity of spy-ing hearts as an exercise in the transcendence of the particularities of politics, as a purely personal activity: "I could wish . . . to spy the *nakedness* of their hearts, and through the different disguises of cus-toms, climates, and religion, find out what is good in them, to fash-ion my own by" (pp. 217–18). In his formulation, through spying one acquires benevolence; in France, however, the meaning of spying is highly politicized. Reactionary and oppressive, the French nobil-ity mistakes benevolence for surveillance, imagining that by spying, Yorick might be attempting to gain some sort of power. It refuses him the prerogative of the gentleman: the power to look into the hearts of others.[40]

And indeed, Yorick needs this power because he cannot take for granted his difference from the poor. Like scores of literary younger brothers and heirs to decayed fortunes, and like the throngs of peo-ple who came to London in the eighteenth century to take advan-tage of new opportunities for making a living, Yorick has to live by his wits.[41] And there are moments in *A Sentimental Journey* when Yorick's status is conflated with that of the poor. When making the rounds of Parisian high life, for example, he has to pay for the main-tenance of his class status by effacing his own character (a phenome-non that in Sterne must always be accompanied by shock):

> For three weeks together, I was of every man's opinion I met. . . . And at this price I could have eaten and drank and been merry all the days

of my life at Paris; but 'twas a dishonest *reckoning*—I grew ashamed of
it—it was the gain of a slave—every sentiment of honour revolted
against it—the higher I got, the more was I forced upon my *beggarly
system*—the better the *Coterie*—the more children of Art—I languish'd
for those of Nature: and one night, after a most vile prostitution of myself to half a dozen different people, I grew sick. . . . (p. 266)

This episode occurs directly after Yorick finds out the secret of the
beggar who asks for charity only of women: " 'twas flattery" (p. 260).
Associated with the beggar through his own "beggarly system" of
flattering people's opinions, Yorick becomes quite seriously dis-
gusted. His "prostitution" in Paris sets up the idealized pastoral that
follows in the countryside, where humble peasants will perform
their sylvan rites and devotions for the delectation of the relieved
tourist.

The passport sequence chronicles Yorick's potential oppression
at the hands of monarchy, in which the benevolist is put into the position of a pathetic victim, a position generally reserved in sentimental literature for the poor. Just as the sentimental novel is figured as
having no moral authority, Yorick himself is frequently figured as socially marginal and powerless. The captive in Yorick's Bastille fantasy,
for example, functions as a figure for Yorick himself as well as for the
sons and daughters of poverty; by drawing a picture of confinement,
Yorick is trying to accustom himself to the idea of his own confinement in the Bastille. Furthermore, the starling, which I have described as a figure for the subversive parodic utterance of servants,
also works as a figure for Yorick in prison. Indeed, the Yorick-figure
is extremely mobile in the novel, moving constantly, as Sedgwick
suggests, between "the fantasy polarities of omnipotence and utter
powerlessness."[42] Yorick's "portrait" of the captive seems at once a
sadistic fantasy of surveillance and a masochistic fantasy of being
looked at. It is telling that when Freud wants to show the susceptibility of an instinct to reversal into its opposite, the instincts he chooses
are sadism-masochism and scoptophilia-exhibitionism: when the
aims are reversed, he writes, "the passive aim (to be tortured, or
looked at) has been substituted for the active aim (to torture, to look
at)."[43] In Sterne, the terms which stand in apposition in Freud—see-

ing and torture—have a direct relation to one another. In psychic terms, Yorick's desires are expressed in the movement back and forth from the "passive aim" of being looked at/tortured to the "active aim" of looking/torturing. In class terms, his status as a gentleman is constituted in the movement back and forth between the fantasy of policing the poor and the fantasy of being policed by the French monarchy.

Yorick's primary tactic in mitigating the problem of his poverty—a tactic generally successful in ensuring his mobility—is his voluntary assumption of the position of the pathetic victim. It is this subjection of himself to the fixing powers of surveillance that makes the novel "self-parodic." Yorick parodies his own marginality by inhabiting and enacting it intentionally. His fantasizing of himself as a pathetic victim—the object rather than the subject of sentimentalism—functions as an apotropaic gesture by which he both rehearses poverty and powerlessness and wards it off, constituting himself as a multivalent and self-ironic gentleman. This maneuver is apparent on a small scale when Yorick renders comic the specter of his imprisonment by pretending that it was his idea all along. Eugenius offers him money to take on his travels, but Yorick refuses, saying "But you don't consider, Eugenius . . . that before I have been three days in Paris, I shall take care to say or do something or other for which I shall get clapp'd up into the Bastile, and that I shall live there a couple of months entirely at the king of France's expence" (pp. 195–96). Through the act of anticipating his own subjection to punishment and surveillance, Yorick preempts the king and thereby mitigates his power; moreover, this anticipatory fantasy enacts his turning imprisonment to his financial advantage.[44]

Nothing quite so clearly shows the way Yorick empowers himself by voluntarily assuming a subordinate position as the way in which he finally obtains the passport that guarantees his freedom. He identifies himself for the Count de B**** as a literary character, Yorick the jester in *Hamlet*. If, as I have argued, the act of biography, or "drawing character" is a form of discipline, Yorick readily submits to being drawn. By being put in the position of the literary character, he achieves his freedom, a freedom that entails his power to travel and to fashion himself by spying the hearts of others. "*Un homme qui rit*, said the duke, *ne sera jamais dangereuz.*—Had it been for any one but the king's jester, added the Count, I could not have got it these two hours" (pp. 226–27). The force of the joke derives from the specific character Yorick ruefully agrees to play: the character of a virtual slave in a feudal system. And the novel's humor derives from Yorick's willingness to achieve freedom by representing himself as a laughing man, a man too servile to pose a danger to the state. The moment Yorick receives his passport he acquires, in the eyes of the Count de B****, the authority to expound upon national character. "And how do you find the French? said the Count de B****, after he had given me the Passport," Yorick says: "The reader may suppose that after so obliging a proof of courtesy, I could not be at a loss to say something handsome to the enquiry" (p. 230).

V. Satire and the Sentimental

As Neil McKendrick has shown, in the eighteenth century England experienced an unprecedented consumer revolution that resulted in the blurring of distinctions among classes:

> These characteristics—the closely stratified nature of English society, the striving for vertical social mobility, the emulative spending bred by social emulation . . . —combined with the widespread ability to spend (offered by novel levels of prosperity) to produce an unprecedented propensity to consume: unprecedented in the depth to which it penetrated the lower reaches of society. . . . [45]

The necessity of emulative spending to capitalist growth was being recognized by the 1770s, but its potential leveling tendencies caused anxiety among the middle classes. Fielding, for example, wrote of the "lower sort" that as a result of the "introduction of trade," "the narrowness of their future is changed into wealth; their frugality into luxury, their humility into pride, and their subjection into equality."[46] I have argued that if the "lower sort" of people parody the wealthy—La Fleur can "do wonders" in handsomely attiring himself with very little money (p. 246)—in *A Sentimental Journey* the unpropertied gentleman counters by parodying poverty.

As Gardner Stout points out, "Yorick's *Journey* was valued by Sterne's contemporaries mainly for its 'tenderness of sentiment' and 'delicacy of feeling' " (Intro., p. 26). And *A Sentimental Journey* has been regarded by many critics as the prototypical sentimental novel. At the same time, critics have always been baffled by the question of the novel's tone, debating whether Sterne intended it to be a straightforward sentimental novel, or a satire of sentimentalism. In this debate the character of Yorick, and his "reliability" as a narrator, have traditionally been deployed as a touchstone to the novel's intentions. Many readings of the novel have concluded with some sort of synthesis of the unstable, contradictory, and self-parodic tones in which Yorick speaks.[47]

This chapter has sought to redirect that argument by claiming not that Yorick's sentimentalism is moral even though it contains satiric elements, but rather that satire is essential to the very production of the sentimental. Self-parody is deployed by the sentimental author as an ideological tactic by which the benevolist rehearses through fantasy his own social victimization and marginalization in order to become a better reader of others' characters, a better connoisseur of sensibility. To put it more strongly, if Yorick begins his sojourn in France by whimsically imagining being robbed by the king, the product that consistently emerges from his fantasies of victimization is a character as diligently acquisitive as any eighteenth-century entrepreneur. Indeed, he is a virtual imperialist of sensibility—a man who "misses nothing he can *fairly* lay his hands on," and who, even in a barren desert, would find some anthropomorphized plant upon which to cut his name (pp. 114–16).

CHAPTER 3

The Satire of Melancholia

'HUMPHRY CLINKER' AND THE AGRICULTURAL REVOLUTION

I believe there is something mischievous in my disposition, for nothing diverts me so much as to see certain characters tormented with false terrors.

—Jery Melford in *Humphry Clinker*[1]

It is as if a humane man could not bring himself to see the real origins of the misery of his time, in the class to which he was directly linked.

—Raymond Williams, *The Country and the City*[2]

Jery Melford's admission of mischievousness may well be Smollett's comic credo, with his elaborate stagings of false terrors and uncomfortable physical situations, his penchant for vomit and diarrhea, his delight in satire that torments. This chapter explores the meanings of Smollett's satire of incorporation and "false terrors" in *Humphry Clinker*, arguing that it should be read in the context of the novel's efforts to absorb, mute, and deny "the real origins of the misery of [its] time." The specific "misery" I address is the fate of the laboring poor under new forms of agrarian social organization in late-eighteenth-century England.

I begin with the premise that while *Humphry Clinker* concludes with not one, but three marriages, it reserves the affective charge of its comic closure for the accounts of two estates—Mr. Dennison's and Mr. Baynard's—recovered by improvement. As the novel winds to a close, Bramble visits his old schoolmate Dennison's overhauled estate and has an access of pleasure far greater than anything he expresses about the weddings: "I could not help breaking forth into the warmest expressions of applause at the beauty of the scene, which is really inchanting" (p. 310). One sees a franker displacement of the marriage plot by the improvement plot in Bramble's description of his old friend Baynard, who, having had his estate ruined by a de-monically—and thoroughly demonized—spendthrift wife, is suddenly freed by her death to improve it. Bramble is quite explicitly celebratory about the fortuitousness of the death, confessing, "I was instantly seized with a violent emotion, but it was not grief" (p. 325). He writes later of Baynard, who, now unencumbered, has been rendered fit for a happy ending:

> He is so pleased with the improvements made on this estate, which is all cultivated like a garden, that he has entered himself as a pupil in farming to Mr. Dennison, and resolved to attach himself wholly to the practice of husbandry. (p. 329)

The shift in attachments made possible by his wife's death turns Bay-nard into a new kind of husband, placing him, in Bramble's figura-tion, in Eden without Eve. Further, upon the marriage of Bramble's niece Liddy—the novel's romantic heroine—her fortune, along with that of other characters, is appropriated towards a loan to Baynard (p. 328), as though the function of the marriage were to free 5,000 pounds for the purposes of improvement. Indeed, so enchanted is Smollett's novel by prospects of improvement that one might regard its multiplication of marriages as a sign of its protesting too much.[3]

Many critics have noticed that *Humphry Clinker* is itself pastoral, or has a relation to the pastoral,[4] and many have suggested that it seeks its solutions to the luxury, unwholesomeness, and class insub-ordination of the city, as well as to the social and cultural threats of mercantile expansion, in the countryside. Focusing more upon the latter part of this novel than upon its memorably lurid city plot, this

chapter complicates the very site of *Humphry Clinker* that critics
have seen as offering its solutions, arguing that if it is about the pastoral it's about the pastoral in a very specific social form: the social
and economic transformation of the countryside in the second half
of the eighteenth century. The intensified influx of city capital into
the country, the development of convertible agriculture, and the expansion of acreage are only a few of the factors that marked this new
agricultural epoch. The most visible and controversial instrument of
this regime was, of course, enclosure, which was strenuously advocated by agricultural writers of the period and whose major purpose
was a more profitable exploitation of the land. *Humphry Clinker* was
written during one of the most concentrated periods of the second
great wave of parliamentary enclosures. While between 1702 and
1760 there were only 246 parliamentary Acts in England, affecting
about 400,000 acres, between 1760 and 1810 they had reached a total
of 2,438, affecting almost five million acres[5]; and of those, some 900
were passed in the 1760s and 1770s.[6]

Matthew Bramble, the landowner whose consciousness domi-
nates *Humphry Clinker*, becomes increasingly interested in enclosure
when his party arrives in Scotland, making casual observations about
the relative unproductiveness of Scottish agriculture, and regarding
Scotland as a site ripe for improvement: "The farms are thinly scattered, the lands uninclosed, and scarce a gentleman's seat is to be seen
in some miles from the Tweed" (p. 201); "Agriculture in this country
is not yet brought to that perfection which it has attained in England.
Inclosures would not only keep the grounds warm, and the several
fields distinct, but would also protect the crop from the high
winds . . . " (p. 208). From Cameron he writes, "The soil of this dis-
trict produces scarce any other grain but oats and barley; perhaps
because it is poorly cultivated, and almost altogether uninclosed"
(p. 237). Later, back in England, Dennison reports being told by his
agricultural consultant Farmer Bland, "With respect to the farm . . .
he said he would willingly take it at the present rent; but at the same
time owned, that if I would expend two hundred pounds in enclosure, it would be worth more than double the sum" (p. 311). Accordingly, Dennison tells Bramble, "I gradually inclosed all my farms, and

made such improvements, that my estate now yields me clear twelve hundred pounds a year" (p. 314).

As these quotations demonstrate, although enclosure is certainly important as a preoccupation in the later part of the novel, it is not very rich as a figure.[7] Finding denser and more suggestive meanings of enclosure in the novel requires looking to more dispersed and mediated effects. In this chapter, therefore, I look to the novel's rich discourse on ghostliness, superstition, and mourning, in order to describe the structure of feeling that organizes its relation to agricultural improvement. Drawing on psychoanalytic texts to describe an ideological process, I suggest that in *Humphry Clinker* the processes of alienation attendant upon the agricultural revolution produce a mental state in the gentry—an ideological formation—one might call melancholia: that melancholia is improvement's ideological mode. As I noted in the Introduction, I follow here from Fredric Jameson's description of narrative form as "an ideological act in its own right, with the function of inventing imaginary or formal 'solutions' to unresolvable social contradictions."[8] Because I take narrative to function as ideological—that is, as a collective fantasy or wish-fulfillment—psychoanalytic concepts are useful to describe it. I use these particular concepts because a certain psychoanalytic description of melancholia and the fantasy called incorporation can quite vividly account for a lot of disparate aspects of this novel—aspects both of content and of form.

I argued in the previous chapter that in *A Sentimental Journey* the gentleman empowers himself by taking on attributes of the poor: it is by enacting poverty that he is able to ward it off. In *Humphry Clinker* gentlemen also take on attributes of the poor, particularly their relation and resistance to dispossession. Here, however, rather than empowering the gentleman, that identification is the result of a radical disavowal, a disavowal hinted at in the notion of "false" terrors, or in Bramble's insistence that in Mrs. Baynard, nothing of value has been lost on the path to improvement. Identification is the magical way the gentleman preserves himself from having to acknowledge the social losses attendant upon the agricultural revolution: from seeing, and particularly from *saying*, the "real origins of

the misery of his time." Taking the concept of incorporation from
Nicolas Abraham and Maria Torok's essay "Introjection—Incorporation: Mourning *or* Melancholia," I argue that incorporation, which
serves the work of melancholia, allows us to connect the novel's per-
sistent disavowal of loss with its satire's centeredness upon the taking
in and the expulsion of food. Finally, I suggest, if the novel's actual
representation of the work of enclosure and improvement is figuratively improverished, that may be because melancholia itself entails a
resistance to the figurative.

I. The Debate on Enclosure

There has been a fierce and complex historical debate about
enclosure's effects on agrarian social relations, particularly about the
degree of economic harm or benefit done to the agricultural labor
force. In 1911 J. L. Hammond and Barbara Hammond argued passionately that enclosure was "fatal" to the small farmer, the cottager,
and the squatter[9]; enclosure history since then has been a protracted
attempt to refute their claims. K. D. M. Snell, one of the most recent
historians of eighteenth-century agriculture, summarizes the refu-
tations of such historians as J. A. Yelling, J. D. Chambers and G. E.
Mingay:

> [E]nclosure brought with it a fuller and more remunerative demand
> for labour . . . , and a feature of this was more regular and seasonally
> secure employment; it alleviated the pauperism and miserable stan-
> dard of living supposedly found in villages before parliamentary en-
> closure; it did not adversely affect the small landowner and tenant
> farmer, whose numbers actually grew in many regions during the
> period of parliamentary enclosure; it did not cause out-migration
> through an ejection of those rural classes previously dependent on the
> commons or open field agriculture; and it was on the contrary con-
> ducive to further and rapid rural population growth in response to its
> associated growing labour requirements.[10]

Snell argues, however, that the conclusions of these historians
about the quality of life of agricultural laborers has been severely
hampered by their limited definition of "employment" as wage-

dependent employment.[11] And if there is one thing that can be agreed upon as a momentous effect of enclosure, it is that by taking away such rights of laboring people as grazing, gleaning, and gathering fuel on common fields and wastes, it forced them into total dependence upon wage labor, or what Raymond Williams calls "the exposure of total hire."[12] David Davies wrote in 1795, "Thus an amazing number of people have been reduced from a comfortable state of partial independence to the precarious condition of hirelings, who, when out of work, must come immediately to their parish."[13] Even such a militantly Whig historian as G. E. Mingay has, ultimately, to account for the radical precariousness of the poor under total hire:

> Positive measures to enable the poor themselves to supplement their incomes, such as the provision of cow pastures and allotments, do not appear to have been widely adopted. Where they were introduced, as in Lincolnshire, they were said to be very effective in keeping labourers off the parish. In only a small proportion of the thousands of enclosures carried out in the later eighteenth century was land put aside for the poor, although occasionally provision was made for erecting a workhouse or school, and the great opportunity of making a large, long-term contribution to poor relief was sadly missed. We cannot put the blame for this on the landlords, however. Farmers were strongly opposed to the idea of giving labourers land because they believed it would make them more independent and careless of their work. . . .[14]

Mingay's admission of the failure to provide for the poor, appearing only in his book's very last pages, is made bearable, one senses, only by his belief in the ruling elite's innocence.

Accompanying and enabling the transformation of once partially independent laborers into a wage-earning labor force was a strident mainstream discourse of morality, in which, as Snell demonstrates, the partial independence of cottagers and laborers was increasingly associated with moral slovenliness, while "a change to wage dependency was equated with an improvement in 'moral' standing, in turn presented as tantamount to an improved standard of living."[15] Attacking those who argued that the poor benefited from the use of commons, John Arbuthnot wrote in 1773,

The benefit which [the Poor] are supposed to reap from commons . . . I know to be merely nominal; nay, indeed, what is worse, I
know that, in many instances it is an essential injury to them, by being
made a plea for their idleness; for, some few excepted, if you offer
them work, they will tell you, they must go to look up their sheep, cut
furzes, get their cow out of the pound, or perhaps, say they must take
their horse to be shod, that he may carry them to a horse-race or
cricket match. . . . If by converting the little farmers into a body of
men who must work for others, more labour is produced, it is an advantage which the nation should wish for: the compulsion will be that
of honest industry to provide for a family.[16]

In Arbuthnot's account the poor's efforts to tend sheep and cut
furzes stand in direct opposition to what counts for him as work: if
you offer them work, they will tell you that they must go do a different kind of work. And that desire to work (to tend their sheep, or
cut furzes) is transformed easily and inevitably into their desire for
recreation, so that they shoe their horse "that he may carry them to
a horse-race or cricket match." (Common lands, as I noted in Chapter 1, were also a site of recreation for rural laborers.) In a rejoinder
to the claim of an anti-enclosure pamphlet that sheep have a roving
nature that requires their grazing on large wastelands, the Rev. J.
Howlett gave a similar account of the poor and their activity on
wastelands, albeit in slightly displaced form:

I see no matter of reason why the poor creatures [the sheep], with
empty bellies and mournful cries, should gallop ten or twenty miles a
day over a barren heath, in quest of a wretchedly precarious subsistence, instead of lying down calm and content and fed to the full; unless, indeed, it were intended to keep them in excellent breathing that
they might at length figure away at Newmarket, or some other of our
public race grounds.[17]

It is hard not to see in Howlett's vision of fat and acquiescent sheep
a fantasy about the poor. And as in Arbuthnot's pamphlet, the quest
for subsistence on the wasteland inevitably gives way to the phan-
tasm of public recreation.

Matthew Bramble is speaking out of the improving morality of
his day, then, when he links the Scottish Highlanders' occupation as

shepherds, whose herds "run wild all winter" on wastelands, "without any shelter or subsistence, but what they can find among the heath," to an essential laziness:

> Perhaps this branch of husbandry, which requires very little attendance and labour, is one of the principal causes of that idleness and want of industry, which distinguishes these mountaineers in their own country—When they come forth into the world, they become as diligent and alert as any people on earth. (p. 245)

That Bramble should also admiringly characterize the Highlanders as "fiery and ferocious" (p. 245) and as lethal and tenacious soldiers, "patient of hunger and fatigue" (p. 246), points to the overweening determining power of labor to determine moral character.

Humphry Clinker does not, however, participate in the dominant farming-interest discourse of its time in any simple way. Rather, with an abiding nostalgia, it represents Matthew Bramble as a landlord who exerts benevolence toward the laborers and poor people in his charge, and who is sensitive to an older code of rights and perquisites. On the one hand, rhapsodizing about Brambleton Hall, Bramble writes, "Without doors, I superintend my farm, and execute plans of improvements, the effects of which I enjoy with unspeakable delight" (p. 118). But he also writes to his neighbor, doctor, and confidant Dr. Lewis at the beginning of the novel:

> Tell Barns I am obliged to him for his advice; but don't choose to follow it. If Davis voluntarily offers to give up the farm, the other shall have it; but I will not begin at this time of day to distress my tenants, because they are unfortunate, and cannot make regular payments: I wonder that Barns should think me capable of such oppression—As for Higgins, the fellow is a notorious poacher, to be sure; and an impudent rascal to set his snares in my own paddock; but, I suppose, he thought he had some right (especially in my absence) to partake of what nature seems to have intended for common use. . . . (p. 16)

Not only is Bramble generous to his smaller tenants, tenants who would be liable to be forced out of their farms by high rents upon enclosure, but when he winks at poaching he also acknowledges and tolerates an older system of common rights. It is worth noting that poaching, besides being an offense against property, was regarded as a threat to labor discipline during the period. In his account of poaching and the social meaning of the game laws, Douglas Hay quotes a 1762 letter from a steward to his lord stating that two poachers, "tho' they have families to maintain & are labourers by Profession are Seldom Seen to Work but are patrolling & Poching in the Night time & in Bed in the Day."[18] Bramble's benevolent paternalism is, no doubt, the mystery Jery alludes to when he says of his uncle, "all his servants and neighbors in the country, are fond of him, even to a degree of enthusiasm, the reason of which I cannot as yet comprehend" (p. 10).

Indeed, in his very first letter Bramble writes to Lewis, "Let Morgan's widow have the Alderney cow" (p. 7). That he gives away a cow is significant because cows were a privileged signifier in the enclosure debates. "There was almost no disagreement," Snell writes, "that enclosure virtually ended the long-established practice of cottagers, squatters, labourers, and other poor people keeping their own livestock"—livestock that made it possible for them to have milk for their children, and whose value Arthur Young estimated as close to the wages of a fully employed laborer. Even the *General Report on Enclosures* of 1808, which fully advocates enclosure, reported great financial hardship to the poor primarily because of their loss of cows.[19] And in Arthur Young's 1801 recanting pamphlet about the effects of enclosure upon the rural poor, he wrote this famous sentence about cows: "The poor in these parishes may say, and with truth, *Parliament may be tender of property; all I know is, I had a cow, and an act of Parliament has taken it from me.*"[20]

Humphry Clinker's general ideological structure concerning improvement asserts at once the benefits of improvement and the total compatibility of improvement with traditional agrarian social relations.[21] Its structural separation of the two by plenty of novelistic space, however—Bramble's adherence to an older patriarchal system is emphasized at the beginning of the novel, while the end emphasizes his development into an enclosure maven—suggests the ideological difficulty of coherently imagining the two together. Also, tellingly, the novel never actually represents Bramble's estate in its narrative present.[22] And despite the fact that Bramble is an improving landlord, Brambleton Hall is quite explicitly and polemically a noncapitalist operation: as Charlotte Sussman suggests, the novel's misogynist loathing for Bramble's sister Tabitha comes from the fact that she sells the products of Brambleton Hall at the local market, thereby "breaking the barriers between Brambleton Hall and the world of commerce."[23]

The moment that separates the novel's nostalgic portrayal of agrarian social relations and its new interest in enclosure is the Bramble party's arrival in Scotland, which, as I have suggested, Bramble regards as a kind of tabula rasa for agricultural innovation. Scotland functions ideologically in a complicated, overdetermined way in this novel. On the one hand, as John Zomchick has argued,

> Because of its more primitive stage of economic development and the survival of 'patriarchal' affiliations, Scotland is a nation at the threshhold of modernity. . . . Because of its transitional status, Scotland does not suffer from the South's problems; rather, it serves as a model for an imaginary solution to the social dislocations accompanying development.[24]

At the same time, it would be wrong not to take seriously the problematical nature of its transitional status. Patriarchal affiliations, for example, survive not as a stable and timeless mode of social being, but as a mode of resistance to the new forms of social organization brought about by the Union. Lismahago is a vociferous spokesman for how much the Scots lost by the Union (pp. 265–69), while Bramble speaks, more ambivalently, about the British legislature's attempt to subdue the Highlanders, and to break their allegiance to their feudal chiefs (pp. 245–48). Indeed, the Highlanders' subjugation by the force of English law is a powerful and suggestive parallel to the subjugation of the English poor by parliamentary acts of enclosure: it is the way the novel speaks of the oppression of the commonality by the law. So while Scotland's transitional status lends itself to a politics of nostalgia—it is unlike, and in some ways superior to, England because modernity has not hit it yet—it just as easily lends itself to mirroring social processes in England, foregrounding the

oppression and dislocation that are represented so much more quietly in the English sections of the novel. That it is alternately portrayed as a place of poverty and a place of plenty suggests the pro-
tean quality of the ideological uses it is put to in this novel. I stress
this point because much of the material I will be drawing upon in
the following sections as crucial to the novel's purpose regarding
improvement occurs in the Scottish section of the novel. While one
would want, to be sure, to respect the specificity of this material's
Scottish content, I treat Scotland as a force field for the projection of
attitudes about the agricultural revolution as it has already been occurring in England as well.

II. Improvement and Melancholia

The category of melancholia is compelling to me because in
each of the scenes of mourning in the novel, the account of the
mourning suggests there is something irrational about it: to the narrator who is the novel's guiding consciousness at that moment, the
mourning always seems rather pathological, unaccountably exceed-
ing the value of its object. At an open house held by the duke of
Queensberry, and attended by the Bramble party, a Scottish gentleman tells a story about an old friend:

> Being on a party of hunting in the North . . . , I resolved to visit an
> old friend, whom I had not seen for twenty years—So long he had
> been retired and sequestered from all his acquaintance, and lived in a
> moping melancholy way, much afflicted with lowness of spirits, occa-
> sioned by the death of his wife, whom he had loved with uncommon
> affection. (p. 260)

The phrase "uncommon affection" is almost a redundancy in this
novel, which love for a wife always takes by surprise; because just
about *any* period of mourning would have been excessive in
Humphry Clinker, the twenty-year moping period creates a kind of
comic wonder. In another minor and casually recounted episode
from the visit to Scotland, Bramble and Jery are invited to "the funeral of an old lady, the grand-mother of a gentleman in this neigh-

borhood." When the large procession arrives at the church, Jery
writes,

> we found we had committed a small oversight, in leaving the corpse
> behind; so that we were obliged to wheel about, and met the old
> gentle-woman half way, . . . attended by the *coronach*, composed of a
> multitude of old hags, who tore their hair, beat their breasts, and
> howled most hideously. (p. 235)

Jery's amused anthropological observation gets its comic force partly
from its alliterative flourishes, but more centrally from the contrast
between the intensity of the grief of the ceremonial mourners and
the rest of the party's cavalier attitude toward the corpse. And late in
the novel, when Clinker carries the unconscious Bramble from the
stream, Bramble's niece Liddy commences a mourning that is similarly irrational and excessive. Her brother Jery writes,

> As for Liddy, I thought the poor girl would have actually lost her
> senses. The good-woman of the house had shifted her linen, and put
> her into bed; but she was seized with the idea that her uncle had per-
> ished, and in this persuasion made a dismal out-cry; nor did she pay
> the least regard to what I said, when I solemnly assured her he was
> safe. (p. 302)

In this scene Liddy is simply mistaken: her uncle has not in fact died.
I'm interested, though, in the fact that when mourning occurs, it
occurs, according to an authoritative voice (in this case Jery's), in the
form of an insane overreaction, Liddy almost "los[ing] her senses."

The novel's climactic instance of mourning is the scene of
Baynard's grief over his wife, a scene that takes place among the
events of the end of the novel, and which I regard as central to its trajectory toward improvement. The improvement of Baynard's estate,
that is, requires not merely his wife's death, but also the process of
melancholia that ensues, a process that I read as constitutive of the
gentry's experience of improvement.[25] Mrs. Baynard has been financially ruining her husband, and Baynard, telling Bramble that
"his wife had such delicate nerves, and such imbecility of spirit, that
she could neither bear remonstrance . . . nor practise any scheme of
retrenchment, even if she perceived the necessity of such a measure,"

has given up and prepared himself for ruin (p. 281). So now that she
has died, Bramble can only regard Baynard as insane, as the bereaved
husband "act[s] all the extravagancies of affliction" (p. 325): weeping
over and clinging to the body, lamenting what a loving wife she was,
claiming that death shall not part them. Between Baynard's excessive
idea of his wife's worth and Bramble's equally insistent assertion of
her worthlessness—an assertion the reader does not question, given
that Mrs. Baynard has been represented to us by Bramble alone—the
novel creates a turbulent, and comic, ambivalence. Finally, "disen-
gage[ing]" Baynard from "the melancholy object" and working hard
to distract him with other topics, Bramble prevails: "In a few hours,
he was calm enough to hear reason, and even to own that Heaven
could not have interposed more effectually to rescue him from dis-
grace and ruin" (pp. 325–26). The grief that the novel rejects as
pathological is powerfully disavowed, to the extent that it is transformed into thankfulness that the wife has died.

Psychoanalytic accounts of melancholia suggest that it differs
from mourning in that it originates from an embattled or ambivalent relation to the lost object. Freud writes in "Mourning and
Melancholia," for example, that in a kind of melancholia that provides a clue for the process of melancholia in general, the object has
not actually died, but "has become lost as an object of love";

> First there existed an object-choice, the libido had attached itself to
> a certain person; then, owing to a real injury or disappointment con-
> cerned with the loved person, this object-relationship was under-
> mined.[26]

In other cases, Freud writes,

> one feels justified in concluding that a loss of the kind has been expe-
> rienced, but one cannot see clearly what has been lost, and may the
> more readily suppose that the patient too cannot consciously perceive
> what it is he has lost. This, indeed, might be so even when the patient
> was aware of the loss giving rise to the melancholia, that is, when he
> knows whom he has lost but not *what* it is he has lost in them. This
> would suggest that melancholia is in some way related to an uncon-
> scious loss of a love-object, in contradistinction to mourning, in
> which there is nothing unconscious about the loss.[27]

The melancholic, then, suffers a loss that challenges his or her love for the object, and that loss is often one that cannot be named or acknowledged.

Nicolas Abraham and Maria Torok describe in even stronger terms the ambivalence and disavowal out of which comes the fantasy of incorporation that makes up melancholia. For them, the work of mourning occurs through a process called introjection, while the fantasy of incorporation is constitutive of melancholia. Their paradigm for introjection is the way the child compensates for its empty mouth when it loses the breast, through "a progressive partial replacement of satisfactions of the mouth filled with the maternal object by satisfactions of the mouth devoid of that object but filled with words addressed to the subject."[28] In introjection, which is the way mourning occurs, the absence of the object is partially replaced by words that express it, and "the original oral void will have found a remedy for all its wants through their conversion in linguistic intercourse with the speaking community." In contrast, incorporation occurs when "the mouth cannot articulate certain words, cannot utter certain phrases," and therefore "in fantasy one will take into the mouth the unspeakable, the thing itself":

> When introjection proves impossible, then, the decisive transition to incorporation is made at the point when the mouth's *words* do not succeed in filling the subject's emptiness, so he fills it instead with an imaginary *thing*.

I will speak in more detail later about the way the fantasy of incorporation works, as well as about the imaginary thing taken into the mouth. For now I want merely to stress that it occurs because the loss cannot be owned:

> One finds that not all narcissistic losses . . . have incorporation as their final fate. *That is so only for losses that cannot—for one reason or another— be acknowledged as losses.*

Incorporation is the very "rejection of mourning": the subject who rejects mourning "contradict[s] the fact of his loss with a radical denial, by pretending to have had nothing to lose." While Baynard does in fact acknowledge and name his loss, crying "O Matthew! I have lost my dear Harriet!" (p. 325), he is eventually led to conclude that it wasn't *really* a loss. But even where gentlemen could be said to acknowledge loss—as, for example, the melancholy gentleman does—the incredulity with which the novel represents those losses creates the aura I call melancholic. That is, while individual characters cry out that they have suffered mortal loss, the collective narrating voices of the novel attempt to create an environment, a cultural attitude, in which such loss may be muted or denied. Another way to describe the difference between individual characters' acknowledgment of loss and the novel's disavowal would be to say that the novel plays mourning and melancholia against one another, as if ambivalent about which better constitutes its relation to loss.[29]

The systematic disavowal of mourning bears a striking resemblance to another mental state in the novel: the disavowal of proletarian fear and loss which the novel enacts by placing them under the rubric of "superstition." The superstition associated with the poor is, of course, a conventional source of satiric amusement in Smollett's (and other eighteenth-century) fiction. It comes in its most typical state in a scene in *Roderick Random*, in which, after a brutal fight with his tyrannical captain, Roderick crawls, wounded and bloodied, into a barn, and catches the attention of a country man when he groans:

> This melancholy note alarmed the clown, who started back, and discovering a body all besmeared with blood, stood trembling, with the pitch-fork extended before him, his hair erect, his eyes staring, his nostrils dilated, and his mouth wide open.—At another time, I should have been much diverted with this figure, which preserved the same attitude very near a quarter of an hour . . . but my tongue failed me, and my language was only a repetition of groans. . . . [30]

The amusement generated by this spectacle is so surefire and automatic that even though he can only groan with pain, Roderick registers the amusement he *would* have felt under normal circumstances.

This stock episode of working-class stupefaction, whose emblematic quality is emphasized by the inordinately long time the man stays frozen in the same position, becomes much more complex and layered in *Humphry Clinker*. For although the famous superstition of the Highlanders is rejected and dismissed by the novel's narrators, it invariably becomes intertwined with the stories gentlemen tell about themselves. In the passage that introduces the tale of the melancholy gentleman, Bramble reflects:

> The longer I live, I see more reason to believe that prejudices of education are never wholly eradicated, even when they are discovered to be erroneous and absurd. Such habits of thinking as interest the grand passions, cleave to the human heart in such a manner, that though an effort of reason may force them from their hold for a moment, this violence no sooner ceases, than they resume their grasp with an encreased elasticity and adhesion.
>
> I am led into this reflection, by what passed at the duke's table after supper. The conversation turned upon the vulgar notions of spirits and omens, that prevail among the commonality of North-Britain, and all the company agreed, that nothing could be more ridiculous. One gentleman, however, told a remarkable story of himself, by way of speculation. . . . (p. 260)

Dismissing the superstitions of the commonality as vulgar and common, this passage nevertheless slides from the idea of "grand passions" to "vulgar notions" as though it does not quite know how to judge these feelings' legitimacy. While it tries to contain the superstitions of the commonality by figuring them as the ridiculous version of a larger and grander mental state, of "such habits of thinking as interest the grand passions," thinking about those superstitions naturally leads Bramble into the account of the story he heard about the grander passions of the melancholy gentleman. Indeed, the novel describes superstition in the same terms that it describes mourning, as something powerfully adhesive, "cleav[ing] to the human heart." Meditating about Baynard's grief, Bramble writes,

> The mind has a surprising facility of accomodating, and even attaching itself, in such a manner, by dint of use, to things that are in their own nature disagreeable, and even pernicious, that it cannot bear to be delivered from them without reluctance and regret. (p. 325)

Like superstition, mourning is a tenacious and irrational attachment to something lost. Such an attachment is also reminiscent of the attachment of the Highlanders to their chiefs despite the dissolution of old ties by the Union:

> The legislature hath not only disarmed these mountaineers, but also
> deprived them of their ancient garb . . . and their slavish tenures are
> all dissolved by act of parliament; so that they are at present as free and
> independent of their chiefs, as the law can make them: but the origi-
> nal attachment still remains. . . . (p. 246)

Bramble figures a social dissolution as the granting of freedom here,
disavowing a loss that he cannot help but notice the Highlanders
regret: he tells several such stories about the Highlanders' refusal to relinquish their attachments to their clans and their chiefs (pp. 246–47).

If the novel represents superstition and mourning in similar
terms, that may be because the superstition attributed to working
people is in fact a relation to something that has been lost: a relation
that expresses itself in the fear or desire that the lost object will return. We may, indeed, connect the famous superstition of the Highlanders—an irrational and powerful attachment—precisely with
their attachment to their old forms of law and property, so that superstition is, here, a form of mourning in the terms of the novel.[31]
Moreover, the novel disavows superstition just as it does mourning,
for the denial of an actual thing-to-be-feared is built into the very
idea of superstition, which refers precisely to an irrational or unrea-
sonable belief. The relation to lost loves is gentle peoples' version of
superstition: they have irrational grief over lost individuals, while
the poor retain an irrational attachment to lost forms of social organization.

Mourning and superstition dovetail in their most complicated
way in the novel's most extended scenario of proletarian superstition, a scene in which Clinker is frightened by a character he takes
to be a ghost. At Cameron House in Scotland, Bramble meets a
character he calls "the admiral," "a person," he writes, "whom I treat
with singular respect, as a venerable druid, who has lived near ninety
years, without pain or sickness, among oaks of his own planting"
(p. 243):

> He was once proprietor of these lands; but being of a projecting spirit,
> some of his schemes miscarried, and he was obliged to part with his
> possession, which hath shifted hands two or three times since that pe-
> riod; but every succeeding proprietor hath done every thing in his

power, to make his old age easy and comfortable. He has a sufficiency
to procure the necessaries of life; and he and his old woman reside in a
small convenient farm-house, having a little garden which he culti-
vates with his own hands. (p. 243)

The admiral has lost his property, but Bramble disavows that loss
through a series of mitigations. Indeed, Bramble gives here what we
may regard as a utopian account of dispossession, in which the man
loses his property because of his own agency, and becoming the
beneficiary of benevolent landlords, leads a life made wholesome by
precapitalist self-sufficiency. Unlike the poacher Higgins, who
thinks "he had some right . . . to partake of what nature seems to
have intended for common use" (p. 16), the admiral has internalized
the concept of private property. Still, one of his chief pleasures is to
imaginatively transcend its bounds; he spends "most of his time in
ranging through the woods, which he declares he enjoys as much as
if they were still his own property" (p. 243). If we imagine such a
declaration from the mouth of a young eighteenth-century landless
laborer—"Gee, I enjoy these woods as much as if they were my own
property!"—we can, perhaps, denaturalize Bramble's characterization, whose complacency is enabled by the admiral's harmless old
age and eccentricity.

But if the admiral is an object of pleasure and respect to Bramble, to Clinker he is positively uncanny[32]:

> Notwithstanding all his innocence, however, he was the cause of great
> perturbation to my man Clinker, whose natural superstition has been
> much injured, by the histories of witches, fairies, ghosts, and goblins,
> which he has heard in this country—On the evening after our arrival,
> Humphry strolled into the wood, in the course of his meditation,
> and all at once the admiral stood before him, under the shadow of a
> spreading oak. . . . [H]e could not stand the sight of this apparition,
> but ran into the kitchen, with his hair standing on end, staring wildly,
> and deprived of utterance. (pp. 243–44)

The classical detail "under the shadow of a spreading oak" makes it
tempting to read this episode as a comic and debased version of
Virgil's first eclogue, in which Meliboeus meets Tityrus "under the
spreading, sheltering beech," and envies him for being able to "seek

out cooling shade."[33] While Tityrus is sheltered by the patronage of Octavian, Meliboeus has had his farm appropriated, and mourns his imminent departure into exile. In Smollett's account the admiral has lost his farm; but the oak he stands under—British neoclassicism's national tree of choice, and one of its characteristic tropes for the benevolence and stability of manorial power—suggests the mitigation of his expropriation by the benevolence of landowners who allow him to remain on his former property.

If the classical allusion reinforces Bramble's conception of the admiral as enfranchised, though, it casts a very different light on Clinker. A "rural proletarian for whom work was varied, seasonal, and uncertain," as John Richetti has characterized him,[34] Clinker belongs to an English labor force whose mobility at least partially resulted from the alienation from the land attendant upon enclosures, higher rents, and other results of agricultural improvement. Richard Halpern has pointed out that this mobility was ideologically reconceptualized by Adam Smith during this period, in the *Wealth of Nations'* angry tirade against the settlement laws. "Movement," Halpern writes, "is no longer seen as a catastrophe inflicted on the working classes by means of their expropriation; instead it is considered an inherent liberty or 'right,' which can be guaranteed only by the free market."[35] The catastrophic nature of this movement is, I think, evoked by the allusion to Virgil, which works as a kind of melancholy shadow effect to this otherwise stock comic episode. One needn't, though, rely solely upon the classical allusion to hear the melancholy that underlies the scene of dispossession; for an earlier episode urges us to read the loss of property in this episode in the light of mortal loss. The admiral's healthy old age contrasts vividly with that of the old friends Bramble meets earlier in the novel, in Bath—especially rear-admiral Balderick, the admiral's explicit counterpart—who are prey to disease and dissatisfaction, but who arouse in Bramble a kind of pleasurable melancholy:

> It was a renovation of youth; a kind of resuscitation of the dead, that realized those interesting dreams, in which we sometimes retrieve our antient friends from the grave. Perhaps my enjoyment was not the less pleasing for being mixed with a strain of melancholy, produced by the

remembrance of past scenes, that conjured up the ideas of some endearing connexions, which the hand of Death has actually dissolved.
(p. 55)

Bramble's meditation on the hand of Death, the dissolution of "endearing connexions," and the fantasy of resuscitating dead loved
ones, all find their way into his account of the ghostly admiral,
where the dissolution of endearing connections is rewritten as an
"obligation to part with his possession," and Death's hand becomes
that of the landlord, as the property "shifts hands." Once again, the
fright Humphry takes from the loss of something social is figured in
the case of gentlemen as the loss of individuals.

The scene of Humphry and the admiral suggests that the lost
object that cannot be named or acknowledged—Clinker is at that
moment "deprived of utterance"—and whose loss therefore produces the melancholia that pervades the novel, has something to do
with the alienation of property. Because the novel represents the admiral and his loss in such ambivalent terms, it is hard to tell what
Clinker recognizes in him: whether he sees in the admiral his own
dispossession regardless of the mitigating light Bramble portrays him
in, or whether he, like Meliboeus, sees a good fortune that oppresses
him with an awareness of his own contrasting poverty. Whatever it
is he sees, though, in running from the woods into the kitchen,
Humphry precisely reenacts the process of alienation that turned
partially self-sufficient laborers into servants.

Even as it suggests that property is the thing lost, though—the
object of what we might call superstitious mourning—this scene is
ambiguous about who is being dispossessed. The admiral, for example, has been a landlord and perhaps a gentleman, and has not lost his
land to enclosure. Moreover, while upon a first reading of the novel
Clinker is at that moment a landless laborer, he is revealed near the
novel's end to be a gentleman's son, and as such one could argue that
he is spooked by a recognition of the dispossession that stripped him
of his rights as a *gentleman*—that is, as Bramble's son—and cast him
into the ranks of the laboring poor. This confusion, or conflation, of
the fates of gentleman and laborer is characteristic of the novel's
treatment of dispossession. In the paragraph immediately following

the episode of Clinker and the admiral, Bramble asks Lewis, "Do you know how we fare in this Scottish paradise? We make free with our landlord's mutton, which is excellent, his poultry-yard, his garden, his dairy, and his cellar, which are all well stored" (p. 244). In his account of this bounty, Bramble represents the food they eat synecdocially, in terms of parts of the estate. His acknowledgment of another's property is emphasized by the (grammatically unnecessary) repetition of the word *his*: but he mentally wanders, in an edenically unhampered and proprietary way, into all of the estate's recesses. He rhapsodizes about his own property, Brambleton Hall, in much the same terms, in one of his letters to Lewis comparing the filth of city life to life in the country: "I indulge with cyder, which my own orchard affords. . . . [M]y bread is sweet and nourishing, made from my own wheat, ground in my own mill, and baked in my own oven; my table is, in a great measure, furnished from my own ground . . . " (p. 118). Like the admiral he has just described, he knows that Cameron House is not his, but he enjoys it as much as if it were. That is, he enacts the relation to others' property performed by someone who has been dispossessed.

Indeed, Bramble's enactment of dispossession is a central part of his character; the complete and generous access of gentleman to one another's estates is a burning issue in this novel, coming in the form of contestation over hospitality. *Humphry Clinker*'s status as a travelogue makes this inevitable, of course; but I would suggest that the novel's obsession with hospitality is the form taken by its obsession with private property. The novel's most violent episode—the Bramble party's revenge after being expelled from Lord Oxmington's estate—should be read in the context of, and in contrast to, their unmediated access to their Scottish host's food and estate. Oxmington, Jery tell us, "considered his guests merely as objects to shine upon, so as to reflect the lustre of his own magnificence— There was much state, but no courtesy. . . . ":

> Before the desert was removed, our noble entertainer proposed three general toasts; then calling for a glass of wine, and bowing all round, wished us a good afternoon. This was the signal for the company to break up, and they obeyed it immediately, all except our 'squire, who

was greatly shocked at the manner of his dismission.—He changed
countenance, bit his lip in silence, but still kept his seat, so that his
lordship found himself obliged to give us another hint, by saying, he
should be glad to see us another time. (p. 271)

Oxmington's shocking dismissal of the gentry from his estate suggests that he regards property in terms of a different paradigm than
they do, a paradigm we might consider in the light of Carole Fabricant's work on domestic tourism in the late part of the century.
Urging us to regard tourism as a cultural institution bound up in
changing ideas about private property—a rigidification she sees as
largely a result of the enclosure movement—Fabricant argues that it
served the ideological function of inviting those of the lower and
middling classes to share aesthetically in what they could not possess
materially: it gave them controlled and highly mediated access to
gorgeous property, training them how to look at it and also how to
respect it. Reading the 1750 version of *The Beauties of Stow*, she
demonstrates that at Stow, like at Oxmington's, "the flow of human
traffic into the house and park was carefully controlled and moni-
tored at the same time that it was actively (indeed, aggressively) promoted."[36] The shock to Bramble's sensibility comes from being
treated as a tourist rather than a gentleman: from actually being expelled from an estate as though his access to estates were attenuated.
He responds by proceeding with a large party, "mounted a-horse-
back, with our pistols loaded and ready primed," which parades
"solemnly and slowly before his lordship's gate," in an extravagant
ritual of the restoration of prerogative (p. 274).

The category of melancholia allows us to posit a relation between the dispossession of the poor and a gentle mentality that has
the fear of dispossession at its center. Arguing that the structure of
melancholia he describes in the 1917 essay "Mourning and Melancholia" becomes for Freud the structure of mourning in general by
the 1923 essay "The Ego and the Id," Judith Butler writes,

> In the experience of losing another human being whom one has
> loved, Freud argues, the ego is said to incorporate that other into the
> very structure of the ego, taking on attributes of the other and "sus-
> taining" the other through magical acts of imitation. The loss of the

other whom one desires and loves is overcome through a specific act
of identification that seeks to harbor that other within the very structure of the self. . . . This identification is not simply momentary or
occasional, but becomes a new structure of identity; in effect, the
other becomes part of the ego through the permanent internalization
of the other's attributes.[37]

While the novel consistently represents the losses of the gentry as
losses in the private sphere rather than the public, Butler's reading
allows us to read the fear of dispossession enacted by the Bramble
party as a magical act of imitation of an entire class. In Freud's account, feelings of poverty and dispossession can be *effects* or *symp-
toms* of melancholia:

> In the clinical picture of melancholia dissatisfaction with the self on
> moral grounds is far the most outstanding feature; the self-criticism
> much less frequently concerns itself with bodily infirmity, ugliness,
> weakness, social inferiority; among these latter ills that the patient
> dreads or asserverates the thought of poverty alone has a favoured po-
> sition.[38]

I am arguing, however, that in Smollett's novel dispossession is the
origin of melancholia: that gentlemen internalize the relation of
the poor to the alienation of their property. While the melancholic,
in Freud's account, usually reproaches him- or herself for a moral
failing, the melancholic abjection of *Humphry Clinker* manifests itself in bodily infirmity, Bramble's valetudinarian status working as
an expression of melancholia.[39] The internalization of attributes of
the poor on the part of the gentle sensibilities of this novel suggests
that the lost object is, in some way, the poor themselves. Or, more
accurately, because the loss that results in incorporation is generally
a "narcissistically indispensable" object,[40] the object mourned by
Humphry Clinker must be some version of the poor indispensable to
the good self-image of the gentry, as though total hire created a nar-
cissistic injury to them. Bramble's contempt for servants is the most
obvious way he registers that the laboring poor have been somehow
transformed. He accounts for the depopulation of farms as follows:

> The plough-boys, cow-herds, and lower hinds, are debauched and se-
> duced by the appearance and discourse of those coxcombs in livery,

when they make their summer excursions. They desert their dirt and drudgery, and swarm up to London, in hopes of getting into service, where they can live luxuriously and wear fine clothes, without being obliged to work; for idleness is natural to man. . . . (p. 87)

For Bramble, the desertion of laborers from their farms is a function of their traitorous *desire* to work under the total hire of servitude.

But alongside this rather obvious instance of blaming the victim, the novel knows that the poor's relation to labor is one to be mourned. Indeed, labor is so wrapped up in death and mourning that this is where the novel lets itself wail—where mourning is its mode, a mourning so implacable it cannot be disavowed.[41] When we first meet Clinker, he is sick from hunger and fever, and explains that

he had been a love begotten babe, brought up in the work-house, and put out apprentice by the parish to a country black-smith, who died before the boy's time was out: that he had for some time worked under his ostler, as a helper and extra postilion, till he was taken ill of the ague. . . . (p. 80)

The nouns denoting professions are immediately followed by modifiers about illness and death. Later, Clinker tells Jery about his quarrel with Jery's servant Dutton:

He has challenged me to fight him at sword's point . . . ; but I might as well challenge him to make a horse-shoe, or a plough iron; for I know no more of the one than he does of the other.—Besides, it doth not become servants to use those weapons, or to claim the privilege of gentlemen to kill one another when they fall out. . . . (p. 203)

Clinker's rich commentary on working and killing serves as an acerbic critique of gentlemanly barbarity, to be sure, as well as of Dutton's lack of useful skills; it also displays a kind of class pride in its elevation of smithing to the level of an aristocratic accomplishment. Most important to me, though, is the way in which, with its cool and weary comparison, it puts smithing and killing on the same level. Finally, in a sentimental set piece about a blacksmith's widow, smithing is even more explicitly associated with death. When the Bramble party's carriage breaks down, Clinker repairs it in the shop of a recently deceased blacksmith, whose widow, "struck with the well-known sound of the hammer and anvil," starts up and, mistaking Clinker for her husband, laments his desertion of her. Jery's claim that "this incident was too pathetic to occasion mirth—it brought tears into the eyes of all present" (p. 180), suggests that it is unassimilable to the wry recuperation of melancholic disavowal—although he registers such a recuperation as certainly *tempting*. And in a sentence that richly evokes the imbricatedness of labor and loss, Jery writes, "As for the tender-hearted Humphry Clinker, he hammered the iron and wept at the same time" (p. 181).

The poor's damaged relation to labor is also indicated by the way in which the romance convention that ultimately reveals Clinker to be a gentleman's son seems insufficient to that problem, in need of ideological supplementation. As Matthew Loyd, Clinker has a new and rather awkward relation to labor that the novel represents as superfluity. Casting around for an appropriate job for him, Bramble suggests to Dr. Lewis that he train him as an apothecary (pp. 329–30); but later he writes:

> What you observe of the vestry-clerk deserves consideration.—I make no doubt but Matthew Loyd is well enough qualified for the office; but, at present, you must find room for him in the house.—His incorruptible honesty and indefatigable care will be serviceable in superintending the oeconomy of my farm; tho' I don't mean that he shall interfere with Barns, of whom I have no cause to complain. (p. 335)

I take Bramble's saying "but, at present," to mean that there already is a vestry clerk, although one that could use replacing; and Barns' good work as a bailiff makes Clinker superfluous even if he could do that job well. The insufficiency of romance to repair the problem of labor manifests itself in an uncertainty about what Clinker should *do* now that he's the son of a gentleman. It doesn't occur to Bramble that it might be appropriate for Clinker to be leisured—indeed, he wants him to be employed so "that the parish may not be overstocked" (p. 329)—but at the same time the novel struggles to figure out how to put him to work. So as it sputters ideologically around romance's inability to address the condition of the laboring

poor, it creates a supplemental figure, one who can absorb and reinvent the problem of labor: Jack Wilson.

Jack Wilson, Dennison's farmer neighbor and close friend, is a
more central figure to the novel's ending than his rather oblique
function in the plot would indicate. It is the Bramble party's fortu-
itous encounter with Dennison's family, not Wilson's, that enables
the marriages at the end of the novel, and even Jack's instrumental-
ity in the improvement of Dennison's farm is displaced a little: he
introduces Dennison to his father-in-law, Farmer Bland, and it is
Bland, not him, who teaches Dennison how to run an estate (pp.
311–12). Wilson's primary purpose in the novel is more affective
than functional: providing an analogy and a corrective to Clinker,[42]
Wilson makes possible the uniting of labor and pleasure.

Striking verbal echoes suggest the analogical status of Clinker
and Wilson. Early in the novel, determining whether to keep
Clinker on as a servant, Bramble asks him, "[W]hat are your qualifications? What are you good for?" Clinker replies with a list whose
length and variedness create a kind of comic braggadocio:

> "I can read and write, and do the business of the stable indifferent
> well—I can dress a horse, and shoe him, and bleed and rowel him;
> and, as for the practice of sow-gelding, I won't turn my back on e'er
> a he in the county of Wilts—Then I can make hog's puddings and
> hob-nails, mend kettles, and tin sauce-pans." Here uncle burst out
> a-laughing, and enquired, what other accomplishments he was master
> of—"I know something of single-stick, and psalmody, (proceeded
> Clinker) I can play upon the Jew's-harp, sing Black-ey'd Susan,
> Arthur- o'Bradley, and divers other songs; I can dance a Welsh jig, and
> Nancy Dawson; wrestle a fall with any lad of my inches, when I'm
> in heart; and, under correction, I can find a hare when your honour
> wants a bit of game." "Foregad! thou art a complete fellow, (cried my
> uncle, still laughing) I have a good mind to take thee into my
> family. . . ."(pp. 81–82)

Later, this list of eclectic skills is reiterated in the context of Jack
Wilson's "qualifications," as recounted by George Dennison:

> Jack is a universal genius—his talents are really astonishing—He is an
> excellent carpenter, joiner, and turner, and a cunning artist in iron and
> brass.—He not only superintended my oeconomy, but also presided

over my pastimes.—He taught me to brew beer, to make cyder, perry, mead, usquebaugh, and plague-water; to cook several outlandish delicacies, such as *ollas, pepper-pots, pillaws, corys, chabobs,* and *stufatas.*—He understands all manner of games from chess down to chuck-farthing, sings a good song, plays upon the violin, and dances a hornpipe with surprising agility. . . . (p. 313)

Though this list has a dose of soldierly cosmopolitanism, the homely hog's puddings of Clinker's account rendered here as the "outlandish delicacies" Wilson has encountered in various colonial enterprises, Jack's skills are quite similar to those of Clinker, down to the syntax. Both of their skills arouse in the gentlemen contemplating them a kind of astonished pleasure. Bramble's laughter at Clinker's skill arises, presumably, from their homeliness and eclecticism, from his hearing them as a debased version of gentlemanly "accomplishments"; but like Dennison, whose appreciation of Wilson's skills comes from his need for such skills as an improving landlord, he also has a general appreciation for work.

What Wilson does for this novel is to bring a consistent pleasure to the labor elsewhere represented as lethal—a pleasure Clinker can only create momentarily, in an ingratiating comic performance intended to land him a job. While Bramble says of Clinker, now Matthew Loyd, "his incorruptible honesty and indefatigable care will be serviceable in superintending the oeconomy of my farm" (p. 355), Dennison says of Wilson that he "not only superintended my oeconomy, but also presided over my pastimes" (p. 313). Jery calls Wilson "an adept in every thing else that can be either useful or entertaining" (p. 318). Wilson becomes the wag of the group at the end of the novel, staging farces and playing tricks on Lismahago and Tabitha after their marriage. And as if to emphasize his role as a restorer of pleasure, everyone keeps talking about how much they like him. When Jery meets him at the averted duel, he says, "Vexed as I was at this adventure, I could not help admiring the coolness of this officer, whose open countenance prepossessed me in his favour" (p. 299). Later, Jery says "I question if ever he was angry or low-spirited in his life" (p. 318), while Dennison goes a step further, telling Bramble:

Wilson is one of the best natured men I ever knew; brave, frank, obliging, and ingenuous.—He liked my conversation, I was charmed with his liberal manner; an acquaintance immediately commenced, and this was soon improved into a friendship without reserve.—There are characters which, like similar particles of matter, strongly attract each other. (p. 311)

Wilson's tendentious likeability—evidently striking enough that Dennison has to try to explain it by general scientific principles—even rubs off on Bramble, who observes, "the scene was much enlivened by the arrival of Jack Wilson, who brought, as usual, some game of his own killing—His honest countenance was a good letter of recommendation.—I received him like a dear friend after a long separation . . ." (p. 316).

In the novel's fantasy of inventing Clinker all over again, it recreates him as a laborer, but this time an independent one: a farmer who both works and hires laborers (p. 312). For much of the novel, a figure called Wilson has haunted Jery by courting his sister Liddy, when Jery is certain he is a vagrant/actor trying to dishonor the family. "Wilson" will turn out to be the young Dennison, a gentleman fit for Liddy's hand. Jery meets the real Wilson, Jack, when he sends a note to a Mr. Wilson challenging him to a duel. Wilson arrives, Jery tells us, at the rendezvous—"an inclosed field at a little distance from the highway"—"wrapped in a dark horseman's coat, with a laced hat flapped over his eyes; but what was my astonishment, when, throwing off this wrapper, he appeared to be a person whom I had never seen before!" (pp. 298–99). In this important scene, an enclosure functions as contested ground, as a site of violent class struggle between a gentleman and an itinerant worker. And Wilson averts violence by dramatically revealing himself to be neither gentleman nor vagrant, but a retired soldier with a small farm. The novel unveils him at this moment, and on this spot, so that he may take over and reinvent the problem of labor, a problem that in its current form threatens to mortally wound both gentleman and laborer.

III. Incorporation, Metaphor, Satire

Because, as I will show in a moment, so many of the scenes of mourning in *Humphry Clinker* are followed by scenes of feasting—because this novel that is so centrally concerned with mourning is also so centrally concerned with consumption—I want here to look more closely at how the fantasy of incorporation works. As Abraham and Torok describe it, incorporation occurs when "the mouth's *words* do not succeed in filling the subject's emptiness, so he fills it instead with an imaginary *thing*," an act that constitutes a denial of the need to mourn:

> [T]he conjunction of urgent demand with the inability to perform a certain mouth activity—talking to others about what has been lost—will turn the subject to another, imaginary activity of the mouth, which is capable of instituting a denial of the very existence of the whole problem. (p. 7)

For them, incorporation involves a literal taking of something into the body rather than a figurative taking-in or swallowing of the loss; it is the refusal or inability to put the original oral void into words, the "very act that makes metaphor possible" (p. 10). It is for these reasons that they regard it as a radically antimetaphorical process:

> The fantasy of incorporation aspires to accomplish [the validation of a loss] by magic, as it were, by carrying out in a literal sense something that has meaning only in a figurative sense. It is to avoid "swallowing" the loss, that one imagines swallowing, or having swallowed, what is lost, in the form of an object. (pp. 4–5)

This account is troubled, I think, by the fact that if metaphoricity is denied on one level—the actual act of swallowing—it is all the more asserted on another. In an analysis of the Wolf Man's sister's swallowing of liquid mercury, for example, Abraham and Torok perform a complex reading of the symbolic meanings of the Russian word for mercury, suggesting that the actual object taken into the mouth may have powerful symbolic significance. One might modify their account by saying that incorporation is an attempt to eradicate—a better word would be *suppress*—metaphor, but that such a suppression can work only locally, at the site of the physical swallowing.

Similarly, in Smollett's novel the passages dealing explicitly with improvement and enclosure have a powerful metaphor-suppressing quality, while the more complex metaphoric resonances of improvement are displaced elsewhere. It is as an effect of incorporation's efforts to suppress metaphoricity that we may read the curious way in which improvement is such a radically antirepresentational project in this novel. I mentioned earlier the relative figurative poverty of Bramble's remarks on enclosure; in the person of Mrs. Baynard we can watch the novel actively eradicate metaphoricity. A veritable fiend of conspicuous consumption, Mrs. Baynard leads her husband to ruin because of her avid pursuit of appearances. Her parlour is "so very fine and delicate, that in all appearance it was designed to be seen only, not inhabited" (p. 279); creating a pleasure ground in a 200-acre farm "to shew her taste in laying out ground" (p. 281), she destroys the gardens and any produce they might have provided: "there was not an inch of garden ground left about the house, nor a tree that produced fruit of any kind . . . " (p. 281). Consequently, one of Bramble's first acts as manager of Baynard's estate after her death is to restore the pleasure ground "to its original use of corn-field and pasture" (p. 328). In this sense *Humphry Clinker* belongs to that tradition of literary works from *To Burlington* to *Mansfield Park* that denounced over-magnificent display, and urged landowners to subordinate show to use. In this tradition the concept *improvement* denoted landscape gardening as well as agricultural production, landscape gardening functioning as the outward sign of improvement's aggressive reshaping of the countryside. In contrast, landscaping is barely tolerated by *Humphry Clinker* at all—barely counts as part of the project of improvement—for Smollett's novel simply does not like signs when it comes to the land. It's as though it is attempting to purge improvement of its representational properties in an ethic of pure production that can mean nothing but production.

It is for that reason that *Humphry Clinker* despises servants even more than most fiction of its time: functioning as mere signs, servants are the very antithesis of labor in this novel. The major symptom of Mrs. Baynard's weakness for representation is her desire for ever more servants, and upon her death Bramble immediately "disband[s] that legion of supernumerary domestics, who had preyed so long upon the vitals of my friend" (p. 326). The portrayal of servants as mere signs is traditional in eighteenth- and nineteenth-century writing, most famously in Marx and Veblen; as Robbins writes: "In describing servants, most authorities agree that nonfunctional symbolism prevails over functional necessity. . . . Economically gratuitous, servants are mere signs of money, itself a sign."[43] Bramble blames their dazzling representational status for the depopulation of farms; in the passage I quoted earlier about the plough-boys swarming to London, what "seduces" them is "the appearance and discourse of these coxcombs in livery." It is, perhaps, to smother the seductive blaze of appearances that the novel gives the farmer who helps Dennison improve his farm the name *Bland*.

If metaphoricity can be suppressed in these scenes of improvement, though, the actual food taken into the mouths of Smollett's gentlemen, in the novel's scenes of ritual incorporation, resonates with very complex, even sometimes contradictory, meanings. Scenes of feasting almost inevitably follow this novel's scenes of mourning. Bramble's happy account of the food his family consumes at Cameron House, for example, directly follows the scene of Clinker's frightened reaction to the admiral, a scene which I have suggested links superstition and mourning, and evokes the dispossession of the poor. Moreover, the Scottish gentleman of the tall tale is not only surprising because he has mourned his wife for twenty years, but also because he has anticipated the arrival of the friend he has not seen for just as long—anticipated him and his party by having dinner prepared and the table set:

> The roads being bad, we did not arrive at the house till two o'clock in the afternoon; and were agreeably surprised to find a very good dinner ready in the kitchen, and the cloth laid with six covers. My friend himself appeared in his best apparel at the gate, and received us with open arms, telling me he had been expecting us these two hours. (p. 261)

This hospitality after his wife's death should be read in contrast to the cold reception the Bramble party receives at the Baynards' when

Mrs. Baynard is still alive: finding at the gate "a great number of powdered lacquies, but no civility," and unable even to keep his balance as he slides along the uncarpeted, "rubbed and waxed" floorboards, Bramble calls the estate "this *temple of cold reception*" (p. 279). And finally, the funeral of the simultaneously mourned and forgotten Scottish grandmother is also followed by a feast, in the form of a conventional comic portrayal of the excessive wake:

> The 'squire and I were, with some difficulty, permitted to retire with our landlord in the evening; but our entertainer was a little chagrined at our retreat; and afterwards seemed to think it a disparagement to his family, that not above a hundred gallons of whisky had been drank upon such a solemn occasion. (pp. 235–36)

The men arise at four in the morning to go hunting, and in Jery's narrative there follows an elaborate inventory of breakfast foods:

> The following articles formed our morning's repast: one kit of boiled eggs; a second full of butter; a third full of cream; an entire cheese, made of goat's milk; a large earthen pot full of honey; the best part of a ham; a cold venison pasty; a bushel of oat meal, made in thin cakes and bannocks, with a small wheaten loaf in the middle for the strangers; a large stone bottle full of whisky, another of brandy, and a kilderkin of ale. (p. 236)

Jery lists the foods in a kind of inventory for anthropological reasons, to show his correspondent Watkin Phillips the customs of the Scottish, just as Smollett describes the foods in France and Italy in his *Travels*. I am interested in the fact that once more, the scene of mourning leads immediately to the scenario of bounteous hospitality.

Food is so overdetermined in Smollet's work that I cannot pretend to say the definitive word about it. One recent essay on *Humphry Clinker* suggests that Smollett's novel "figures the process of inter-cultural exchange as a kind of poisoning, newly possible at the domestic table,"[44] and creates a fantasy of pure English food to compensate for its anxiety about the effects of the products of mercantile accumulation on English bodies. Similarly, another equally persuasive essay, focusing on alimentary violence and sexuality in Smollett's novels, argues that rituals of incorporation register "the

vague sense that the European self and social order is being transformed from a system of *anthropemy* to one based on the incorporation of dangerous or resistant elements."[45] I too wish to examine rituals of incorporation, but in keeping with my focus upon the domestic, I would like to think about the meanings of food in the
context of the intensified production created by the agricultural
revolution. For regardless of the light in which they regard the social
consequences of this production, and regardless of the fact that the
distribution of food was catastrophically unequal, everyone agrees
that the dramatically beneficial change brought about by it was England's capacity to stockpile food, and its consequent invulnerability
to famine.

I suggest that the feasts in Scottish and English country houses
be read as descendants of the genre of the country house poem,
which praised a particular house and its owner in order to express
larger social and moral values. As Raymond Williams has shown,
such poems as Jonson's *To Penshurst* and Carew's *To Saxham* celebrated the way of life of the benevolent country gentleman in contrast to the ambition and vice of the court and the city, and con-
tained—though not without a consciousness of the poor, and an
anxiety that charitable landowners may be exceptions to the rule—
"a willing and happy ethic of consuming, made evident by the or-
ganisation of the poems around the centrality of the dining-table."[46]
Williams argues that this charity at the level of consumption covers
over "a charity of production—of loving relations between men actually working and producing what is ultimately, in whatever proportions, to be shared." Indeed, the actual work of laborers is absent
from the poems, the work performed by a magical natural order,
and the laborers appearing as "rurall folke" who are the objects of
charity.[47]

In Smollett's novel, scenes of disavowed mourning are followed
by scenes that, with a kind of hyperbolic emphasis on plenty, mark
the consumption of food. To be sure, those moments of feasting occur primarily in Scotland, a place not yet affected by the intensifica-
tion of agricultural production, and are often intended ostensibly to
mark the old-fashioned values and hospitality of a *pre*-capitalist soci-

ety. The plenteous consumption to follow upon Baynard's grief is only implied and projected into the future, in the reference to his estate being "all cultivated like a garden." But since Scotland figures so prominently in the novel as territory-to-be-improved, and since it functions, as I have suggested, as terrain through which the novel often expresses more vividly or explicitly the social dynamics at work in England, I would argue that these scenes of consumption may be read as part of a general pattern of loss, disavowal, and eating in the novel—an ideological pattern which is, as I've suggested, central to the agricultural improvement so strenuously advocated in the novel's second half. In that context they constitute scenes of melancholic incorporation. These scenes swerve from the conventions of the country house poem by omitting the poor altogether, and one might argue that it is that very absence, that resolute silence, that produces melancholia. Because *Humphry Clinker* "cannot articulate certain words, cannot utter certain phrases"[48] about the social losses brought about by the agricultural revolution, the gentry fills its collective mouth, as it were, with food. One is not allowed to be frightened or grief-stricken in this novel, but one *is* allowed to be hungry.[49] And it is the very telos of the agricultural revolution—swallowing food, appeasing hunger—that substitutes, in this novel, for "swallowing" the loss that is the transformation of the poor under total hire. The consumption of food is the activity that abolishes metaphoricity, which is a way of rejecting mourning itself:

> To absorb what has just been lost in the form of food, real or imagined, when the psyche is plunged into mourning, is to *reject mourning* and its consequences; it is to refuse to take within oneself the part of oneself contained in what has been lost, to refuse to admit the true meaning of that loss, which if admitted would make one different. . . . (pp. 4–5)

The project of improvement is the origin of the ego-wounding transformation of the poor: the way it becomes imagined, or rendered *ideological*, by the collectivity that is the novel's consciousness, functions as a rejection of mourning and its consequences.

Of course, in a novel with so many conflicted attitudes about food—with food more often than not figured as filthy and noxious and foreign, as a physical and cultural threat[50]—it is not *always* effective as an object that blocks certain kinds of recognitions from happening. It is only in the fantasy that organizes its relation to agricultural improvement that food—specifically, British food—can work this way. I conclude this chapter by looking at a few of the satiric set pieces that deal specifically with food, in order to examine the relation between melancholic incorporation and satire in this novel.

At an inn at Harrigate, a Scottish lawyer named Mr. Micklewhimmen retaliates for a practical joke in which Jery steals away the bottle he claims contains stomach medicine, discovers it to be "excellent claret," and passes it around to the rest of the company, by saying "it was a vara poorful infusion of jallap in Bourdeaux wine; at its possable he may ha ta'en sic a dose as will produce a terrible catastrophe in his ain booels—" (p. 169). A clothier from Leeds, whom Jery considers "a great coxcomb in his way," and who has drunk most of the contents of the bottle, panics:

> He began to spit, to make wry faces, and writhe himself into various contorsions. . . . [H]e retired, roaring with pain, to his own chamber . . . the doctor [was] sent for; but before he arrived, the miserable patient had made such discharges upwards and downwards, that nothing remained to give him further offence; and this double evacuation, was produced by imagination alone; for what he had drank was genuine wine of Bourdeaux, which the lawyer had brought from Scotland for his own private use. (p. 169)

Similarly, at the table of a country squire named Burdock, a justice named Frogmore is terrified by a facetious doctor friend of the master of the house, who suggests that the mushrooms he just ate are "of the kind called *champignons*, which in some constitutions has a poisonous effect." Frogmore retires to his room, "not without marks of terror and disquiet," is given various lubricating medicines and laxatives, and makes his terrified final confession while "enthroned on an easing-chair, under the pressure of a double evacuation" (pp. 287–91).

Although they quite clearly deal with the bodily incorporation of substances, the relation of these satiric moments to the melancholic fantasy of incorporation is a complex one. First, it is hard to tell whether vomiting and diarrhea would constitute *part* of the fantasy of incorporation (Abraham and Torok suggest they do),[51] or whether, being modes of expulsion, they would constitute a negation of incorporation. Second, that the object of terror is food *itself* seems complicated in a context where food is usually the thing swallowed so that terror and grief need *not* be "swallowed." In this way, these scenes would seem to operate antithetically to the scenes of feasting that work as moments of incorporation. One reason for this contradiction is that the substances swallowed here (jallap, Bordeaux, champignons) are decisively foreign, and swallowed in a xenophobic context. But I think it is also important to note that in *Humphry Clinker* the use of food as a block to grieving is not seamless: rather, it seems to require a labor that these scenes perform. These scenes set up an ambivalent relation to food, posing the question of whether or not it is dangerous. Ultimately, they tell us, "It's not poison, just mushrooms—not a purgative, just a nice Bordeaux!" They are moments in which the novel rehearses, then resists, its own phobias about food.

But while these scenes suggest what kinds of obstacles must be overcome in order for the fantasy of incorporation to work—suggest, that is, the fragility of that fantasy—they function in another sense as paradigmatic melancholic moments. One often wonders, reading Smollett, what is so funny about watching someone stricken with terror that he is about to die; one tends to attribute (Pollyannishly, perhaps) the pleasure in such sadism to a different historical sensibility, a sensibility critics like to call "robust." But why the novel might find these satiric moments so appealing becomes clearer if we read them as rituals of disavowal, rituals that perform the work of instantiating terrors as "false" terrors, "produced by imagination alone." Indeed, they are even more pleasurable than the spectacle of a spooked rustic because the audience watching the emotional butt of the joke knows *for sure* that there is nothing to be afraid of: the joke is created around that knowledge. These scenes, in which the novel's ideology-forming powers exercise themselves in the form of a hazing ritual, are the most explicit example of what we might think of as *Humphry Clinker's* role in the agricultural revolution. Smollett's novel creates a collective gentlemanly ethos whose aim is to discipline those suffering fear or grief, to teach them that they have lost nothing after all, or nothing, at least, worth mourning. Such a denial generally has the tone of a manly stoicism, an amused reasonableness, but the satiric set pieces betray a greater effort, the pedagogy of denial becoming concerted and ferocious.

I argued in the previous chapter that in *A Sentimental Journey* parody is essential to the production of the sentimental. In *Humphry Clinker*, conversely, melancholia is essential to the production of satiric humor: while we might intuitively expect humor to serve as an *antidote* to melancholia, the comic effect of the novel's treatment of emotive excessiveness is created by ambivalence over loss. It is worth noting in this context that *Humphry Clinker* has been regarded as Smollett's kinder, gentler novel. As Rothstein notes, contrasting Clinker's persuasive nature to Bramble's harsher and more violent one, "the redemptive way is not the way of Juvenalian fury. In this novel violent satire informs us, perhaps gratifies us, but does not make anyone better."[52] That softening may come from the fact that in order to disavow, one must have an intimation of the disaster the disavowal is intended to block from consciousness. In *Humphry Clinker* the spectacle of some rustic staring at what he thinks is a ghost, his hair standing on end, and his mouth agape, can no longer produce a pleasure that is simply malicious. For while the disavowal of grief with which Smollett's final novel responds to the social transformation of the countryside generates satiric humor, the glimmer of that grief also tempers it.

CHAPTER 4

'This Dream of Fancied Sorrow'

FEMALE AFFECTIVITY AND

THE LABORING POOR IN

FRANCES BURNEY'S 'CECILIA'

At one point late in Frances Burney's *Cecilia* (1782), the heroine has been humiliated by a failed clandestine marriage attempt she has made against her own best judgment and sense of propriety. The family of her aristocratic lover, Mortimer Delvile, opposes the marriage because Cecilia's possession of an estate of £3,000 per annum, which she has inherited from her uncle, depends upon the stipulation that she "annex[ ] her name, if she is married, to the disposal of her hand and her riches"[1]—a stipulation unthinkable to the proud Delviles. She has sworn, therefore, out of respectful obedience to Mrs. Delvile, whom she loves, not to see Mortimer anymore. When she receives a letter from Mrs. Delvile thanking and praising her for giving him up, she responds like this:

> The attempted philosophy, and laboured resignation of Cecilia, this letter destroyed: the struggle was over, the apathy was at an end, and she burst into an agony of tears, which finding the vent they had long sought, now flowed unchecked down her cheeks, sad monitors of the weakness of reason opposed to the anguish of sorrow! (p. 701)

As she is experiencing the "monitors" of reason's weakness, the man who is soon to call himself her monitor (pp. 709, 790) enters the room. The monitors that flow from the private female body—reminders that the "anguish of sorrow" is supreme—will be rejected by this stern monitor, this representative of the poor, a man who has devoted his life to "seek[ing] the distressed where-ever they are hid, [and following] the prosperous to beg a mite to serve them" (p. 708).

Albany, a prophetic madman taken to infiltrating fashionable gatherings and uttering stentorian moralisms like "Oh vassals of famine and distress! Come and listen to this wantonness of wealth!" (p. 67), has taken a shine to Cecilia and her generosity. But seeing the marks of tears on her face, he begins to question her to see if she deserves his pity; and learning that she has neither "lost by death the friend of [her] bosom," nor dissipated her fortune, nor "been guilty of some vice," he addresses her harshly:

> His countenance now again resumed its severity, and, in the sternest manner, "Whence then," he said, "these tears? and what is this caprice you dignify with the name of sorrow?—strange wantonness of indolence and luxury! perverse repining of ungrateful plenitude!—oh hadst thou known what *I* have suffered!—" (p. 703)

Cecilia's grief and Albany's almost comically self-aggrandizing repudiation of it are both striking and familiar, recalling the dynamic in *Humphry Clinker* in which voices in one strand of the novel express grief, while those in another contest and repudiate it. Albany continues:

> "I will tell thee my own sad story. Then wilt thou find how much happier is thy lot, then wilt thou raise thy head in thankful triumph. . . . [T]o awaken thee from this dream of fancied sorrow, I will open all my wounds, and thou shalt probe them with fresh shame." (p. 704)

Representing her feelings as a mere "dream" or "fancy," Albany competes with Cecilia over the legitimacy of female sorrow. Indeed, this chapter argues that in its lush portrayal of the emotions of feminine grief and shame, *Cecilia* is centrally concerned with both the production and the containment of female affect.

To briefly summarize this only recently semicanonical novel: Cecilia is the sole survivor of the Beverly family, and has inherited two components of their fortune: £10,000 from her parents, and an estate of £3,000 per annum from her uncle. There is one restriction to her ownership of the estate, however: the stipulation that her husband take her name.[2] The novel represents Cecilia's relation to her inheritance as a solemn "sense of DUTY"; she regards it as a "debt contracted with the poor" (p. 55). But while Cecilia's fondest desire is to figure out a sensible and effective scheme of charity, the novel concertedly denies her that desire. In the first half of the novel she loses the money she has inherited from her parents, through a series of extortions by a spendthrift and criminally irresponsible guardian who ultimately kills himself. In the second half of the novel she loses her estate, not long after she actually comes into possession of it. For Cecilia falls in love with—and marries in a disastrously clandestine way—precisely the man who cannot possibly take her name: Mortimer Delvile. Cecilia eventually loses her entire fortune and goes insane: hallucinating that Delvile has been wounded by an imagined rival; mistaken for a woman who has escaped from Bedlam; locked up in a room in a pawnshop while raving and running a dangerous fever. At the very end, though, the novel allows her a recovery and also rustles up a little surprise inheritance from one of Delvile's aunts to settle the exhausted couple with.

Cecilia contains many long scenes that vigorously satirize the affectation and love of show of various vacuous fashionable acquaintances of Cecilia. But as Terry Castle has described it, "Any comic précis of Cecilia must necessarily exclude much, notably the current of uneasiness and melancholia that eddies through the book. The novel often lapses into bizarre and hectic melodrama."[3] And Catherine Gallagher has written of this plot, "Perhaps no book in the annals of the English novel succeeds as thoroughly as this one does in focusing our apprehensive attention on a character's property. We do not often fear for Cecilia, but we are kept in a state of perpetual anxiety about the fate of her money."[4]

Cecilia's loss of property is best read, I believe, in the context of Nancy Armstrong's claim that the domestic woman was created by eighteenth-century authors of fiction and conduct literature as a figure defined by subjectivity rather than by status or rank:

> In place of the intricate status system that had long dominated British thinking, these authors began to represent an individual's value in terms of his, but more often in terms of her, essential qualities of mind.

Literature devoted to producing the domestic woman thus appeared to ignore the political world run by men. Of the female alone did it presume to say that neither birth nor the accoutrements of title and status accurately represented the individual; only the more subtle nuances of behavior indicated what one was really worth. In this way, writing for and about the female introduced a whole new vocabulary for social relations, terms that attached precise moral value to certain qualities of mind.[5]

I take the term "the domestic woman" to comprise those women in classes that had already been defined, or were coming to be defined, as leisured. It was as a way of establishing middle-class power, Armstrong suggests, that a set of moral norms was created to privilege the domestic woman, who was valued for her "depths" rather than her surface, over the aristocratic woman, who was regarded as having a degraded investment in self-display.[6] In *Cecilia* the concerted stripping away of the heroine's property and status may be read as a savage commentary on the formation of the domestic woman. For Cecilia goes from being a woman of property to a woman of affect; she remains with nothing *but* her subjectivity, in the form of insanity.

Indeed, while the sense of an inner self came to be regarded as a primary attribute of middle-class and gentle women, contemporary writing on grief—one of the period's major synecdoches for emotion—also suggests a powerful anxiety about female subjectivity, about uncontrolled affect that threatens to wrest the woman from the social realm. We know this anxiety primarily from the literature of sensibility. John Mullan has shown that in these texts sensibility often threatens to turn into illness, and the conservative reaction to sentimental and gothic literature in the 1790s constantly urged reason as a necessary modulating force on the emotions.[7] And Claudia L. Johnson has argued that in novels by Wollstonecraft, Radcliffe, and Burney, "the flagrancy of suffering so copiously represented . . . is surpassed only by the strenuousness of the heroines' inhibitions about articulating it, for under sentimentality the prestige of suffering belongs to men."[8] In *Cecilia* anxiety over emotional excess is most luridly expressed in the portrayal of headstrong aristocrats, who not only ride roughshod over and ultimately destroy a paragon of modest virtue, but who do so by virtue of the violence of their emotions. Delvile's passionate impulsiveness is often coded as "violent"; Cecilia comes to "dread[] his impetuosity of temper" (p. 858), and his kinswoman Lady Honoria, jokingly suggesting how Cecilia could annul the disastrous marriage, says, "You have only, you know, to take an oath that you were forcibly run away with; and as you are an Heiress, and the Delviles are all so violent, it will easily be credited" (p. 933). The uncontrollable Mrs. Delvile, meanwhile, literally bursts a blood vessel when her desires are thwarted, blood gushing from her mouth as if to literalize the expression of her inner self. Later, praising Cecilia's feminine self-command, she laments that her own health "is the sacrifice of emotions most fatally unrestrained" (p. 700).

At least until these aristocrats drive her mad, Cecilia's subjectivity expresses itself as the struggle to contain emotion, or to have socially responsible emotion. As Lady Honoria exclaims, "Lord, how you are always upon your guard! If I were half as cautious, I should die of the vapours in a month" (p. 935). Part of this chapter is about that effort. But I also want to shift the emphasis from the way in which the domestic woman was created in opposition to an aristocratic model, in order to emphasize another crucial—and perhaps more immediate—influence on the formation of her subjectivity: the crucible of the relation between leisured women and the poor, a relation mediated by charity. Like that in *Humphry Clinker*, the current of melancholia that runs through *Cecilia*—as well as its related affect, shame—emerges, I will argue, out of the reorganization of labor practices in the late part of the eighteenth century. As actual labor becomes increasingly stigmatized for middle-class as well as already leisured women, it becomes these women's job to take on and express the emotions attendant upon the reorganization of labor. Indeed, the figure of the gentlewoman stripped of her property and left with her affect alone may be regarded as analogous to one of the great economic accomplishments of the eighteenth century: the divorce of workers from ownership of the materials of production, leaving them with their labor power as their sole form of property.[9] Affect is precisely the gentlewoman's form of labor. But it is not merely that these emotions exist and leisured women take on the burden of bearing them: as I will show, the emotions themselves are imagined through the very tropes used to describe labor in this period.

It was charity, the conventional form of contact between gentlewomen and the poor, that was offered as a putative solution to the problem of excessive grief. The fact that during this period women begin to become the major agents of charity—a trend that reaches its peak in the evangelical organizations of the nineteenth century—is partly, I would argue, a function of this anxiety about excessive emotion. That is, charity functions as the social act that authorizes and controls the expression of emotion. But while charity promises to be a social cure for the excessively personal behaviors of grief and shame, it also *creates* a new and damaging surplus of emotion.[10] In my reading of *A Sentimental Journey* I demonstrated how the gentleman constitutes himself as such in the act of charity. In contrast, in *Cecilia* the task offered to women as the very expression of feminine propriety ends up being deeply damaging to female reputation, making the gentlewoman virtually disintegrate. The creation of the domestic woman must be read in relation to the explosive interaction between leisured women and the poor, then, at a moment when such interaction was both encouraged and unviable.

I. Labor and Charity in the Age of Manufactures

Because the proto-industrial period, the period roughly spanning 1780–1820, was so profoundly transitional, and because the industrial period that followed seems to stand in such stark and defined contrast to what preceded it, contemporary historians continue to debate the character of economic organization and practices in this period.[11] Most recently, Maxine Berg's *The Age of Manufactures* has challenged conventional models of describing what she calls "the age of manufactures." Berg resists reading the proto-industrial period teleologically from the point of the factory, refusing the perspective that reads backward into the eighteenth century for "examples of the 'modern,' for instances of striking increases in productivity, and for some clearly defined path into nineteenth-century industrial greatness."[12] Instead, she attempts to create a nuanced picture of the proto-industrial period that can account for the richness and variety of industrial forms in this period: for the way, for example, the factory and the domestic system often coexisted side by side, even within the same industry; for the way in which some industries declined while others grew; and for the fact that industrialization during this period comprised both mechanization and alternatives to it, such as improved hand techniques, the use of cheap labor-saving materials, and the division of labor and simplification of individual tasks.[13] Moreover, evoking Marx's definition of the manufacture stage in the development of capitalism as "the process through which the division of labour splits up productive activity into component parts, separating workers into skilled and unskilled, thereby creating a hierarchy of labour powers," Berg stresses that it was not technical innovation alone that enabled increases in productivity over this period, but also the more efficient division of labor, and greater exploitation of the labor force.[14]

Changing industrial practices during this period of transition required a huge supply of unskilled mobile labor, not only for the factory, but for its adjuvant sites of production as well. Indeed, as Berg argues, a large force of underemployed domestic workers complemented factory labor throughout this period, cutting the costs of full mechanization and offsetting the effects of cyclical fluctuations; this was a part-time and flexible force of laborers supplementing meager family incomes earned in agriculture, mining, or fishing. So, Berg writes, "while highly organized groups of skilled artisans in both town and country areas fought the displacement of their skills by new machinery, large groups of underemployed domestic workers helped to shore up the new technology by reducing risks and costs."[15] She stresses that if labor was exploited in the factory, it was exploited with equal intensity in domestic and workshop manufacture, particularly the labor of women and children.[16]

This large, mobile, and flexible labor force was created in part, as I discussed in the previous chapter, by enclosure; and the repeal of the Statute of Artificers and Apprentices (5 Elizabeth, 1563) in 1814 was a decisive step in removing legislative limitations on the labor market, one fiercely resisted by organized skilled labor, which appealed to the protective functions of the state.[17] As labor was being reorganized, commodified, rendered more efficient, a new historical sociology tried to reconceptualize the problem of labor: what the experience of labor is like and why men work. Donna Andrew dates this writing from the mid-1770s to the early 1790s, and calls it a new psychology of labor. Rather than arguing that men are driven to work by fear and hunger, as earlier theorists had, such philosophers and political economists as Hume and Adam Smith hinged man's drive to work upon self-interest, and the passion for self-betterment. These theorists, Andrew suggests, "held that labor, or the steady, repetitious exertion at the same task, was a forced activity, inherently unpleasant and unnatural to man";[18] there was considerable anxiety in this period, most famously expressed by Adam Smith, about the corrosive and stupefying effects of the division of labor, an anxiety I will return to in the next section. The hope of the political economists was that the appeal to self-betterment could offset the unpleasant character of labor and make "free" laborers work as much as they were able. Consequently, they emphasized man's desire for freedom, which to them meant "the enjoyment of the fruits of property," and urged high wages as the best incentive to labor.[19] Andrew suggests that "this sociology was among other things a critique of the use of fear to motivate men. The use of fear to extract labor was seen to characterize primitive societies; in this new sociology it was the lessening of coercion and the growth of individual freedom that indicated historical progress from one epoch to another."[20]

The attempts of these theorists to ally labor and freedom indicate just how difficult and volatile the idea of "freedom" was during this period. As John Rule describes the ethos of the skilled artisans, they had a morally informed conception of their freedom: "Adam Smith's view that apprenticeship offended against the 'most sacred and inviolable' property which every man had in his own labour to exercise in whatever manner he thought fit without injury to his neighbour, was in direct contradiction to the view of the skilled workers. They saw completion of apprenticeship as conferring a very special property right."[21] The idea of the laborer "free" in his or her labor power also came up jarringly against the concept of "freedom" implicit in *laissez faire*. Showing how the concept of freedom could resonate for working people, E. P. Thompson argues about a slightly later period,

> We are so accustomed to the notion that it was both inevitable and "progressive" that trade should have been freed in the early 19th century from "restrictive practices," that it requires an effort of imagination to understand that the "free" factory-owner or large hosier or cotton-manufacturer, who built his fortune by these means, was regarded not only with jealousy but as a man engaging in *immoral* and *illegal* practices. The tradition of the just price and the fair wage lived longer among "the lower orders" than is sometimes supposed. They saw *laissez faire*, not as freedom but as "foul Imposition."[22]

And as Thompson argues, the agitation that began to erupt among working people following the French Revolution had its roots in popular notions of the birthright of the "free-born Englishman."[23]

Labor's commodification and reorganization, then, were accompanied by an attempt by political economists to wrest some kind of ideological compromise between the demands of labor and the demands of freedom. And if ruling-class writers expressed acute ambivalence about labor, they also had complicated attitudes about leisure. As I argued in the introduction, via Gertrude Himmelfarb, it was at this time that the concept of the "laboring poor" began to be pried apart, a process that would culminate in the Poor Law of 1834. The ideological force of the distinction between "laborer" and "poor," Himmelfarb suggests in her reading of Burke—one of the first to insist upon such a distinction—is to resuscitate labor, refashioning it into a universal condition rather than one to be pitied. And indeed, in *Cecilia* the force of the redefinition of freedom through labor overwhelms not just working people, but all people; one of the primary urges of Burney's novel, I will argue, is to catapult people (that is, male people) into labor. When the novel's most vivid figure for the perils of leisure and conspicuous expenditure, the fashionable gentleman Harrel, becomes overwhelmed with debt from dissipated living and commits suicide, he blames his ruin on his own idleness. Harrel writes in his suicide note: "Had I a son, I would bequeath him a plough; I should then leave him happier than my parents left me. . . . Idleness has been my destruction; the want of something to do led me into all evil" (p. 431). It is no doubt partly as a function of this cultural revulsion toward leisure that at late century, as Beth Fowkes Tobin argues, there was an attempt by the middle classes "to discredit the landed upper classes as managers of the rural economy and to promote the talent, intelligence, and expertise of the middle classes in the regulation of the countryside and its people."[24] These middle-class writers, Fowkes Tobin writes, portrayed the leisured classes as "careless, self-indulgent, and incompetent managers of their property and the people who occupied it."[25]

Tellingly, this anxiety about leisure occurs coterminously with the creation of a whole new leisured class of middle-class women, whom increased wealth allowed to withdraw from all connection from business. Armstrong shows that such women were not merely released from the performance of labor, but rather actively enjoined not to engage in labor, which was figured as a stain upon their characters. Claiming that in the conduct books any proximity to labor made women seem sexually compromised, and arguing that the governess was a particularly volatile case in point, Armstrong writes, "She seemed to call into question an absolutely rigid distinction between domestic duty and labor that was performed for money, a distinction so deeply engraved upon the public mind that the figure of the prostitute could be freely invoked to describe any woman who dared to labor for money."[26] In her own reading of eighteenth-century conduct books and treatises on female education, Kristina Straub argues that domestic duty itself was entangled in ideological contradiction. The middle-class woman, she writes, "learns to see herself in part through the performance of ritual social occupations that she is, in turn, discouraged from seeing as valuable."[27] Straub describes the keen cultural ambivalence toward the more "genteel" female employments; while writers such as Richard Lovell Edgeworth and Maria Edgeworth believed that women should "be encouraged . . . to cultivate those tastes which can attach them to their home, and which can preserve them from the miseries of dissipation," they wrote contemptuously about what women actually produced with their needles.[28] Alongside the contradictory demands of labor and freedom, then, arose even more dizzying contradictions surrounding middle-class women and work: insistence on middle-class women's leisure and a concomitant cultural attitude of revulsion against leisure, and disparagement of the very employments women were enjoined to perform to combat the dissipating effects of leisure.

These attempts to reconfigure both the character and the ideology of labor, as well as the ideology of freedom, brought about shifts in the practice of charity. Andrew has shown that charity on the institutional level underwent a severe crisis of confidence between 1770 and 1790, and she suggests two major reasons for this crisis. First, theories about the benefits of a large population changed in the 1770s. More important, the political economists regarded such practices as the acceptance of alms, the workhouse, and the Law of Settlement as degradations and infringements upon the freedom of the autonomous laborer. As the concept of freedom became ideologically transformed, "institutions or laws that shackled men to each other by noncommercial bonds, such things as the Poor Law or voluntary charities, were . . . seen to be retrogressive, a return to pre-modern forms of dependence."[29]

Not surprisingly, perhaps, it was at this time, as charity was falling into disrepute as an illegitimate form of social connection, that middle-class and gentlewomen became the major agents of charity in the culture. *Cecilia* was written on the cusp of the age of the charitable society, the institution through which women came into their own as social organizers.[30] Leisured women come to take charge of charity, then, at a moment of acute ideological struggle over the concepts of labor, leisure, and freedom. And as *Cecilia* shows us with an almost vicious insistence, they could not be asked to manage a more difficult and damaging range of social contradictions. It is, I argue, in conjunction with and in response to these social and economic events that the gentlewoman's interiority is created in *Cecilia*. In the following two sections I discuss two primary affects of Burney's heroine, grief and shame, showing how the rhetorics that

describe them borrow from and interweave with contemporary
rhetorics of labor and charity. Although it is slightly artificial to separate two such interrelated affects, each one evokes such a complicated chain of socio-economic associations that they require separate treatment; I will bring them back together at the end of the
chapter.

II. Grief and the Division of Labor

When Albany rebukes Cecilia, in the paragraphs with which I
opened this chapter, he's worrying melancholically, as many did during this time, about grief's excessiveness and inappropriateness. The
century's most eloquent philosopher of sorrow, Dr. Johnson, wrote
in the *Rambler* essay entitled "The Proper Means of regulating sorrow" about grief's intractability; for Johnson, too, the problem of
sorrow is the problem of excessive or inappropriate sorrow:

> It seems determined, by the general suffrage of mankind, that sorrow
> is to a certain point laudable, as the offspring of love, or at least par-
> donable as the effect of weakness; but that it ought not to be suffered
> to increase by indulgence, but must give way, after a stated time, to so-
> cial duties, and the common avocations of life. It is at first unavoidable,
> and therefore must be allowed, whether with or without choice; it may
> afterwards be admitted as a decent and affectionate testimony of kind-
> ness and esteem; something will be extorted by nature, and something
> may be given to the world. But all beyond the bursts of passion, or the
> forms of solemnity, is not only useless, but culpable; for we have no
> right to sacrifice, to the vain longings of affection, that time which
> providence allows us for the task of our station. Yet it too often hap-
> pens that sorrow, thus lawfully entering, gains such a firm possession
> of the mind, that it is not afterwards to be ejected. . . . [31]

Johnson's dry and careful "It seems determined, by the general suffrage of mankind" qualifies the truth-value of his statement that
grief often becomes excessive; one senses that for him, it cannot help
but be so. What I want to stress here is that the anxiety that sorrow
will reach excessive proportions is characteristic of mid- to late-
eighteenth-century English culture. "The general suffrage of man-

kind": a certain amount of grief is all that the general culture will allow.[32]

Moreover, as Johnson suggests, a measure of sorrow's appropriateness is its capacity to "give way, after a stated time, to social duties." The threat of excessive sorrow is that it will grip the mind so powerfully that it will unmoor the individual from the social. If sorrow is a debt to the world—"and something may be given to the world," Johnson allows—it also takes one away from the "task of our station." As Mullan has argued of eighteenth-century medical literature about "passion," "the tendencies which can enhance sociability can also turn the individual inwards and away from all society by becoming illness."[33] One senses that in this period emotion always carries the threat of turning the individual away from society.

If contemporary writers worried about middle-class and gentle women turning away from society, that's because in a sense they were, in their withdrawal from economic activity. It is both customary and useful to read, as Mullan does, eighteenth-century "nervous disease" as a malady of removal from the marketplace; "the exclusion of the wives and daughters of the ruling class from economic activity and from the management of assets outside a narrow domestic realm has the unwarranted effect of rendering them more liable to such 'Disorders.' "[34] And as Armstrong points out, affectivity was attributed to middle-class and gentle women at the same time that an acute stigma was brought upon those of them who actually labored. Grief, then, is regarded as an effect of withdrawal from labor; Albany is certainly blaming Cecilia's grief on leisure when he calls it the "strange wantonness of indolence and luxury." But what is striking about Burney's novel is that in its withdrawal from the social, grief bears an uncanny *resemblance to* labor.

In *Cecilia* labor could not be farther from a collective or social act. Belfield, the character most enveloped in a labor plot and most philosophical about labor, imagines it as a near-total seclusion from the world. The novel's object lesson in the wrongness of aspiring above one's station, Belfield is a linen-draper's son who has been given by his father a genteel education, and who consequently develops a disdain for his father's trade. When the father dies the busi-

ness goes under since Belfield is incompetent to save it, and his fool-
ish doting mother and her remaining dependent daughter Henrietta
fall into poverty. Belfield is still aided and abetted in his aspirations,
however, by his mother, who would rather see herself and Henrietta
starve than give up her illusions about her son's gentility. After a
long and fruitless period of attempting to gain gentle patronage,
Belfield disappears and later surfaces thanks to that reliable engine
of eighteenth-century novel plots, the carriage breakdown. Unrec-
ognized in the darkness by Cecilia, he helps repair the carriage,
wounding his foot when it catches under a wheel; later Cecilia goes
to thank the man who has been reported to be a day laborer, and
discovers that it is Belfield himself. Attempting to account for this
turn in his fortune, Belfield announces in an extravagant apostrophe
to happiness, "mankind seems only composed as matter for thy experiments, and I will quit the whole race. . . . "

> "Is then the great secret of happiness," said Cecilia, "nothing, at last,
> but total seclusion from the world?"
>   "No, madam," answered he, "it is Labour with Independence."
> (p. 659)

Here Belfield figures labor as that which mitigates utter solitude. At
first, he tells Cecilia, he sought "a total seclusion from society," but
then, reflecting upon the perils of solitude, and reading Johnson's
Life of Cowley, he has realized "the vanity and absurdity of *panting
after solitude*" (p. 663) and become a day laborer, living in "a cottage,
situated upon a common" (p. 657). Echoing Harrel's suicide note
about the dangers of idleness, Belfield says, "I am here out of the
way of all society, yet avoid the great evil of retreat, *having nothing to
do*" (pp. 663–64).

But although he argues that labor helps him avoid solitude, labor is most repeatedly and resoundingly figured in this sequence as
seclusion, as "giving up the whole world" and "out of the way of all
society" (pp. 661, 663). Of course, one might take the expressions
"the world" and "society" in their narrow definition of the *beau
monde*; but this scene wants to at least evoke a broader withdrawal in
the phrase "*all* society," and in Belfield's answer to Cecilia's confused

question why, if the life of a laborer is so happy, "we [have] so many complaints of the suffering of the poor": "Oh had they known and felt provocations such as these, how gladly would their resentful spirits turn from the whole unfeeling race, and how would they respect that noble and manly labour, which at once disentangles them from such subjugating snares, and enables them to fly the ingratitude they abhor!" (p. 665). At a moment in which the viability of non-commercial bonds between people is challenged by the logic of the market, "independent" labor is figured as a disentangling from the snares of collectivity that results in utter solitude. When the novel shows us Belfield working, he is alone in a garden; when it shows us Belfield renouncing his harebrained scheme later on, it has him exclaim that "the life I led at the cottage was the life of a savage; no intercourse with society, no consolation from books . . . " (p. 738).

Although the strand of the novel represented by Albany, then, regards grief as an effect of withdrawal from labor and the market, there is an equally strong urge in this novel to figure grief and labor as equally solitary pursuits. And indeed, during this period the language used to describe labor in its specialized state is strikingly similar to that used to describe grief. In his history of the experience of death in European cultures, Philippe Ariès has argued that during this period there occurred a shift in modes of experiencing grief:

> In our former, traditional societies affectivity was distributed among a greater number of individuals rather than limited to the members of the conjugal family. It was extended to ever-widening circles, and diluted. . . . Beginning in the eighteenth century, however, affectivity was, from childhood, entirely concentrated on a few individuals, who became exceptional, irreplaceable, and inseparable.[35]

In the *Rambler* essay entitled "The contemplation of the calamities of others, a remedy for grief," Johnson uses just such a rhetoric of concentration and dissipation when he writes of the grieving person meditating upon others' sorrows:

> The first effect of this meditation is, that it furnishes a new employment for the mind, and engages the passions on remoter objects. . . . The attention is dissipated by variety, and acts more weakly upon any

single part, as that torrent may be drawn off to different channels, which, pouring down in one collected body, cannot be resisted.[36]

In this passage, it is as though Johnson is marking and resisting the change in the nature of mourning documented by Ariès. For Johnson the concentration of grieving attention on a single object is unbearable, and conjuring a variety of objects beneficial because it dissipates the attention.

The rhetoric of singleness and variety, direction and dissipation, is also central to contemporary descriptions of the division of labor. According to Adam Smith, the division of labor increases the dexterity of the worker "by reducing every man's business to some one simple operation, and by making this operation the sole employment of his life."[37] One beneficial result of such concentration, Smith argues, is that it motivates workers to invent new kinds of machinery. He describes the psychology of worker initiative as follows:

> Men are much more likely to discover easier and readier methods of attaining any object, when the whole attention of their minds is directed towards that single object, than when it is dissipated among a great variety of things.[38]

But of course, in Smith there is the concomitant awareness of the harmful effects of concentrating attention upon a single object. As he writes, in the famous comparison of the agricultural worker and the worker in manufactures:

> The common ploughman . . . is less accustomed, indeed, to social intercourse than the mechanic who lives in a town. His voice and language are more uncouth and more difficult to be understood by those who are not used to them. His understanding, however, being accustomed to consider a greater variety of objects, is generally much superior to that of the other, whose whole attention from morning till night is commonly occupied in performing one or two very simple operations.[39]

Both grief and labor in its most efficient form, then, are states in which the attention is focused too intently upon one object. The narrowing of the attention to one object recalls John Barrell's argument that in the eighteenth century the condition of being a gentleman was defined precisely by the capacity to see a wide vista. For gentlewomen, then, having one's view narrowed by grief is a form of deracination.

Pressuring the overlap of the rhetorics of grief and labor reveals the profound ambivalence at the heart of late-century thought about labor. First, in a similar dynamic to that in *Humphry Clinker*, the overlap has the effect of casting a shadow of grief over labor: the focus of one's attention on a single object becomes the very figure of mourning. The wound to Belfield's foot neatly sums up the way labor impairs in Burney's novel. Second, though, the rhetorical overlap also expresses a need to figure affectivity as a form of labor—a need that indicates an anxiety about the condition of leisure. It is in this context that we may read the rather fantastical portrayal of Belfield's passage into labor: his use of the language of gentlemanly retirement to describe his experience, his reading of Johnson in preparation for field labor, his insistence on the originality of his action ("servility of imitation has ever been as much my scorn as servility of dependence" [p. 663]). It is a little tempting to read his quixotic behavior as a function of the naïveté of a genteel woman novelist—akin to the novel's periodic assertion that the cause of poverty is the refusal of gentlemen to pay workers the wages owed to them. But the imaginative overlap between retirement and labor is worth taking seriously. The character Burney's novel imagines subjected to the rigors of labor is one whose life was defined by an aspiration to be a gentleman; Belfield does not simply go from being a linen-draper's son to falling into poverty and then needing to labor, but goes through the route of gentlemanly aspiration and pursuit. It is because he has wanted to be a gentleman that Belfield must labor—and, persisting to the bitter end, he imagines that labor will constitute his apotheosis as a gentleman. If the novel expresses a knowledge that labor is stupefying, it also conveys a considerable ambivalence toward leisure.

In *Cecilia*, female subjectivity—the sense of depths—is not just constituted in opposition to an aristocracy obsessed with surfaces and out of control of its own emotions. Feminine grief is an emotion whose very shape is imagined in relation to the language of the division of labor. And it is charity, in its capacity to offer a variety of images to the mind, that functions as a solution for the hyper-privatizing and deracinating effects of grief. Attempting to get over Delvile, Cecilia meditates, "Nothing, therefore, appeared to her so indispensable as constant employment, by which a variety of new images might force their way in her mind to supplant the old ones, and by which no time might be allowed for brooding over melancholy retrospections" (p. 790). In this she echoes Johnson, who wrote, "The safe and general antidote against sorrow, is employment. . . . Sorrow is a kind of rust of the soul, which every new idea contributes in its passage to scour away. It is the putrefaction of stagnant life, and is remedied by exercise and motion."[40] The form of employment most available and appropriate to Cecilia in her search for new ideas and images is charity. She seeks out Albany, and together they embark upon a charity mission that lasts for the first winter of her majority.

For Albany, the charitable impulse legitimates sorrow. It is when Cecilia transforms private grief into public work that he begins "to compassionate the sadness which hitherto he had reproved," exclaiming, "Oh sacred be thy sorrow, for thou canst melt at that of the indigent!" (p. 769). The charitable impulse authorizes sorrow, bringing it from being wanton and perverse to being sacred. Albany also believes that wounds can be healed by charity, saying, when Cecilia goes on his "rambles" with him, succoring the deserving poor, "The blessings of the fatherless, the prayers of little children, shall heal all your wounds with balm of sweetest fragrance. When sad, they shall chear, when complaining, they shall soothe you" (p. 710). If there is a vague contradictoriness to the proposition that charity both legitimizes sorrow and cures it—both makes its existence acceptable and gets rid of it—that contradictoriness is, we shall see, a symptom of the circular logic of charity in this novel.

It is a commonplace of late-eighteenth-century English culture that one can heal sorrow by helping the poor. Charity, contemporaries thought, served the threefold function of providing employment for the mind, reminding one that one was not that badly off, and giving one an opportunity to exercise Christian virtue.[41] It is difficult to pry apart the ideological structure that says that social action can help cure sorrow—difficult, that is, to recognize such an idea as ideological, because it seems so commonsensical. But what is *not* necessarily commonsensical is how this works the other way around: that during this period the sorrow of the gentlewoman donor functions in fact as a precondition of charity. When, for example, Dr. Gregory addresses the issue of charity in *A Father's Legacy to his Daughters* (1774), he begins as follows:

> Your whole life is often a life of suffering. You cannot plunge into business, or dissipate yourselves in pleasure and riot, as men too often do, when under the pressure of misfortunes. You must bear your sorrows in silence, unknown and unpitied. You must often put on a face of serenity and cheerfulness, when your hearts are torn with anguish, or sinking in despair. Then your only resource is in the consolations of Religion.
>
> The best effect of your religion will be a diffusive humanity to all in distress. Set apart a certain proportion of your income as sacred to charitable purposes. . . . [42]

Gregory's discussion of the ethics and mechanics of female charity is predicated upon a claim about the inevitability of female sorrow. Similarly, in one of the *Cheap Repository Tracts* about a charitable woman who brings discipline and relative prosperity to a poor parish, Hannah More opens with a death and a mourning. Mrs. Jones, "a great merchant's lady" whose husband dies after his business fails, retires to a small village on a small income, where she indulges a grief represented as excessive:

> Though a pious woman, she was too apt to indulge her sorrow; and though she did not neglect to read and pray, yet she gave up a great part of her time to melancholy thoughts, and grew quite inactive. . . . [S]he was not aware how wrong it was to weep away that time which might have been better spent in drying the tears of others. [43]

Under the influence of a wise vicar, Mrs. Jones bestirs herself to educate and discipline the community, and at the end of the story the vicar asks triumphantly, "Well, madam . . . which is best, to sit down and cry over our misfortunes, or to bestir ourselves to do our duty to the world?"[44] It clearly cannot happen in these tracts—or, for that matter, in novels like *Clarissa* or *Millenium Hall*—that the gentle-woman simply be rich and content and give to the poor, as Cecilia does in the beginning of Burney's novel. The act of charity seems not to make ideological sense when it works that way; something about the always-excessive sorrow of the heroine is indispensable to making sense of the whole project of charity.

Hence that famous cruel scene in which the novel sets up char-ity and grief as a mutual fantasy. Albany figures Cecilia's sorrow as a mere dream to be awakened from into charitable action; several pages later, though, the terms are reversed, when Cecilia wakes from a dream of fancied charitable activity into actual mortal loss. After she leaves the Harrels' and before she can take possession of her own home, Cecilia has been taking refuge with an older woman, Mrs. Charlton, whom she has known since she was a child. After seeing Albany, "Cecilia passed the rest of the day in fanciful projects of beneficence," and when she goes to sleep, has a powerful dream:

> At night, with less sadness than usual, she retired to rest. In her sleep she bestowed riches, and poured plenty upon the land; she humbled the oppressor, she exalted the oppressed; slaves were raised to digni-ties, captives restored to liberty; beggars saw smiling abundance, and wretchedness was banished the world. From a cloud in which she was supported by angels, Cecilia beheld these wonders; and while enjoy-ing the glorious illusion, she was awakened by her maid, with news that Mrs. Charlton was dying! (p. 711)

As critics have pointed out, this passage echoes the prophetic injunc-tions of Anchises to Aeneas in Book VI of the *Aeneid*.[45] Cecilia's dream of fancied imperialism is immediately deflated by the novel, which has her awake cruelly into mortal loss. "She started up, and, undressed, was running to her apartment,—when the maid, calling to stop her, confessed she was already dead! (pp. 711–12). The novel makes her run around in deshabille, as though she might have some agency, and then deflates that fantasy too.[46] The narrator comments, "Happily and in good time had Cecilia been somewhat recruited by one night of refreshing slumbers and flattering dreams, for the shock she now received promised her not soon another" (p. 712). Charity,

the social act meant to heal fancied sorrow, has become itself a "flattering dream" that dissolves in the face of real, implacable sorrow.

It is not difficult to see, in even the most cursory reading of
Cecilia, that as a cure for sorrow charity fails resoundingly. The novel
cues us with an explicitly skeptical rhetoric of fantasy, figuring
Cecilia's desire to give charity, for example, as a pleasing "fancy" that
"enrapture[s] her imagination" (pp. 55–56). My point here is the
contradictoriness of charity: the way in which charity is figured as a
cure for female grief, but in fact depends upon such grief as its indispensable precondition. A form of "employment" that functions
as a phantasmatic solution to a condition already figured as labor,
charity is as much designed to ensure the existence of painful affect
as it is to assuage it. Indeed, as I will show in the following section, it
actively produces the novel's most devastating crises.

III. 'You must try to think less of him': Shame and Charity

Cecilia's grief may struggle for expression in the face of Albany's melancholic challenge, but Burney's heroine also has a strong
melancholic impulse of her own; she testily shrugs off the grief of
poor women throughout the novel, especially that of the mothers of
laboring sons.[47] Mrs. Hill, the wife of the carpenter working on the
dissipated guardian Harrel's pleasure gardens, and Cecilia's first object of charity in the novel, is taking care of her husband, who is
dying of injuries sustained from this "very hard work . . . which I
am sure will cost my husband his life" (p. 73). But she chiefly mourns
her son Billy, who died at seventeen of a consumption. At first she
tells Cecilia, "I have quite left off grieving for him now" (p. 72), but
in her second meeting with her benefactress it becomes clear that
leaving off her grief isn't that easy: "I have been blest enough to-day
to comfort me for every thing in the world, if I could but keep from
thinking of poor Billy! I could bear all the rest, madam, but whenever my other troubles go off, that comes back to me so much the
harder!" (p. 78). Cecilia responds, "There, indeed, I can afford you no
relief . . . but you must try to think less of him, and more of your
husband and children who are now alive" (p. 78). Later, she steps up

her efforts at toughlove; "Try, however, to think less of him" (p. 86), and finally, "I cannot bear this! . . . you must tell me no more of your Billy" (p. 87). Mrs. Belfield too has trouble letting go of her son. She has pampered Belfield throughout his life, squandering the respectable trading family's resources by insisting on raising him as a gentleman. When Cecilia tells her one day how wonderful she thinks Henrietta is, Mrs. Belfield says, "But what is a daughter, madam, to such a son as mine?" (p. 315), which Cecilia calls "the unjust partiality shewn to her brother" (p. 317). When Belfield gets a job in a nobleman's family—a job that will be a godsend to his impoverished family but that might take him abroad—Mrs. Belfield can't accept parting with him; her daughter comments, "And so, if my mother can but reconcile herself to parting with him, perhaps we may all do well again" (p. 338). Cecilia has little patience for this maternal grief: "You must endeavor to reconcile yourself to parting with him" (p. 316), she says, to which the distraught mother replies, "Yes, but how am I to do that, when I don't know if ever I shall see him again?" (p. 317).

So the novel also feels very melancholic in the tension between intense maternal grief for sons, and Cecilia's repudiation of that grief, her demand that they get used to it. The novel scapegoats Belfield's mother because she insists that he's a gentleman—that is, that he should not be subjected to labor. When Belfield goes off to work as a day laborer, he doesn't tell his mother where he's going. For in this novel mothers hold onto their sons for dear life. Contemplating the possibility that her son will go abroad as the nobleman's companion, Mrs. Belfield laments, "it half drives me out of my senses to have him taken away from me at last in that unnatural manner" (p. 341)—the plaintive *at last* suggesting the long-standing success of her clinging to her son. And the novel wants rather nastily to say "Stop complaining and give him up already!" Margaret Doody argues that "in a novel that displays the patriarchal, the real emotional power and the only true acknowledged authority belong to the matriarchy."[48] But I believe that in *Cecilia* the emotional power of maternity is powerfully troubled, for it is as the familial drama of the mother's sacrifice of the son that this novel most intensely fig-

ures the socioeconomic drama of the reorganization and commodification of labor. It's as though the novel is eager for that decisive
moment when labor will be freed; it is eager for it because, strangely,
that is the moment when daughters will be restored to mothers. The
figuring of sons being released into labor as a drama of mother-loss
explains something about the intense solitude of Belfield's labor,
and the wound to his leg, which seems to literalize "the wound his
sensibility had received" (p. 667). It also leads us to another way in
which upper-class female affectivity is formed in relation to labor
and the poor: to the shame affect so prominent in the novel.

While Cecilia loses everything in this novel—her money, her
name, even her sanity—the thing that is represented as the final and
fatal loss is that of her self-regard. After she agrees to a clandestine
marriage to Delvile, she enters into a kind of hallucinatory state
where "all that had passed for a while appeared a dream" (pp.
575–76)—even her own sorrow. The narrator explains:

> Hitherto, though no stranger to sorrow, which the sickness and early
> loss of her friends had first taught her to feel, and which the subse-
> quent anxiety of her own heart had since instructed her to bear, she
> had yet invariably possessed the consolation of self-approving reflec-
> tions: but the step she was now about to take, all her principles op-
> posed; it terrified her as undutiful, it shocked her as clandestine, and
> scarce was Delvile out of sight, before she regretted her consent to it
> as the loss of her self-esteem, and believed, even if a reconciliation
> took place, the remembrance of a wilful fault would still follow her,
> blemish in her own eyes the character she had hoped to support, and
> be a constant allay to her happiness, by telling her how unworthily she
> had obtained it. (p. 576)

In this passage, shame is set into opposition with sorrow, much worse
and much more lasting; Cecilia has already gone through the school
of sorrow, which is represented as a closed circuit at this point.

When the chairs arrive to take her to church, her shame intensifies:

> The greatness of her undertaking, the hazard of all her future happi-
> ness, the disgraceful secresy of her conduct, the expected reproaches
> of Mrs. Delvile, and the boldness and indelicacy of the step she was

about to take, all so forcibly struck, and so painfully wounded her, that the moment she was summoned to set out, she again lost her resolution, and regretting the hour that ever Delvile was known to her, she sunk into a chair, and gave up her whole soul to anguish and sorrow. . . . [A] sudden horror against herself had now seized her spirits, which, exhausted by long struggles, could rally no more. (p. 624)

In her recent work on shame, Eve Kosofsky Sedgwick describes the psychiatric account of the genesis of shame as follows:

Recent work by theorists and psychologists of shame locates the proto-form (eyes down, head averted) of this powerful affect—which appears in infants very early, between the third and seventh months of life, just after the infant has become able to distinguish and recognize the face of its caregiver—at a particular moment in a particular repeated narrative. That is the moment when the circuit of mirroring expressions between the child's face and the caregiver's recognized . . . face is broken: the moment when the adult face fails or refuses to play its part in the continuation of mutual gaze; when, for any one of many reasons, it fails to be recognizable to, or recognizing of, the infant who has been, so to speak, "giving face" based on a faith in the continuity of this circuit.[49]

The person of whom Cecilia is most frightened when she begins to lose her self-regard is precisely a mother, one whose gaze she depends on: she quails beneath the idea of "the expected reproaches of Mrs. Delvile." The very first description of Mrs. Delvile foregrounds her gorgeous and piercing eyes, which, "though they had lost their youthful fire, retained a lustre that evinced their primeval brilliancy." Here is the account of their first impressions of one another:

The surprise and admiration with which Cecilia at the first glance was struck proved reciprocal: Mrs. Delvile, though prepared for youth and beauty, expected not to see a countenance so intelligent, nor manners so well formed as those of Cecilia: thus mutually astonished and mutually pleased, their first salutations were accompanied by looks so flattering to both, that each saw in the other, an immediate prepossession in her favour, and from the moment that they met, they seemed instinctively impelled to admire. (p. 155)

With its emphasis on the striking immediacy of their contact ("an immediate prepossession," "from the moment they met"), its focus on the gaze ("the first glance," "looks so flattering"), and its insistence upon the "reciprocal" and "mutual" nature of their approval for one another, this passage suggests the utopian circuit of gazing between mother and child. Sedgwick quotes Michael Franz Basch as saying that "shame-humiliation throughout life can be thought of as an inability to effectively arouse the other person's positive reactions to one's communications."[50] At this moment, Cecilia is astonished by her discovery of a mother with hyperbolically positive reactions to her communications. And as though drawn instinctively to a scenario of the newly born, Delvile will later say of Cecilia and his mother, "You seem, indeed, born for each other" (p. 518).

As it is the mother who so lovingly expresses her approval, so it is she who could wither Cecilia with a glance at any moment. When considering whether to marry Delvile against his parents' wishes, Cecilia meditates, "In accepting him, she was exposed to all the displeasure of his relations, and, which affected her most, to the indignant severity of his mother . . . " (p. 622). The eye of the mother might turn out to be "wrath-darting" rather than approving:

> Her praises, her partiality, her confidence in her character, which hitherto had been her pride, she now only recollected with shame and with sadness. The terror of the first interview never ceased to be present to her; she shrunk even in imagination from her wrath-darting eye, she felt stung by pointed satire, and subdued by cold contempt. (p. 577)

I will argue later that one thing that satire might be said to be in this book is the opposite of the loving and approving eye of the mother, the mode of inducing shame. Later, after the clandestine marriage attempt fails, Cecilia meditates painfully on the news arriving to the Delviles, and says "How will his noble mother disdain me! how cruelly shall I sink before the severity of her eye!" (p. 617). And indeed, Cecilia has forfeited the approbation of the mother. She tells Mrs. Delvile that she hopes to regain her good opinion, and Mrs. Delvile replies, "the fault was my own, in indulging an expectation of perfection to which human nature is perhaps unequal" (p. 637):

> Ah, then, thought Cecilia, all is over! the contempt I so much feared is incurred, and though it may be softened, it can never be removed! (p. 637)

Mrs. Delvile's remark that she should not have expected Cecilia to be absolutely perfect is actually rather generous; that Cecilia experiences it as devastating is a measure of the intensely idealized quality of their bond, a bond that until this point has evidently had the magical effect of making Cecilia feel absolutely perfect. She tells Mrs. Delvile too, "I pine, I sicken to recover my own good opinion" (p. 637). And a little later, when she has given Delvile up: "she had sacrificed the son, she had resigned herself to the mother" (p. 647).

Cecilia, then, longs for a mother who will return her hungry gaze at the same time that she repudiates maternal connection with sons, demanding that mothers "sacrifice the son." It is, after all, that "unjust partiality" shown to sons that keeps damaging daughters. Henrietta Belfield lives in poverty because all the family's money has been put to the son's use so that he can continue to be leisured; the "sacrifice" that Mrs. Belfield will not perform is releasing her son into labor. And Mrs. Delvile's "idolotry" of Mortimer makes it impossible for Cecilia to marry him—makes it impossible for her to be the daughter she wants to be. In this sense the sentence "she had sacrificed the son, she had resigned herself to the mother" (p. 647) may be read as a utopian promise in the guise of a renunciation. For it is by sacrificing her lover, "the son," that Cecilia hopes to be cured of shame, restored to the mother's loving gaze.

As the Delvile plot suggests, the refusal to let sons go is a trans-class phenomenon in *Cecilia*; indeed, at many points the novel satirically figures men of all classes as babies, or as unnaturally attached to their childhoods.[51] To foreground and pressure the accounts of those sons who labor, however, and to read the anguish of mother-loss as a richly displaced evocation of the "release" of laborers into the labor market affords us a compelling route into the shame response so central to the dynamic of charity. Shame is, of course, a staple of the paternalistic charitable transaction in the eighteenth century: "head down, eyes averted" might be said to be the exemplary response of the recipient of charity. Miss Belfield does this wonderfully; presented to Cecilia by Albany as a poor person in need of aid, she seemed "overwhelmed with shame and chagrin" (p. 207). Her brother, too, feels the shame of dependence. Talking to Cecilia about the laboring poor who have never known a different life from the day labor he now performs,[52] Belfield represents his situation as a crisis of looking: "had they seen an attentive circle wait all its entertainment from their powers, yet found themselves forgotten as soon as out of sight, and perceived themselves avoided when no longer buffoons!" (p. 665). The formative moment of Belfield's decision to become a day laborer occurs when, broke and shabbily dressed, he sees a gentleman he knows thrown from his horse, and rushes to help:

> He knew me, but looked suprised at my appearance; he was speaking to me, however, with kindness, when seeing some gentlemen of his acquaintance gallopping up to him, he hastily disengaged himself from me, and instantly beginning to recount to them what had happened, he sedulously looked another way, and joining his new companions, walked off without taking further notice of me. . . . Here finished my deliberation; the disgust to the world which I had already conceived, this little incident confirmed. . . . (p. 662)

It is a moment of tentative and shaky recognition, followed by the abrupt and "sedulous" breaking of the gaze, that sends Belfield into the fields.

This is a different dynamic from that of the disciplinary gaze in *A Sentimental Journey*—its absence an expression of rupture between the poor and those who care for them. Indeed, because, as Fowkes Tobin argues, the spread of disciplinary mechanisms and techniques during this period entailed the gradual withdrawal of face-to-face contact between paternalists and the poor, this novel represents gazing between actual people with longing and nostalgia. Psychoanalytically speaking, the shame response might be said to be the response of those who have been disconnected from the mother's life-giving gaze, and who now rely upon others to give them life. And interestingly, in *Cecilia* it is on the level of the psychic process of the gentlewoman that this drama of mother-loss and consequent shame is enacted in the most powerful and sustained way. Indeed, what seems to mark this period, in which charity has fallen into disrepute as a mode of social connection, is not any kind of heightened expectation of the shame of the recipients of charity—the shame of the poor is a standard-issue requirement throughout the early modern period—but rather the expectation that the *donor* be suffused with shame. It somehow becomes the gentlewoman's job to bear and express the shame of those classes that have been cut off from the life-giving gaze of the culture. This shame, I would suggest, is the shame of transition. It comes from mothers' attempts to hold onto sons by looking away from daughters; it would be assuaged by the release of the sons into labor.

In its substitution of other caregivers for the primary caregiver, charity may be regarded as a way to repair or mitigate the shame of the fracture of the mother's gaze. But as in the case of grief, the performance of charity has the effect of exacerbating Cecilia's shame, of producing fresh reserves of shame. For in Burney's novel, charity is nothing less than the occasion to disastrously confuse an economic issue with a sexual one.[53] Cecilia is taken to be unchaste precisely because of her benevolence: indeed, nothing could be more mutually exclusive than the claims of benevolence and the claims of feminine propriety. When Delvile learns that Cecilia has contracted with a "Jew" moneylender to save her guardian Harrel from ruin, he writes of his mother, "How grieved [she will be] that your own too great benevolence should be productive of such black aspersions upon your character!" (p. 808). And the novel's most fatal misunderstandings are caused by Delvile's mistaking of her charitable ministrations to Henrietta Belfield for a liaison with her brother. Early in the novel, before they have acknowledged their love for each other, Cecilia bumps into Mortimer at Belfield's, and when he behaves coldly toward her, "she now saw with some alarm the danger to which benevolence itself, directed towards a youthful object, might expose her" (p. 229). Even quite late in the day, when she and Mortimer are already married and she has been expelled from her home for violating the name clause on his behalf, the novel's most gothic turn is kicked off by Delvile's surprising her at Belfield's house, and storming off in a temper tantrum because he thinks she is carrying on an illicit relationship with him (pp. 885–87). If in *A Sentimental Journey* the gentleman constitutes himself as such every time he gives charity, in *Cecilia* it is—in one of those neat vicious double binds so characteristic of late-eighteenth-century culture's construction of women—the condition of femininity to have one's character assassinated at the very moment one is performing the duties of feminine virtue.

The charity plot and the courtship plot split a powerful ambivalence toward the mother; in the courtship plot Cecilia adores Mrs. Delvile, while in the charity plot she despises Mrs. Belfield. It is Belfield's mother who insists upon misunderstanding charitable ministrations as sexual advances; Mrs. Delvile, the idealized mother, is the one who wants to keep Cecilia *apart* from her son. Indeed, I would argue that Mrs. Delvile is idealized *precisely because* she demands that Cecilia sacrifice the son and resign herself to the mother. There's something inherently scandalous and stigma-producing about Mrs. Belfield's regarding her son as a sexual object rather than as an instantiation of labor power. For the scandal of cross-class love lies in its capacity to interrupt the process of creating labor power.[54]

⁓✥⁓

We generally think of charity as paternalistic, paternalism being that cluster of attitudes and practices that attempted to counter the encroachment of the impersonal logic of the market. In the dynamic in *Cecilia* that I've been describing, paternalism constitutes an attempt to salve the trauma of the fracture of the maternal bond. But paradoxically, as Belfield's experience and the shame response intrinsic to receiving charity suggest, it is also a form of repetition compulsion, in which that fracture is repeatedly re-evoked and re-enacted. I will conclude this section by reading Albany's story as a parable of paternalism. That Albany is a lunatic—"certainly," according to Gosport, "confined, at one part of his life, in a private mad-house" (p. 291) and referred to by the "young ladies" as "the *crazy-man*" (p. 66)—does not in the least disqualify him for the position of the novel's resident paternalist; Burney has little use for fathers throughout her *oeuvre*, and I take Albany to represent the lunacy at the heart of paternalism. The quotation with which I opened this chapter hints at the nature of Albany's pathology: "[T]o awaken thee from this dream of fancied sorrow," he tells Cecilia, "I will open all my wounds, and thou shalt probe them with fresh shame" (p. 704). Albany is purportedly referring to Cecilia's shame, but there is also ambiguity there, for it is shame that has caused his wounds, and the word *fresh* suggests the fresh bleeding of newly opened wounds. Albany, that is, conflates Cecilia's affect with his own. And indeed, the sad story he finally tells her provides a kind of allegory for the way paternalism borrows from and depends upon female affect.

In his youth, Albany tells Cecilia, he beat and destroyed his lover, a villager's young daughter, because she became the mistress of his best friend while he was settling his affairs in Jamaica after his father's death. She disappears, "terrified with expectation of insult" and Albany, chastened by "the softness of her sorrow" (p. 706), finds her two years later, walking the streets at midnight and entering a "house of infamy" (p. 706). He drags her away and settles her in a house in the country, and when her health begins to fail he tries to comfort her. At first she has screamed and wept; now, however, "I spoke . . . to a statue . . . she seemed deaf, mute, insensible, her face unmoved, a settled despair fixed in her eyes" (p. 707). She reveals finally that "she had made a vow, upon entering the house, to live speechless and motionless, as a pennance for her offences!" (p. 708). Later in the novel, Cecilia will experience a nearly identical insanity. "Senseless, speechless, motionless, her features void of all expression, her cheeks without colour, her eyes without meaning" (p. 918): at the climax of her madness, Cecilia embodies a radical vacancy, a terrible void in the place of voice, expression, animation. Insanity in this novel is the limit case of affect itself, characterized by a tension between an excess of emotion, in which Cecilia raves, screams, and hallucinates, and something like the opposite of subjectivity, a system shutdown. Like the villager's daughter, when Cecilia goes mad, she performs the double gesture of being the epitome of female affectivity and of refusing affect altogether.

Doody argues of Albany's destroyed lover, "her stern-willed penance for her life seems a hostile parody of what men want women to be (deaf, mute, anorexic, motionless)."[55] While Doody's comment expresses a kind of conventional wisdom about patriarchy's effects on women, I have argued that on the contrary, the demand on women is that they bear certain affective burdens, which is why even the social act designed to calm strong emotion keeps producing more strong emotion. When the villager's daughter dies, Albany goes insane. As he describes it, "I kept her loved corpse till my own senses failed me,—it was then only torn from me,—and I have lost all recollection of three years of my existence!" (p. 708). Albany's clasp on the corpse transmits its speechlessness and motionlessness to him; there is a kind of rigorous logic to his "I kept her loved corpse till my own senses failed me,—it was then only torn from me," as if he is saying, "It could be torn from me only when my own sense failed." He hangs onto the corpse until he himself becomes one. The form Albany's insanity takes is his imitating women's grief and shame; and it is this insanity that leads to his charity work:

> The scene to which my memory first leads me back . . . is visiting her grave; solemnly upon it I returned her vow, though not by one of equal severity. To her poor remains did I pledge myself, that the day should never pass in which I would receive nourishment, nor the night come in which I would take rest, till I had done, or zealously attempted to do, some service to a fellow-creature. (p. 708)

Albany's story of the pathos of the patriarch—the story that is supposed to be so much more heartrending than Cecilia's own sad story—suggests that paternalistic charitable endeavor originates in the "poor remains" of a woman. It originates in a substitution: a vow to perform service to fellow-creatures in exchange for a vow to live stricken by grief and shame. It is worth noting two things about this substitution. First, Albany's commitment to the vow, his promise that if his lover becomes stricken by grief and shame he will reciprocate by dedicating his life to succoring the poor. Second, one might consider the resemblance between charity work and paralysis to be sufficiently faint to make the claim of similitude feel tendentious; Albany's assertion that he behaved just like his lover demonstrates a rather strained commitment to imitating her. Doody claims that "Albany's moral worth, his capacity to castigate others and make them give, is founded . . . on mistreatment of a woman."[56] But just as in *Humphry Clinker* it's not just the woman dying but in particular excessive, egregious grief for the woman being expressed and denied, that is ideologically necessary for improvement to happen, I think that here it is not only that women have to be abused and killed for patriarchy to take care of its poor, but that silent wounded women—women stricken by grief and shame—need to be harbored within the very structure of its ego.

This is a more complicated dynamic than the melancholic structure of *Humphry Clinker*. In Burney's novel paternalism requires women as an intermediary to absorb and to shape into emotion the impact of the reorganization of labor practices and the concomitant wound to the laboring poor. It is also a more chaotic dynamic— indeed, a maddening circle of cause and effect. Gentlewomen feel grief and shame, perform charity to get over their emotions, and find that charity only produces fresh grief and shame; the paternalist incorporates the figure of the stricken woman, which in turn enables him to be a paternalist—that is, to give charity. In this moment of transition, as political economists are trying to wrest labor and freedom into an ideology of the free laborer, charity is not completely devalued; indeed, in *Cecilia* it is clearly highly cathected as a form of social connection. But it does have to take a circuitous route and perform fresh functions. No longer merely a way of succoring those who have been cut off from the life-giving gaze of the culture, charity has also become a catalyst for female emotion: for the psychic work of grief and shame that accompanies and enables sending sons into labor.

The opening of Nichols and Wray's 1935 *The History of the Foundling Hospital* gives an account of that charity's inception that richly evokes the dynamic of maternal rupture and paternalist response:

> An old sea captain, returning early in the eighteenth century from the illimitable and untouched areas of the New World, where human labour was the greatest need, saw newly-born children left deserted, to die, on the dunghills in and around London.
>
> This horrible waste of human life filled him with indignation and fury. Thomas Coram, the sea captain, made up his mind that this practice should be ended.
>
> And that was the beginning of the Foundling Hospital.[57]

The notion of "horrible waste" derives its force not from any general sense of the indispensability of human lives, but rather from the need for labor in the New World; this account of the founding of the hospital, which raised and educated abandoned newborn children for apprenticeship or service, represents paternalist practice as the effective joining of the two social loose ends of abandoned children and the need for labor. At the Foundling Hospital, mothers quite literally relinquished their infant children to labor. From 1756, when the hospital began its policy of indiscriminate admissions, they brought their children and placed them in a basket outside the hospital gates, along with, in accordance with regulations, "some particular writing, or other distinguishing mark or token."[58] Intended not only to identify the infants, but also to help acquit the mothers should they be accused of infanticide,[59] these distinguishing marks helped sustain a perhaps tenuous boundary between killing infants and giving them over to labor.

Tellingly, the Foundling Hospital was one of the charities hardest hit by the decline in institutional charity in the 1770s and 1780s. Andrew writes that while the governors of the hospital

> had originally maintained that as many exposed and deserted children as the hospital could support should be admitted . . . they now saw their responsibility to lie only with the care of those children whose sponsors could offer proof that they would otherwise perish. It must have been exceedingly difficult to offer such proof. However, by these new regulations the hospital tried to dispel widely held fears that its existence was encouraging the working poor to idleness by giving them an easy refuge and escape from their legitimate responsibilities.[60]

The justifications for this retrenchment (so acutely suggestive of the rhetoric of the U.S. Congress about welfare in 1995–96) suggest that even the project of training children to labor could backfire, if it was thought to result in dependence on the part of their parents. The Hospital would revive later, but its decline suggests that the paternalist response to maternal rupture could itself function as a threat to the process of creating autonomous laborers. In *Cecilia* paternalism might elaborately and painfully shape its woman donor as a suffering subjectivity in order to do its work; but the fate of the

Foundling Hospital shows us that the demands of a market economy intent on creating "free" labor were paramount, heedless of the
tortuous paths taken by those trying to resist it.

IV. Labor, Satire, and the Figure of Hope

In a novel so focused upon gazing and the gaze's rupture, satire—a practice of exposure—has a special resonance. The novel's
most extended satiric scenes center around Cecilia's dread of exposure. On her highly charged clandestine journey to London to meet
Delvile, she passes a carriage that has broken down and is roped into
helping a parcel of fashionable acquaintance. Summoned by Miss
Larolles, Cecilia cries, "And how should she know me? . . . I am
sure she could not see me" (p. 592); she is deeply upset by this "un-
seasonable" meeting, having "particularly wished to have escaped all
notice" (p. 593). To make things worse, she is teased by the novel's
resident satirist, Mr. Gosport, who, getting a whiff of her anxiety,
launches into a witty and damning similitude between architecture
and female character. The novel then proceeds to engineer a new
sequence of suspense by having Delvile gallop by "much muffled
up, his hat flapped, and a handkerchief held to his mouth and chin"
(p. 602); he is chased and hounded by the bored males in the party,
while Cecilia waits in a paroxysm of anxiety that he will be discovered. In a later, critical scene in the novel, Cecilia visits Henrietta,
who leads her into a back room that Cecilia doesn't realize belongs
to her brother—whereupon Delvile's father, who has come to in-
quire whether she is indeed involved with Belfield, arrives unex-
pectedly at the Belfield residence. Hiding in an agony of suspense,
Cecilia is forced to overhear a humiliating exchange—one of what
Johnson calls "those quintessentially Burneyan scenes of preposter-
ous embarrassment"[61]—in which the vulgar Mrs. Belfield compla-
cently wreaks havoc on her character in the presence of the haughty
and increasingly scornful aristocrat. And Cecilia is eventually discovered: "Such was the situation of the discovered, abashed, per-
plexed, and embarrased! while that of the discoverers, far different,
was bold, delighted, and triumphant!" (p. 785).

I suggested earlier that the flip side of Mrs. Delvile's loving gaze is her "wrath-darting" eye, which Cecilia fears will sting "with pointed satire"; and indeed, in these scenes satire is a mode of looking antithetical to the maternal gaze, an act of triumphant discovery rather than loving recognition. At the same time, one important characteristic of fashionable society in this novel—as Belfield's anecdote of the gentleman thrown from his horse suggests—is precisely the failure to look. The coolest possible member of the *ton*, Mr. Meadows, is described by Miss Larolles as "so remarkably absent" (p. 402) and "so excessive absent" (p. 605):

> Why he's at the very head of the *ton*. There's nothing in the world so fashionable as taking no notice of things, and never seeing people, and saying nothing at all, and never hearing a word, and not knowing one's own acquaintance. All the *ton* people do so. . . . (p. 605)

Satire, then, is activated in the interstices of the fear of being exposed and the fear of not being seen at all.

These extended satiric set pieces hold us, as well as Cecilia, hostage to long and annoying suspense, and to the nonsensical chatter and unmeaning stunts of shallow fashionable characters; at these moments Burney stalls the plot in a way that feels almost wanton. In *Cecilia* satire disrupts forward journeys, and prevents loved ones from finding each other, in the interests of exposing character. Although Burney mercilessly savages people in the business classes for loudly insisting that they have personalities,[62] I want to focus on the satire leveled at fashionable society's famously tenuous hold on the connection between surfaces and depths. Satire is, of course, a congenial form for ridicule of the fashionable, in its exposure of hypocrisy, the willful failure of correspondence between surfaces and depths. In policing the relation between inside and outside, satire speaks on behalf of a self constituted by depths that correspond to surfaces—on behalf, in this case, of the creation of the domestic woman. At the same time, however, the interminability of these scenes, Burney's rigorous and agonizing drawing out of every single satiric possibility, suggests a certain commitment to incongruity. It is as though the novel wants to attack and expose these characters, but also needs to dwell among them at length.

The masquerade is a privileged figure for such incongruity, and the novel's most utopian site of satiric pleasure. Until she gets harrassed and attacked by an aristocrat dressed as Lucifer, Cecilia has a singular experience there: fun. She remarks to Gosport, who is gussied up as a schoolmaster for the occasion,

> "To own the truth . . . the almost universal neglect of the characters assumed by these masquers, has been the chief source of my entertainment this evening: for at a place of this sort, the next best thing to a character well supported, is a character ridiculously burlesqued" (p. 113).[63]

Although she stipulates that "neglect of character" be bounded to "a place of this sort," and judiciously names "character well supported" as the best delight, Cecilia's pleasure comes from her ridicule of fashionable thoughtlessness and incongruity. That incongruity produces a sense of riotous variety:

> Her expectations of entertainment were not only fulfilled but surpassed; the variety of dresses, the medley of characters, the quick succession of figures, and the ludicrous mixture of groupes, kept her attention unwearied: while the conceited efforts at wit, the total thoughtlessness of consistency, and the ridiculous incongruity of the language with the appearance, were incitements to surprise and diversion without end. (p. 106)

As a satirist, Cecilia knows "surprise and diversion without end" because she is provided with a variety of images. One might argue, then, that the satiric moment comes in sharp contradistinction to the grief/division of labor dynamic that constricts the scope of vision, and that is so central to the construction of the domestic woman. It is worth contrasting Cecilia's experience, and her legitimacy as a satirist in this scene, with Lady Honoria, "a relation of the Delviles, and of a character the most airy and unthinking" (p. 354)—the delight of whose life, according to Mrs. Delvile, is "to create wonder by her rattle" (p. 464). Lady Honoria is a false satirist, and a clue to her failure lies in her comment, "You must know my eyes tire extremely of always seeing the same objects" (p. 465). Her "unthinking" satire, dismissed as "incorrigible levity," comes out of a bored exhaustion redolent of grief; satire, in other words, fails at the evocation of the rhetoric of grief and the division of labor. For good satire depends upon incongruity of character, which is associated with a pleasurable surfeit of images.

As they contemplate a "figure of Hope" who is "expressive of despondency," Cecilia and Gosport have a conversation that further emphasizes the mutual exclusivity of satiric commentary and the trope of labor. Gosport comments that "the assumed character is always given up, where an opportunity offers to display any beauty, or manifest any perfection in the dear proper person!" and Cecilia responds as follows:

> "But why," said Cecilia, "should she assume the character of *Hope*? Could she not have been equally dejected, and equally elegant as Niobe, or some tragedy queen?"
>
> "But she does not assume the character," answered the schoolmaster, "she does not even think of it: the dress is her object, and that alone fills up her ideas." (p. 121)

In the midst of this standard satiric critique of dress and show, Cecilia offers an aesthetic helpful hint that also happens to be an infanticidal fantasy—a fantasy about a mother's excessive attachment to her children, and their consequent murder. For Niobe had a dangerously arrogant pride in her fourteen children, boasting,

> My very abundance has made me safe. I am too great for Fortune to harm; though she should take many from me, still many more will she leave to me.[64]

When Niobe publicly taunts the goddess Latona for having only two children, Latona responds by murdering all fourteen of Niobe's children. At the end there remains one daughter, whom Niobe pleads for: "Oh, leave me one, the littlest! Of all my many children, the littlest I beg you spare—just one!"[65] Poignantly evocative of Cecilia's desire to dwell alone in the mother's gaze, that daughter too is killed. And Niobe turns into a staring vacant figure reminiscent of both the villager's daughter destroyed by Albany, and Cecilia herself:

> Now does the childless mother sit down amid the lifeless bodies of her sons, her daughters, and her husband, in stony grief. Her hair stirs not in the breeze; her face is pale and bloodless, and her eyes are fixed

and staring in her sad face. There is nothing alive in the picture. Her
very tongue is silent, frozen to her mouth's roof, and her veins can
move no longer; her neck cannot bend nor her arms move nor her
feet go. Within also her vitals are stone. But still she weeps . . . and
even to this day tears trickle from the marble.[66]

It is the figure of weeping stone, "the picture of utter grief," that Cecilia recommends to solve a failure to "support character." A mother
losing her children, so central to this novel's imagination of the laboring poor, becomes the figure that enables the creation of interiority; it is only when the children are sacrificed—given over to labor, given over to death—that there emerges a self whose surface
corresponds to its depths.

So it is no wonder that Burney's novel is committed to the
practice of satire—nor that such practice feels so adamant and tax-
ing. Satire is insistent here, and in its best moments utopian, because
it has the power to hold off the creation of the domestic woman and
the process of the reorganization of labor that such creation entails.
That Cecilia is devastated by it, caught between the rock of exposure and the hard place of neglect, does not make it any less utopian.
She is exposed to the novel's punitive energies at the moment the
son returns—the moment, for example, that Belfield comes back
into the sphere of the mother. The domestic woman is shown to be
flawed and hypocritical herself when the process of labor is dis-
rupted, for as I have argued, her creation and the reorganization of
labor are mutually constitutive. When satire takes furious aim at the
domestic woman, it does so on behalf of halting the processes attendant upon the development of a market economy. That is why at
the masquerade—the moment of its apotheosis—satire is allied
with the figure of Hope.

Conclusion

LABOR AND SATIRE
AT THE CENTURY'S END

In highlighting different focal points in each novel—literacy in *Joseph Andrews*, charity in *A Sentimental Journey*, labor and enclosure in *Humphry Clinker*, and labor and charity in *Cecilia*—I have been guided by my sense of where each novel devotes its primary energy in relation to the poor. This way of proceeding has suggested the increasing centrality of labor to the portrayal of the poor in the novel as the century progresses, and its increasing capacity to generate considerable cultural anxiety.[1] The sheer force of complication in the later novels—in which the circuits of identification between gentle and poor become both more mediated and more contradictory as labor is introduced—indicates the complexity of the ideological web woven around labor, and consequently, around leisure. It is instructive in that regard to look at the briefer and less concerted representations of labor in *Joseph Andrews* and *A Sentimental Journey*, and to juxtapose these novels with what is perhaps eighteenth-century England's most extraordinary novel about labor: Burney's *The Wanderer*. Burney began her dreary and implacable final novel in the late 1790s, but published it only in 1814. Delayed by the death of her beloved sister Susanna and her own mastectomy for breast cancer, written in both England and France, *The Wanderer* is well suited to conclude this study, for it imagines a post-French-revolutionary

world rendered starkly dystopian by an imperative to labor so powerfully universal it overwhelms gentle identity.

I argued in Chapter 1 that *Joseph Andrews* imagines literacy as the
engine of upward mobility. Joseph is portrayed from the beginning
of the novel as disarmingly disqualified from labor. Bound apprentice to Sir Thomas Booby at the age of ten, he promptly and charm-
ingly fails at various forms of labor because of the sweetness of his
voice. He is set to keeping birds from the crops, for example, but his
voice is "so extremely musical, that it rather allured the Birds than
terrified them" (*JA*, p. 21), and when he is placed as a "whipper-in"
under the huntsman, "for this Place likewise the Sweetness of his
Voice disqualified him: the Dogs preferring the Melody of his chid-
ing to all the alluring Notes of the Huntsman. . . . "[2] Joseph is therefore initially represented as a poor boy whose sweet voice makes him
unfit for various forms of labor—although he succeeds as a jockey
for Sir Thomas' racehorses, and is from there promoted, at the age of
seventeen, to the role of footman to Lady Booby. As a footman, especially when Lady Booby moves to London, Joseph's life parodies
genteel pursuits, and once more, the novel connects voice to leisure:
in London, "He applied most of his leisure Hours to Music, in which
he greatly improved himself, and became so perfect a Connoisseur
in that Art, that he led the Opinion of all the other Footmen at an
Opera . . . " (*JA*, p. 27). As voice functions in the case of Fanny
as literacy's antithesis and antidote, in the case of Joseph it militates
against labor. One might argue that in Fielding's novel, voice is the
antidote to upward mobility, but also a form of protection from labor. It would be overstating the case to say that Joseph never labors in
Fielding's novel. But it is worth noticing that when Joseph gets fired
from Lady Booby's employ, he does not worry about finding work,
but instead decides to set out to look for his girlfriend; and in the nu-
merous scenes in which he and Adams come up short with their inn
bills, the novel does not imagine their having to work for the money.
Instead, Adams tries to procure money from benevolent people, an
act that serves as the occasion for various ethical arguments about
works vs. faith. Indeed, in *Joseph Andrews* the problematic of *works*
has the emotional energy and complexity that the problematic of

work will take on in the later novels, which suggests that it may be fruitful to think of the ideological knot of labor and leisure in the later part of the century as a secular form of that debate.

Interestingly, Joseph is also protected from labor by his status as a servant. As we have seen, Robbins argues that the English novel has characteristically used servants to represent labor. For Robbins, labor functions as the ideological pressure point between rulers and ruled, "common ground where ruptures, recognitions, and renegotiations can take place between them."[3] In the Victorian period, he suggests, these ruptures and recognitions occur partly through the eroticization of labor. We get a foretaste of this in Fielding's first description of Fanny, which describes her extreme beauty as both tempered and amplified by the signs of labor upon her hands: they are "a little redden'd by her Labour" (*JA*, p. 152), but their redness sets off the whiteness of her neck—with a similar logic to how the small-pox mark on her chin, which "might have been mistaken for a Dimple" (*JA*, p. 153), sets off the dimple on her left cheek. The marks of labor on Fanny are a vital part of her attractiveness. But if it is as workers that servants are eroticized in the novel, insofar as they function as signs for conspicuous consumption, they also represent leisure. They are liminal figures not only in their capacity as intermediaries between classes, but also in their capacity to straddle the leisure/labor divide. And indeed, in *Joseph Andrews* being a servant functions as a kind of protection against labor. Not only does Joseph's job as a footman in London entail leisure pursuit, but he has trouble shedding his status as a servant even after he is fired by Lady Booby. As readers of *Joseph Andrews* know, Fielding makes a narrative error by having Joseph stripped of his livery when he is fired from Lady Booby's (*JA*, p. 47), but later recognized by it at an inn, after he has been stripped of it once more by robbers (*JA*, p. 64). If Fielding was in fact nodding there, the effect is nevertheless rich: Joseph's trouble definitively shedding his livery, I believe, suggests something about the novel's commitment to preserving his status as a servant.

Like most novels of its genre, *A Sentimental Journey* is more interested in those poor on the fringes of society—disabled military men, seduced and abandoned young women, the semi-insane—

than in the laboring poor. But near the end of the novel, when Yorick decides to leave France for Italy because he is sick and tired of his life in the French *monde*, a life he calls a "vile prostitution,"[4] a vision of labor comes to refresh him. Sterne's portrayal of the vintage in Bourbonnais is highly stylized and romanticized—and, typically, interrupted:

> I never felt what the distress of plenty was in any one shape till now—to travel it through the Bourbonnois, the sweetest part of France—in the hey-day of the vintage, when Nature is pouring her abundance into every one's lap, and every eye is lifted up—a journey through each step of which music beats time to *Labour*, and all her children are rejoicing as they carry in their clusters—to pass through this with my affections flying out, and kindling at every group before me—and every one of 'em was pregnant with adventures.
>
> Just Heaven!—it would fill up twenty volumes—and alas! I have but a few small pages left of this to croud it into—and half of these must be taken up with the poor Maria my friend, Mr. Shandy, met with near Moulines. (pp. 268–69)

The scene cuts away to Maria, the pathetic object *par excellence*, supposedly because labor provides too plenteous an array of objects for representation. But it is not hard to see that the laborers are in fact less interesting than Maria, because they don't function as objects of compassion. One might argue that labor fails to capture the imagination of Sterne—that instead, the most cathected bodily moment in *A Sentimental Journey* occurs when the body is held still for visual or tactile scrutiny. When Yorick finds Maria she is sitting under a poplar: "she was sitting with her elbow in her lap, and her head leaning on one side within her hand . . . " (p. 270). Later, when fantasizing about a peasant tending a herd of sheep, Yorick arrests this potential portrayal of labor with a sentimental posture similar to Maria's: imagining the peasant finding a dead lamb from another flock, Yorick writes, "This moment I beheld him leaning with his head against his crook, with piteous inclination looking down upon it . . . " (p. 279). Sterne transforms the body engaged in the movement of labor into a body in studied repose.

For if the body is laboring, it is not holding still enough for the intense scrutiny that reading character requires. One might press this point and argue that one of the ideological burdens of Sterne's novel is precisely to hold bodies still. Not only does the legibility of character depend upon it, but it's also instrumental in the identification of gentlemen with the poor. That is, not only does Yorick find his anxious-making double in the non-laboring poor, but the novel consistently makes this process possible by producing the poor as images of non-labor. Identification is predicated on the likeness of gentle and poor in leisured postures. In contrast, in Smollett's and Burney's novels, the gentry's identification with the poor hinges upon the crisis point of the moment of labor's inauguration: in *Humphry Clinker* the gentle return obsessively to the alienation from the land that led to total hire, while the gentlewoman's torment in *Cecilia* is produced by the agonizing wait for the release of the sons into labor. There's a sense, then, in which one might view the earlier two novels as not so much uninterested in labor, as in attempting to ward it off.

ᘏ᙭ᘏ

At late century, as I have argued, the processes of reorganizing and commodifying labor were accompanied by a rhetoric of labor's universality and a concomitant strain of antipathy toward leisure. Burney's *The Wanderer; or, Female Difficulties* depicts a late-century limit case of this rhetoric. Margaret Doody writes of Burney that she "employed her imagination on women's work, and on work in general, with an intensity and disillusion not usually to be found until the social novels of the late 1830s and early 1840s."[5] Of all Burney's novels, it is her novel of the French Revolution that meditates on labor with the most intensity and disillusion, as well as with an almost encyclopedic variety and exactness. If *Cecilia* is about the effort to keep sons from laboring, *The Wanderer* is about a gentlewoman's inexorable and harrowing fall into labor. In the opening scene of this ponderous novel—which Claudia Johnson aptly calls "a work of gigantic ambition and bewildering failure"[6]—Burney's heroine escapes from the Terror in France anonymous and disguised, and during most of the 900-page novel she cannot reveal her identity, because, we learn only near the end, a beloved elderly male guardian will be killed in France if she does. Like so many of Burney's heroines with name-trouble, this one, provisionally called Ellis, is not given her real name, Juliet, for most of the novel, and the story concerns her struggle to simultaneously survive and maintain a feminine propriety whose rules could not be more exacting, when she cannot reveal either her connections or her gentle status—although discerning eyes can tell she is a gentlewoman from her beauty and cultivation.

The Wanderer is not easy to categorize ideologically among the polemical fiction of the 1790s. While its first sentence sets it "during the dire reign of the terrific Robespierre" (p. 11), Burney seems to have known and loved too many French people to be able to demonize the Revolution in any simple way. The Revolution wreaks considerable havoc in the novel—havoc of family, fortune, and religious faith—and late in her story, Juliet recounts her traumatic memories of the Scene of the Guillotine, whose frenzy and gore terrified her into her (luckily unconsummated) marriage. At the same time, Burney has the heroine's friend Gabriella, a virtuous fallen French aristocrat, utter a densely ambivalent statement about the Revolution's effects:

> Alas! whence I come, all that are greatest, most ancient, and most noble, have learnt, that self-exertion can alone mark nobility of soul; and that self-dependence can only sustain honour in adversity. . . . Ah, Sir, the French Revolution has opened our eyes to a species of equality more rational, because more feasible, than that of lands or of rank; an equality not alone of mental sufferings, but of manual exertions. (p. 639)

As Doody argues, in *The Wanderer* "the French Revolution has had the invigorating effect on its surviving victims that the pro-Revolutionary theorists designed for themselves."[7] Doody points out too that "throughout the novel, the English characters are complacent, politically obtuse, and xenophobic . . . through that group of provincials England is presented as an affluent society turned in upon itself and withering away."[8] For these reasons, and also because it was published in 1814, right after the defeat of Napoleon, when the tide of conservative feeling was high, the novel was roundly disparaged by reviewers, who regarded it as subversively democratic.[9]

Gabriella's equation of "mental sufferings" and "manual exertions," and her extolling the beneficial effects of self-exertion only after first crying "Alas!" are symptomatic of *The Wanderer*'s complex relation to labor. On the one hand, the novel's hero and strongest moral authority, Harleigh, agrees with Gabriella in insisting that the French Revolution has had a salutary and invigorating effect on people of rank by rousing them into labor, citing this lesson as the moral of the novel:

> [The French Revolution] has not operated more wonderfully upon the fate and fortune, than upon the minds and characters of those individuals who have borne in it any share; and who, according to their temperaments and dispositions, have received its new doctrines as lessons, or as warnings. Its undistinguishing admirers, it has emancipated from all rule and order; while its unwilling, yet observant and suffering witnesses, have been formed by it to fortitude, prudence, and philosophy; it has taught them to strengthen the mind with the body; it has animated the exercise of reason, the exertion of the faculties, activity in labour, resignation in endurance, and cheerfulness under every privation; it has formed, my Lord Melbury, in the school of refining adversity, your firm, yet tender sister! . . . (p. 869)

At the same time, in the phrase "in the school of refining adversity" we can see something of the ambivalence over labor's effects: it alludes to a process of purification, but also suggests Harleigh's hope that labor could render the gentle even more gentle. For the imperative to labor gradually overwhelms the gentlewoman: what *The Wanderer* imagines is the incremental but inexorable breakdown of her activity from leisured accomplishment into something that can be regarded as labor proper. And despite its moral of a fortunate fall, the novel comes to a virtual ideological standstill in an astounding anti-pastoral sequence that suggests that labor is so numbing and degraded that it can only be compensated for in the afterlife.

As the novel's subtitle suggests, its major concern is the condition of women. Burney has Ellis/Juliet meditate explicitly about female difficulties; she exclaims, for example, "how insufficient . . . is a FEMALE to herself! How utterly dependant upon situation—con-

nexions—circumstance! how nameless, how for ever fresh-spring-
ing are her DIFFICULTIES, when she would owe her existence to her
own exertions!" (p. 275). The problem of female genteel poverty—
bereaved gentlewomen and the female dependents of merchants—
shoots through the tracts on female education that proliferated in
the years following the French Revolution. A work like Mary Ann
Radcliffe's *The Female Advocate*, for example, which advocates for
poor women locked out of the professions of millinery and mantua-making by men she views as contemptibly feminine, presup-
poses a prior gentility for these women.[10] Women of means fallen
into poverty were a compelling figure for both conservative and
progressive writers desiring to show the deleterious effects of too
much or the wrong kind of education for women—or, in the case
of tradesmen's daughters, the effects of not deigning to teach a
daughter anything about the family business. Indeed, when I talk
about the leisured woman, I by definition refer to the middle-class
woman *tout court*, for in this period she too is defined by her leisure.

For these reasons the excellent criticism written on *The Wanderer* has been primarily feminist, focusing on the various double
binds that both constitute and trouble femininity.[11] Without any
claims to superseding or correcting that criticism, my brief reading
foregrounds the class allegory of the novel, reading it as a meditation
upon labor and gentility, and its choice of a female protagonist as a
strategy for heightening the stakes of imagining the gentle at work.
For Burney's novel is specifically about a gentlewoman, and as in all
her novels, there is a categorical difference between gentlewomen
and the leisured wives and daughters of tradesmen: in *The Wanderer*,
for example, the tradesman's daughter learning to play the harp may
as well be a barking seal, so little do her capacities resemble those of
the heroine. Moreover, as I argued in the previous chapter, in the
earlier industrial period the gentry and the working middle classes
struggled among themselves for moral legitimacy. In the last decades
of the eighteenth century, middle-class men and women argued for
their own greater competence in managing land and laborers, figuring the landed classes as self-indulgent and morally unqualified by
virtue of their leisure.[12] For the purposes of this study, then, I read
The Wanderer as a fantasy about the gentry, although certainly its hy-

perbolic effect is partly created by putting at its center a woman, whom the claims of gender make intensely vulnerable.

The novel's force is to enact, volume by volume, a rigorous and inexorable breaking down of the distinction between accomplishments and labor. In Volume I, the heroine takes precarious protection with the family of an arrogant and tyrannical gentlewoman named Mrs. Maple, and this volume, progressing as a series of accidental revelations of her accomplishments, worries the problem of accomplishments. Ellis/Juliet instinctively sits down to play the harp when the family goes out to dinner, but their hostess being seized with a sudden indisposition, they arrive home earlier and catch her playing. To the hero, the discerning Harleigh, "her language, her air, and her manner, pervading every disadvantage of apparel, poverty, and subjection, had announced her, from the first, to have received the education, and to have lived the life of a gentlewoman. . . . " (p. 75). And later, he is once more surprised by her gentility:

> Harleigh, who had not seen the stranger turned into the closet, now entered it, in search of a pencil. Not a little was then his surprize to find her sketching, upon the back of a letter, a view of the hills, downs, cottages, and cattle, which formed the prospect from the window.
>
> It was beautifully executed, and undoubtedly from nature. Harleigh, with mingled astonishment and admiration, clasped his hands, and energetically exclaimed, "Accomplished creature! who . . . and what are you?" (p. 88)

Aside from their prim class consciousness, what is a little craven about these and many other similar moments of astonishing gentility is the clumsiness of the machinations that allow Ellis/Juliet to display herself without intending to display herself.[13] That clumsiness suggests a tension inherent in accomplishment: by definition it entails display, but it also elicits a cultural antipathy to leisured accomplishments precisely for its element of display. Of course, the idea of gentility being unable to help revealing itself is a time-honored romance convention. But in this novel female gentility hides itself partly because it is under siege; to reveal it is to be at once sexually charismatic and sexually compromised.

After the heroine has repeatedly, and always unintentionally, revealed herself to be of gentle birth, the second volume of *The Wanderer* focuses upon the double binds inherent in trying to parlay accomplishments into work. Threatened to be expelled from Mrs. Maple's house, Ellis/Juliet longs to be financially self-supporting: "Her many accomplishments invited her industry, and promised it success; yet how to bring them into use was difficult" (p. 146). And later,

> How few, she cried, how circumscribed, are the attainments of women! and how much fewer and more circumscribed still, are those which may, in their consequences, be useful as well as ornamental, to the higher, or educated class! those through which, in the reverses of fortune, a FEMALE may reap benefit without abasement! (p. 289)

She tries to give music lessons to young ladies, but finds that the outlay for decent clothes and a rental harp is formidable, and that because they are characters in a Burney novel, the gentry refuse to pay what they owe.

Ellis/Juliet's attempt to straddle the realm of gentility and work produces two debates about labor and accomplishment. In the first, a gentleman named Mr. Giles Arbe—one of Burney's philanthropists *manqué*, a man who has spent a lot of money helping the poor but who suffers from absentmindedness so acute that its effects on Ellis/Juliet are vicious—argues with some society people who disdain genteel labor on the grounds that it does not constitute labor. A man named Mr. Scope calls Ellis/Juliet an "artist of luxury" and asks, "you do not hold it to be as essential to the morals of a state, to encourage luxuries, as to provide for necessaries?" Mr. Arbe retorts,

> Luxury? What is it you all of you mean by luxury? . . . because you, at idle hours, and from mere love of dissipation, lounge in your box at operas and concerts, to hear a tune, or to look at a jump, do you imagine he who sings, or who dances, must be a voluptuary? No! all he does is pain and toil to himself; learnt with labour, and exhibited with difficulty. The better he performs, the harder he has worked. (p. 325)

Burney's novel strains to imbue gentle accomplishment with the exertion of labor, to demarcate it as a realm from which one could receive, and deserve, wages.[14]

Meanwhile, though, there is another pull on Ellis/Juliet, a pull that comes from the threat that her music lessons will resemble labor too *much*, and will consequently threaten her status as a gentle-woman. Although it wounds her sensibility, she reluctantly agrees, in order to pay off her creditors, to perform with her students, young ladies of fashion, in a series of subscription concerts held in private homes. And here she is passionately besieged by Harleigh on behalf of her class status as a gentlewoman. He begs that "your accomplishments should be reserved for the resources of your leisure, and the happiness of your friends, at your own time, and your own choice . . . " (p. 338), and although he does not yet know her circumstances, he argues on behalf of her possible genteel family:

> If, then, there be any family that you quit, yet that you may yourself desire should one day reclaim you; and if there be any family—leave mine alone!—to which you may hereafter be allied, and that you may wish should appreciate, should revere you, as you merit to be revered and appreciated—for such let me plead! Wound not the customs of their ancestors, the received notions of the world, the hitherto acknowledged boundaries of elegant life! (p. 343)

The labor/leisure contradiction works particularly viciously for Ellis/Juliet, her accomplishments viewed at once as contemptible because leisure activities, and as dangerous to a vulnerable gentility because of their status as labor.

The third volume drives Ellis/Juliet incrementally into labor proper. An extended meditation on the experience of labor, it opens with Ellis/Juliet's providential encounter with her old friend Gabriella at the grave of her child, an encounter that brings up material about grief and labor with which we are familiar from the previous chapter. Gabriella's fall into labor is represented as simultaneous with the loss of a son:

> not alone bowed down by the general evils of revolutionary events . . . not only driven, without offence, or even accusation, from prosperity and honours, to exile, to want, to misery, and to labour; but suffering, at the same time, the heaviest of personal afflictions, in the immediate loss of a darling child. . . . (p. 390)

Labor takes place over the sign of this dead son, Gabriella ritualisti-
cally visiting his grave every morning before work. Together, she
and Ellis/Juliet try to earn a living by doing needlework, an effort
that evokes the familiar account of labor as similar to grief, "neither
seek[ing] nor mak[ing] observation"—as an oppressive riveting of
the attention in one place:

> Yet, it was with difficulty that they learnt to enjoy each other's soci-
> ety, upon such terms as their altered condition now exacted; where
> the eye must never be spared from laborious business, to search, or to
> reciprocate a sentiment. . . . The lively intelligence, the rapid concep-
> tion, the arch remark, the cordial smile; which gave grace to kindness,
> playfulness to counsel, gentleness to raillery, and softness even to re-
> proach; these, the expressive sources of delight, and of comprehen-
> sion, in social commerce, they were fain wholly to relinquish; from
> the hurry of unremitting diligence, and undivided attention to man-
> ual toil. (pp. 394–95)

Labor is deracinating, then, not only because it marks poverty, but
also because undivided attention to it shuts down the expressiveness
so integral to gentility.

Finally, after working in a milliner's shop and at mantua-making,
running a haberdasher's shop for a brief while before it fails, and en-
during an excruciating stretch as a humble companion, Ellis/Juliet
is chased down by the brutal Frenchman who claims to be her husband, and goes on the lam into the New Forest. This scene opens up
a new picture of degradation, and the novel's most despairing meditation on the laboring poor. It is hard to think of another eighteenth-century novel in which it is so frightening to be among the
poor; at every turn, potential rapists and murderers threaten the bodily safety and integrity of the gentlewoman. Passing by a field during
the hour of repast, she is harassed by laborers whose "mental lassitude . . . made them ready for any dissipation that might divert
their weariness" (p. 668); passing by two woodcutters in the New
Forest she is nearly raped (pp. 688–89). She takes refuge with a coarse
and brutal family whose mother puts suspicious food on the table
(pp. 678–79) and who terrify her by bringing a bag with a body inside into the house in the middle of the night (p. 682)—learning
only later that they are poachers rather than murderers. Later,

Ellis/Juliet lives briefly with a family of day laborers who live in a "beautifully picturesque cottage in the neighborhood." And though somehow still expecting a scene of pastoral pleasure to open up before her, she learns that while the day laborer is not subject to the same anxieties as those who work their own land, "he waked not to active hope; he looked not forward to sanguine expectation" (p. 698). Nor could "the wide spreading beauties of the landscape . . . charm . . . the labourer":

> Those who toil, heed them not. Their eyes are upon their plough; their attention is fixed upon the harvest; their sight follows the pruning hook. If the vivid field catches their view, it is but to present to them the image of the scythe, with which their labour must mow it. . . . (p. 701)

The laborer, in Burney, can see nothing but images of labor, and can find no rest, only a corrupting lassitude. Ellis/Juliet's sojourn with the laboring poor is a dystopia of constricted vision and consciousness.

This powerful antipastoral sequence concludes with an exclamation by the heroine:

> [W]ho can examine and meditate upon the uncertain existence of thy creatures,—see failure without fault; success without virtue; sickness without relief; oppression in the very face of liberty; labour without sustenance; and suffering without crime;—and not see, and not feel that all call aloud for resurrection and retribution! that annihilation and injustice would be one! and that Man, from the very nature of his precarious earthly being, must necessarily be destined, by the All Wise, and All Just, for regions that we see not; for purposes that we know not;—for Immortality! (pp. 701–2)

If in *Humphry Clinker* labor is necessarily bound up in mortal loss, Burney's last novel gestures toward the life to come as the only solution for the suffering it imposes. In doing so, *The Wanderer* intersects lightly with the millenarian fantasies of social equality in the afterlife that proliferated in the last five years of the eighteenth century, fantasies that found poetic form in the work of Burns and Blake, and that, in the words of E. P. Thompson, expressed "an indefinite social optimism of the credulous which was kin to the revolutionary aspirations of the more sophisticated."[15]

The belief in labor's capacity to invigorate the gentle expresses itself in other novels between *The Wanderer*'s composition and publication, expressing itself in different moods. It finds, for example, hyperbolic expression in the gothic villain, who is typically a younger son; the villainy of Radcliffe's Schedoni comes not only from his assault on primogeniture, but more importantly from his determination to remain leisured. At the same time, in Jane Austen the gentleman's need for a vocation becomes a commonplace; the tones here range from gentle irony in *Sense and Sensibility* over the passivity of Edward, who characterizes himself as "an idle, helpless being" and who suffers from a "want of spirits," to the offstage drama of Tom's illness and recovery into a useful heir in *Mansfield Park*, which makes Sir Thomas acknowledge "the advantages of early hardship and discipline, and the consciousness of being born to struggle and endure" that the Prices bring into the Bertram family.[16] The variety of intensity on this issue's emotional continuum suggests ideology in flux.[17] It is *The Wanderer*'s peculiar achievement that it has a powerful vision of the actual experience of labor, and that it represents the catastrophic nature of this issue to inhere not in leisure itself, but rather in the attempt to ameliorate the problems of leisure. For if Burney's novel insists that the gentle need to labor in order to be roused into virtuous activity, it also insists that labor is irredeemably damaging. By using a woman protagonist to double the stakes, and by portraying the hardship of labor as hopeless and brutalizing, Burney's novel makes the conflicting urges about labor and leisure in English culture of the 1790s catastrophically collide.

❦

I conclude with a striking scene late in *The Wanderer*—a scene unlike any other in Burney's novels—which brings together this dynamic of labor and the problem of satire. Ellis/Juliet has been revealed as Juliet Granville, and her brutal supposed husband catches up with her and threatens to capture her. Luckily, a peace officer arrives on the scene to arrest the false husband on charges of smuggling and other crimes. Faint with fear and misery, Juliet is aided by an old, feeble, whimsical gentleman named Sir Jaspar Herrington, who addresses her by her real name and offers to escort her to her newly discovered noble relatives. It is in his carriage that she finally reveals the story of the French-revolutionary-gothic machinations that have forced her into a marriage and secrecy about her identity. But then, to her dismay, she finds that in rescuing her, Sir Jaspar has not acted upon the authority of her family, as she assumed he did, but rather has acted out of a fit of infatuation. Tormented by yet an additional access of wounded propriety, Juliet is brought first to Wilton, the mansion of the Earl of Pembroke, whose magnificent art gallery elicits only a "morbid insensibility," "a nearly torpid state" from the frightened heroine (p. 760). Then, because, he says, "I have all my life . . . fostered, as the wish next my heart, the idea of being the object of some marvellous adventure" (p. 767), Sir Jaspar brings her to Stonehenge. In this extraordinary scene we see the fate of satire in a period in which the imperative to labor has become so overwhelming that it swamps leisure itself.

By thrusting Juliet into the protection of Sir Jaspar, Burney initiates one of those painful satiric interludes with which we are familiar from *Cecilia*.[18] Representing both privilege and impotence, Sir Jaspar is rather severely satirized for being old, his age linked to the luxury for which the upper classes are traditionally criticized:

> Not even the delight of thus victoriously carrying off a disputed prize, could immediately reconcile Sir Jaspar to the fear of even the smallest disorder in the economy of his medicines, anodynes, sweetmeats, and various whims; which, from long habits of self-indulgence, he now conceived to be necessaries, not luxuries. (p. 737)

Sir Jaspar's excellent adventure is like a scene in a sentimental novel in which the hero encounters a woman in distress—but it is the feminist version, told from the woman's point of view. Regarding him as crazy and a little dangerous, Juliet has to keep reminding herself "that . . . with all his gallantry, he was not only aged and sickly, but a gentleman in manners and sentiments, as much as in birth and rank of life" (p. 769).

Not only is Sir Jaspar a parody of a benevolist, but he is also a packed figure of satire.[19] For one, his actions, he says, are guided by imaginary sylphs and imps that evoke *The Rape of the Lock*. Moreover, his account of his youthful failure to find a wife "without a blot" harks back to the Juvenalian strain of Augustan poetry, and indeed, to Juvenal's Sixth Satire on women, which tried to persuade men stricken by love that they could extricate themselves from marriage if they relinquished their illusions about women.[20] Sir Jaspar explains:

> The wicked little imps who then guided and goaded me . . . urged me to pursue the glowing Beauty, whose vivid cheeks, crimsoned by the dance, had warmed all my senses at a ball, to her alighting from her carriage, at her return home, with the livid hue of fatigue and moonlight! They instigated me to surprize, when ill-dressed, negligent, and spiritless, the charming face and form that, skilfully adorned, had appeared to me Venus attired by the Graces. They twitched me on to dart upon another, whose bloom had seemed the opening of the rose-bud, just as an untoward accident had rubbed off, from one cheek, the sweet pink which remained undiminished upon the other! . . . They led me to overhear the softest of maidens insult a poor dependent; they shewed me a pattern of discretion, secretly involved in debt; and the frankest of human lasses, engaged in a clandestine affair! They whisked me, in short, into every crevice of female subtlety. (pp. 631–32)

Having played the severe and misogynist satirist, however, Sir Jaspar now regrets not finding a wife: "Alas, my fair love, my history is but that of half the old bachelors existing! . . . after having wasted our early life in conceiving that no one is good enough for us, we consume our latter days in envy of every married man!" (p. 632). One might claim that Sir Jaspar has not been well served by the little imps who act as the wicked agents of Augustan satire. Moreover, the placement of his satiric impulse into his distant past makes it seem antiquated. Indeed, I would argue that in this impotent and superannuated gentleman who is a figure for Augustan satire, Burney creates a figure for the outdatedness of satire itself.

    And it is this figure who brings Juliet to a sublime vision of human labor, the scene of Stonehenge. Juliet arrives at "a stupendous assemblage of enormous stones":

> though each of them, taken separately, might seem, from its astonishing height and breadth, there, like some rock, to have been placed from "the beginning of things;" and though not even the rudest sculp-

ture denoted any vestige of human art, still the whole was clearly no phenomenon of nature. The form, that might still be traced, of an antique structure, was evidently circular and artificial; and here and there, supported by gigantic posts, or pillars, immense slabs of flat stone were raised horizontally, that could only by manual art and labour have been elevated to such a height. Many were fallen; many, with grim menace, looked nodding; but many, still sustaining their upright direction, were so ponderous that they appeared to have resisted all the wars of the elements, in this high and bleak situation, for ages. (p. 765)

Symbolically speaking, it is a complex structure, not denoting art in any of its parts, yet as a whole evidently the product of "manual art and labour." Doody points out too that the circular nature of Stonehenge echoes in magnified form the seaside grave of Gabriella's son, which is "encircled by short sticks, intersected with rushes" (p. 385); she suggests that "the circle is a place of the Mother."[21] As such, Stonehenge might be read as a stupendous monument to the son whose separation from his mother marks, in Burney, labor's inauguration. Moreover, describing the stones as seeming to have been placed from "the beginning of things," Burney places Ellis/Juliet and Gabriella's labor into what Doody calls "the realm of deep time, of measureless antiquity."[22] Indeed, Burney takes labor and imagines it in relation to all conceivable time, stretching back over a vast past, and receiving its just recompense in the afterlife, an unending futurity. The work of this vision is to utterly universalize labor.

This complex scene of labor evokes a mental state unlike any other I have described in the book:

[T]he nearly savage, however wonderful work of antiquity, in which she was now rambling; placed in this abandoned spot, far from the intercourse, or even view of mankind, with no prospect but of heath and sky; blunted, for the moment, her sensibility, by removing her wide from all the objects with which it was in contact; and insensibly calmed her spirits; though not by dissipating her reverie. Here, on the contrary, was room for "meditation even to madness;" nothing distracted the sight, nothing broke in upon attention, nor varied the ideas. Thought, uninterrupted and uncontrouled, was master of the mind. (p. 766)

The portrayal of Juliet's interiority is in one sense familiar, in that she experiences the "blunted sensibility" characteristic of labor, and in that although it is a wide prospect, Burney describes its effects on her consciousness in terms of constriction: "nothing broke in upon attention, nor varied the ideas." Here though, as with so many of the scene's effects, this one is heightened; it is as though rather than blunting her consciousness, the scene of wildness and labor intensifies it. Also, interestingly, Burney does not portray Juliet's thought as having any particular content: it is rather the fact of rampant thought itself that brings her close to madness. The mind in a striking state while contemplating a wild and desolate natural scene on Salisbury Plain; it is not implausible to argue, as Doody does, that we have moved into the realm of Romanticism. It is the colossal monument to labor that creates an interiority so uncontrolled that it verges on madness. But interestingly, as raw and dystopian as this vision is, the state of semi-madness feels oddly comforting to Juliet, "insensibly calm[ing] her spirits." This is not the madness of Cecilia, a madness that expressed a certain panic about the inner life of the domestic woman. Rather, the half-mad interiority associated with the vision of labor's universality finds a certain equipoise, as though getting ready for or getting used to its own untrammeled state.

Sir Jaspar's comic approach breaks the grandeur of the scene and interrupts this uncontrolled expression of thought: "Here, in deep and melancholy rumination, she remained, till she was joined by the Baronet; who toiled after his fair charge with an eager will, though with slack and discourteous feet" (p. 766). While in *Cecilia* satire is allied with the figure of Hope, functioning as a respite from the rigors of the construction of the domestic woman, here it hobbles in as a weak and annoying anachronism. To be sure, Sir Jaspar successfully interrupts the domestic woman's thought, to the degree that this paragon of punctilio "tried, but vainly, to make a civil speech" (p. 766). But in a world in which the imperative to labor has become so powerful that even the accomplishments that define the gentle are contested and redefined by its rubric, satire has been rendered impotent, toiling in with slack and discourteous feet. Even the word "toiled" seems to add insult to injury, a mocking allusion to the processes of labor that satire tries, but fails, to block.

༈

Because *The Wanderer* appeared in 1814, just after the defeat of Napoleon, most critics figured Burney's novel itself as outdated. The conservative critic John Wilson Croker went so far as to counter her portrayal of superannuated satire by figuring Burney herself as an anachronism, marshaling satiric rhetoric of decaying women's bodies to do so: "The Wanderer has the identical features of Evelina—but of Evelina grown old; the vivacity, the bloom, the elegance, 'the purple light of love' are vanished; the eyes are there, but they are dim; the cheek, but it is furrowed; the lips, but they are withered."[23] Croker's vigorous use of this rhetoric suggests a commitment to the relevance of satire. And indeed, even as Burney was figuring satire as anachronistic, there was a notable outbreak of satire in writing of all kinds in the polemical decade of the 1790s.[24] That it happened in both progressive and conservative writing suggests that it was reacting to a social and economic process more overwhelming than could be comprehended by either side alone. If we regard it through the symbolic framework Burney offers us, the explosion of satire may be read as a last-ditch attempt to ward off the processes of the division and reorganization of labor.

By 1814 the literary establishment wanted to put the social world depicted by *The Wanderer* behind it. But Burney's huge and awkward failure of a novel provides a vivid and moving set of images for a culture on the threshold of industrialization—a vision of mother-love, mortal loss, magnificent and debilitating labor, impotent satire, and a staunch semi-madness.

Reference Matter

Notes

Introduction

1. Bond, ed., *The Spectator*, no. 130, II.15–16.
2. Ibid., II.16–17.
3. See McKeon, Rawson, and Watt, *The Rise*.
4. Nancy Armstrong, for example, suggests that "novels rewarding self-assertion on the part of those in an inferior position undoubtedly provided the middle-class readership with a fable for their own emergence" (p. 51). Only Davis attempts to interweave the presence of the lower classes with the rise of the novel, arguing that the early novel was partly definable by its fascination with criminality, which expressed the political aspirations of the poor. See *Factual Fictions*, esp. Chapter 7.
5. Robbins, p. 80. Robbins argues that there occurred a "symbolic *volte-face* [in] 1848, in which the bourgeoisie backed away from its identification with the servant figure as it achieved hegemony and began to fear the militant masses beneath it . . . " (p. 81).
6. From Robbins' beautiful book, which shows how in English novels servants make claims on behalf of lost forms of social organization, I take the disposition to read these four novels as engaged in negotiating lost pasts.
7. Bond, ed., *The Spectator*, no. 107, I.444.
8. For an account of a more skillful and sometimes subversive mimicry of ruling-class culture, see Landry (chapter 1) on the appropriation of neo-classical poetic forms in the poetry of eighteenth-century working-class women.
9. According to Castle, for example, at the eighteenth-century mas-

querade, which she describes as "a meditation on cultural classification," the gentry often masqueraded in the dress of the working orders, and " . . . the provocative travesties of rank and occupation intimated a potentially disarming fluidity in the realm of social circumstance, as critics of the masquerade throughout the century were obsessively to point out" (pp. 6, 63).

10. Stallybrass and White, p. 2.

11. Ibid., p. 6. While my book focuses on the gentry, *The Politics and Poetics of Transgression* is about bourgeois culture in the most general sense; for Stallybrass and White, all ruling-class subjectivity participates in this process. Our projects also differ in that Stallybrass and White take their examples of seventeenth- and eighteenth-century high culture from Restoration theater and Augustan satire. Satire is a congenial form to explore for their theory, because the expression of disgust in it is so extreme, and its taxonomic and hierarchical impulse so powerful, and they are interested in the extremes of high and low. "If," they write, "we can grasp the system of extremes which encode the body, the social order, psychic form and spatial location, we thereby lay bare a major framework of discourse within which any further 'redress of balance' or judicious qualification must take place" (p. 3). It is perhaps for this reason that they go from Jonson to the Restoration stage, to Swift, Pope, and then Wordsworth, leaving out the novel. The novel is, I would suggest, uncongenial for the purposes of their argument because high and low are not so starkly delineated in the novel. And indeed, my own project is an exercise in what they would call "judicious qualification," distinguishing both between monied and landed people and landed and unlanded gentlemen, and dealing with modes of incorporation that do not have to do so much with filth as with various kinds of social alienation.

12. Kraft, pp. 13, 28. See also Campbell, which I discuss in detail in Chapter 1.

13. Mullan, *Sentiment and Sociability*, pp. 15–16. For Claudia L. Johnson the cult of sensibility, particularly in the literature of the 1790s, came at the expense of women, whose feelings were represented as the extreme and pathological outer limit of more legitimate feeling in men.

14. Mullan, *Sentiment and Sociability*, p. 213.

15. I mean by *affect* the expression of emotions, and sometimes use it interchangeably with *emotion* and *feeling*. By the terms *consciousness* and *subjectivity* I mean the self as it is constructed by the social: the self-in-culture.

16. Thompson, "Eighteenth-Century English Society," p. 151.

17. During one congressional debate, for example, Representatives Barbara Cubin (R-Wyo.) and John L. Mica (R-Fla.), referred to women on welfare as "wolves" and "alligators." See Pollitt, p. 58. Pollitt also points to conservative nostalgia for Victorian methods of poor-relief (p. 60).

18. Fielding, *An Enquiry into the Causes*, p. 108.
19. Dorothy Marshall, pp. 1–2.
20. Slack, pp. 32, 30.
21. Ibid., pp. 30, 28.
22. The best critique of Himmelfarb I have read is by Schwarzbach, who argues that her book "rigorously depoliticiz[es] the problem of poverty," and is at the same time undertheorized: although she has "quite clear ideological and methodological positions, . . . they remain implicit" (pp. 102–3). And while Himmelfarb routinely makes gestures eschewing the "Whig position" of history, Schwarzbach rightly calls her actual position "a modified version of the Whig interpretation—things were getting better (although not quickly or for all social and occupational groups), even if contemporaries can be excused for failing to appreciate this" (p. 103).

The conservative and undertheorized nature of Himmelfarb's argument leads her into what is for a critic with any Marxist training an almost comic pattern. Most strikingly in the early chapters, and in the chapter on Adam Smith, she discovers seemingly insoluble contradictions. How can one reconcile, she asks, Smith's "dismal portrait of the industrial worker reduced to a state of torpor, stupidity, and ignorance, lacking in judgment, initiative, courage, or any 'intellectual, social, and martial virtues'—all this because of the division of labor—with the earlier image of the 'hearty,' 'cheerful' worker who, as a result of the same division of labor, received a 'plentiful subsistence,' enjoyed 'bodily strength,' was 'active, diligent, and expeditious' . . . " (p. 57)? How could Burke believe, in the *Reflections on the Revolution in France*, in a natural, hierarchical, traditional God-given social order, while in "Thoughts and Details on Scarcity" he argued strenuously against the phrase "labouring poor" and spoke of " 'labour' as a 'commodity' or 'article of trade' whose price was determined not by the 'necessity of the vender' (otherwise known as 'subsistence') but by the 'necessity of the purchaser' . . . " (p. 71)? Because, as Schwarzbach points out, her intellectual history is so dissociated from its historical context—because her model for explanation is primarily biographical and because she will not use any (say, Marxist) theory that would enable her to deal with the category of contradiction—Himmelfarb can only come down weakly on one side. About Smith, for example, she comes down on the side of the "optimistic" image of the worker, because it "informs by far the largest part of the book and . . . bears the largest weight of the argument" . . . (p. 57)—as though the louder the optimism the truer it is.

23. See, for example, Slack. The most influential study of the impact of population growth is Wrigley and Schofield.
24. As Berg argues of the proto-industrial period, " . . . [T]here is an urgent need for enquiry into the social realities behind 'increases in produc-

tivity.' It is beyond doubt that the technical, organizational and structural changes behind increases in labour productivity involved the dislocation of labour and communities" (p. 318).

25. Christopher Hill, pp. 266–68.

26. See Williams, p. 66; and for a more contemporary and properly historical account of the effects of enclosure upon the laboring poor, Snell.

27. Dorothy Marshall, p. 5.

28. Thompson, "Eighteenth-Century English Society," p. 158.

29. Malcomson, *Life and Labour*, pp. 45–46.

30. Ibid., p. 126. See also Halpern, p. 75; and Rule, who argues that skilled workers viewed completion of apprenticeship as conferring upon them a property right in the exclusive exercise of their trades (p. 106). For me the most telling symptom of the way Himmelfarb's untheorized conservatism hurts her argument is her unexamined use of the concept of "freedom." She ventriloquizes Smith on freedom, for example, without the least exploration of what that term might mean: "All that was necessary was to free people—all people, in all ranks and callings—so that they could act on their interests. From these individually motivated, freely inspired actions, the general interest would emerge without any intervention, regulation, or coercion" (p. 53).

31. Thompson, "Patrician Society," pp. 383–87.

32. McKendrick, p. 11.

33. Sekora has a useful summary of this body of writing (pp. 63–66).

34. Robbins, pp. 111, 151–52.

35. See Slack, pp. 22–32; and Sedgwick, *Epistemology*, pp. 40–48. As I was revising this Introduction, Michael Massing published his article "Ghetto Blasting," which argued that contemporary journalistic writing on the inner city has tended to champion inner-city children while pathologizing their parents. Here the universalizing and minoritizing instincts get split generationally, the children regarded as innocent victims of social circumstance, while the adults are regarded as *causing* their poverty through their behavior.

36. Mayhew, vol. 1, p. 2.

37. McKeon, pp. 161–62.

38. Barrell, *English Literature in History*, p. 33.

39. Ibid., pp. 39–40.

40. McKeon, p. 218.

41. Stone and Fawtier Stone, pp. 5–6, 229.

42. Ibid., p. 229.

43. Defoe, p. 18. All further quotations are from this edition and cited in the body of the text.

44. Much of the force of Defoe's tract comes from a voice that is positively Swiftean in its savage deadpan volatility. In the library edition I have used, a previous reader commented anxiously in the margin of a passage in which Defoe compares the ordering of social status to the order of the lights God has placed in the firmament: "he probably means to refute this." To add to the vertiginousness of tone, McKeon notes that "Defoe was obsessed with the illusion of his own gentility, and at various stages in his career he proudly rode the livery of his merchant's company, outrageously inflated his ancestry, and . . . employed the medium of print to become armigerous and to aristocratize his name from Foe to De Foe" (p. 326).

45. See Stone and Fawtier Stone on younger sons in trades (pp. 233–39), as well as *The Spectator*, no. 108, in which the Spectator pities Will Wimble, the younger brother of a baronet, for wasting away his life in idle pursuits when he is "perfectly well turned for the Occupations of Trade and Commerce" (I.449).

46. Other than writing, the main occupations providing an outlet for younger sons were the Church, the armed services, and the law (Stone and Fawtier Stone, pp. 228–33).

47. Andrew, pp. 136–45. Andrew dates this writing from the mid-1770s to the early 1790s, and calls it a new psychology of labor.

48. Burke, "Third Letter," p. 355. See also his "Thoughts and Details on Scarcity" (1795), p. 121.

49. Barrell, *English Literature in History*, p. 38.

50. Burney, *Cecilia*, p. 431. See Mayhew: "It has been said that there is a close resemblance between many of the characteristics of a very high class, socially, and a very low class. Those who remember the disclosures on a trial a few years back, as to how men of rank and wealth passed their leisure in card-playing—many of their lives being one continued leisure—can judge how far the analogy holds . . . " (vol. 1, p. 12).

51. Isaac Barrow's sermon on the text "Rejoice evermore" (1 Thess. 5:16), quoted in Tave, p. 4.

52. Seidel, *Satiric Inheritance*, pp. 6–8. Paulson writes of *satura lanx* that it suggests "a form at least roughly dramatic into which almost anything can be poured, a form with a sociolegalistic content and even (it is impossible not to conclude) a preoccupation with food as symbol." *Satire and the Novel*, p. 21.

53. Tave, p. 23.

54. Paulson, *Satire and the Novel*, p. 61.

55. Tave, p. viii.

56. Paulson, *Satire and the Novel*, p. 16. See also Carnochan's interesting article on the eighteenth century's abiding preference for Juvenal over Ho-

race, and the way contemporaries had to read him as a sentimentalist in order to do so.

57. Paulson, *Satire and the Novel*, p. 62.

58. Bond, ed., *The Spectator*, no. 2, I.8.

59. Ibid., no. 544, IV.445–46.

60. Tave, pp. 104, 264.

61. Ibid., p. 104.

62. Bond, ed., *The Spectator*, no. 517, IV.339–40.

63. In a footnote to the episode of the prostitute, which he argues was written by Steele, Bond writes, "Budgell has recorded (*The Bee*, No. 1, Feb. 1733) that Addison 'was so heartily vexed when he read this Paper, that he immediately called a Coach, went to his Friend Sir *Richard*, and never left him, till he had made him promise that he would meddle no more with Sir *Roger*'s Character' " (ibid., III. p. 531). Here too the tension in Sir Roger's character is externalized as the tension between two separate men.

64. Tave, pp. 97–98. Tave is quoting from Hazlitt's *Comic Writers*.

65. Malcomson, *Popular Recreations*, p. 68. Quoted in Stallybrass and White, p. 86.

66. Stallybrass and White, p. 86.

67. Tave, pp. 57–58.

68. Fielding, *Joseph Andrews*, p. 9.

69. Stallybrass and White describe Augustan satire, for example, as "the generic form which enabled writers to express and negate the grotesque simultaneously. It was the natural site for this labour of projection and repulsion upon which the construction of the public sphere depended" (p. 106).

70. Seidel, *Satiric Inheritance*, pp. 21, 18.

71. Ibid., p. 3.

72. Ibid., p. 21.

73. Freud, "Mourning and Melancholia," pp. 166, 170. I elaborate upon the idea of melancholia in Chapter 3.

74. Jameson, p. 79.

Chapter 1

1. See Altick; Cressy; Hunter; Neuburg, chapters 1, 4; Spufford; and Watt, *The Rise*.

2. Fielding, *Joseph Andrews*, p. 9. All further references to the Preface and *Joseph Andrews* are cited parenthetically in the text (*JA*).

3. See Battestin; Paulson, *Satire and the Novel*; Reed; Watt, *The Rise*.

4. Stallybrass and White, pp. 5–6.

5. Paulson, *Popular and Polite Art*, pp. 15–16.

6. Ibid., p. 13.

7. See Spufford. Comparing the definitions of the burlesque in the 1694 and 1776 editions of the *Dictionnaire de l'Académie Françoise*, Dane suggests that it became increasingly regarded as a literary form during the course of the eighteenth century (pp. 123–24).

8. Loftis et al., pp. 250–51.

9. Rivero, p. 4. In his readings of various prefaces and prologues of Fielding's plays, Rivero makes similar attempts at generic distinction as Fielding does in the Preface, distinguishing between "comedy" and "entertainment" in the preface to *Love in Several Masques* (p. 7) and between "comedy" and "farce" in the prologue to *The Lottery. A Farce* (1732) (p. 39).

10. Rivero, p. 21. For another excellent study of Fielding's plays, by a theater historian who contextualizes them within the theatrical, economic, and political conditions of the London theater, see Hume.

11. Stallybrass and White, pp. 83, 112.

12. Loftis, pp. 14–15; Loftis et al., pp. 19–21, 24.

13. Fielding, *Tom Jones*, p. 640.

14. Stallybrass and White, pp. 93, 87.

15. Malcomson, *Popular Recreations*, p. 16. While Malcomson dates the beginning of this oppression at around 1750, there is plenty of evidence, especially in the history of the theater, to suggest that it began earlier. Bakhtin also discusses the encroachment of the state upon "festive life" in seventeenth- and eighteenth-century Europe (p. 33).

16. Liesenfeld, p. 24.

17. Ibid., pp. 27–28, 24–26.

18. Ibid., p. 73, chapter 3.

19. Robbins discusses the "discrepancy between the class-bound harshness of actual proposals and the stylizations of fiction" in Defoe and Fielding, suggesting that it "would seem less dependent on genre than on the local, transgeneric workings of comic rhetoric" (p. 13).

20. Fielding, *An Enquiry into the Causes*, p. 77. All further references are cited parenthetically in the text (*Enquiry*).

21. Paulson has noted the link between this social affectation in the *Enquiry* and affectation as the source of the ridiculous in the Preface (*Popular and Polite Art*, pp. 3–4).

22. Fielding, "An Essay on the Knowledge of the Characters of Men," p. 155.

23. Castle, p. 63.

24. See McKeon, pp. 162–67. McKeon writes of Fielding's ambivalent relation to the possibilities afforded by English commercialism, "Attracted . . . to the energy of the career open to talents, Fielding was appalled

by the vanity and pretension of those who enacted that career with any success or conviction" (p. 408).

25. The classification and discipline of persons in the eighteenth century is, of course, documented in Foucault. See the section entitled "Proposals for Erecting a County Work-house, etc.," in Fielding's "A Proposal
for Making an Effectual Provision for the Poor," in Fielding, *An Enquiry*,
pp. 237–55. This section is a veritable cornucopia of Foucaultian disciplinary techniques.

26. Altick, pp. 51–52; Hunter, p. 266. *Joseph Andrews* would have been
expensive for a servant, the first edition selling for 6s (Battestin, p. xxix).

27. Fielding, "An Essay," p. 162.

28. Stallybrass and White, pp. 5–6.

29. Campbell argues that this passage "draws a limit to the legitimacy of
satire's practice of exposure" (p. 660).

30. Pope justifies satire of the poor along similar but more punitive
grounds: " . . . [P]overty itself becomes a just subject of satyre, when it is
the consequence of vice, prodigality, or neglect of one's lawful calling. . . .
For men are not bunglers because they are poor, but they are poor because
they are bunglers" (p. 15).

31. Freud, *Jokes and Their Relation to the Unconscious*, p. 103.

32. Amory; Rothstein, "Framework," p. 381; and Watt, "*Shamela*." These
readings point toward specific historical referents for the characters, and
concern the political conflict between Walpole and the Opposition. One
problem with this kind of reading is that the figure of Walpole acquires a
truly dreamlike overdetermined status—that is, *all* the characters turn out
to be Walpole.

33. McKeon, p. 396. See also Eagleton. Richardson's biographers comment irately that Fielding, "as an educated man, disapproved of Richardson's detailed realism and of his 'lowness' and thus can be regarded as a reactionary classicist who failed to see the freshness of *Pamela*." Eaves and
Kimpel, pp. 128–29.

34. Robbins, p. 6. Robbins argues that servants occupy a "sliding, inde-
terminate ideological position . . . a position which is both popular and
political to the extent that it articulates a variety of ideological aspirations
and disturbances that 'represent' the people without being exclusive to or
defining them" (54). See also Richetti.

35. Hecht, pp. 121, 206–24.

36. Fielding, *The Grub-Street Opera*, pp. 70–73. The promise of feasting
on the pig recalls the swineherd Eumaios' offer to the disguised Odysseus of
a fattened pig, which is generally meant for the aristocratic suitors, rather
than a young pig, which is food for the servants. Robbins writes of the
scene in the *Odyssey*: "Eumaios' hospitable gesture has an apocalyptic ex-

cess. In its generosity it delivers the right to enjoy the fruits of the land to everyone, Odysseus and servingmen alike" (p. 29).

37. Fielding, *The Grub-Street Opera*, pp. 67, 59.

38. Amory, p. 244. They seem, however, to be missing something important about the text's affect: it is hard to ignore that Fielding's Lord of Misrule scenario is often rather genial about the incipient class-consciousness of the servants, and contains elements one might call, after Robbins, utopian.

39. McKeon, pp. 373, 371; Richardson, p. 20.

40. Fielding, *Joseph Andrews and Shamela*, p. 308. All further references are cited parenthetically in the text (*S*).

41. Richardson, p. 83.

42. Ong, p. 209.

43. Some verbal echoes: While in *Shamela* Fielding writes that "the thought is everywhere exactly clothed by the expression; and becomes its dress as *roundly* and as close as Pamela her country habit" (*S*, p. 304), Fanny is dressed "close": "so plump, that she seemed bursting through her tight Stays, especially in the Part which confined her swelling Breasts" (*JA*, p. 152). Fanny's "swelling Breasts" likewise recall Booby's confused exclamation to Shamela—"I know not whether you are a man or a woman, unless by your swelling breasts" (*S*, pp. 313–14)—which we can in turn refer back to Joseph's dismayed insistence to Lady Booby that he does not "know whether any Maid in the House is Man or Woman" (*JA*, p. 334), and Adams' vow when he is caught accidentally in bed with Fanny: "As I am a Christian, I know not whether she is a Man or Woman" (*JA*, p. 334).

44. Richardson, p. 10.

45. Bourdieu characterizes this kind of reading as a "popular aesthetic": "Popular taste . . . performs a systematic reduction of the things of art to the things of life. . . . Intellectuals could be said to believe in the representation . . . more than in the things represented, whereas the people chiefly expect representations and the conventions which govern them to allow them to believe 'naively' in the things represented" (p. 5).

46. One is reminded of Derrida's account of the ideology of "natural writing": "There is therefore a good and a bad writing: the good and natural is the divine inscription in the heart and soul; the perverse and artful is technique, exiled in the exteriority of the body" (p. 17). Joseph's song in the reunion scene is also crucially about images: about the "dear Image" of Chloe in his breast, which he alternately defends (" . . . no Tyrant's hard Power, / Her Image can tear from my Breast"), bemoans ("How can it thy dear Image be, / Which fills thus my Bosom with Woe?"), and repudiates as "Counterfeit" because it brings him grief rather than joy.

47. Campbell, p. 651.

48. Ovid, vol. 2, p. 83.

49. Ibid., vol. 1, p. 153.   50. Ibid.

51. Ong, p. 251.   52. McKeon, p. 408.

53. Campbell, p. 653.

54. In this otherwise extremely persuasive account of Fielding's critique of conventional masculinity and his valorization of the feminine, it is telling that Campbell's argument deals very little with Fanny. For in feminist terms, Fanny looks something like a severe backlash against that very valorization. More often than not referred to as "poor Fanny," she exists in the novel to be buffetted about by male violence, a target of repeated rape attempts; and these scenes conceal their own pleasure as badly as do the scenes in which Mr. B attempts to rape Pamela.

55. Spufford, chapter 5. My thanks to Douglas Patey for suggesting that I read Fielding's pedlar in the light of Spufford's account.

Chapter 2

1. Sterne, *The Life and Opinions of Tristram Shandy*, vol. 1, pp. 82–83. All further page numbers are from vol. 1 of this edition and will be cited parenthetically (*TS*) in the text.

2. Sterne, *A Sentimental Journey*, pp. 217–18. All further page numbers are from this edition and will be cited parenthetically in the text. In this, and in all subsequent chapters where I extensively cite a single novel, citations appear simply with a page number and without identifying abbreviation.

3. Stout, "Introduction" to Sterne, *A Sentimental Journey*, pp. 33–34.

4. Felsenstein, "Introduction" to Smollett, *Travels Through France and Italy*, p. lxi.

5. Poovey, "Ideology," p. 98.

6. Eagleton writes, "Pity, pathos and the pacific, 'womanly' qualities suppressed by a warring nobility, became the hallmarks of a bourgeoisie whose economic goals seem best guaranteed by political tranquility" (p. 15). Claudia L. Johnson argues that in the 1790s, this dynamic was reversed— that rather than entailing the feminization of culture, "sentimentality entailed instead the 'masculinization' of formerly feminine gender traits, and . . . the affective practices associated with it are valued *not* because they are understood as feminine, but precisely and only insofar as they have been recoded as masculine" (p. 14).

7. Markeley, pp. 217–18.

8. Van Sant, pp. 19, 26–27. In her book, Van Sant rehearses many of the arguments I made in the article version of this chapter (*ELH* 55, 1989), particularly my emphasis on vision as a technique of sentiment and my claim that the aim of sentimental vision is to reveal character.

9. Orr, pp. 1–3.

10. Ibid., p. 4.

11. Van Sant's argument that the poor are exposed to vision in order to have their characters revealed seems to me to stall there. For her, the point of philanthropic institutions displaying the poor is to "create pity and to demonstrate that their social experiments worked" (p. 31). The idea of a social experiment being created in order to prove that the social experiment works is tautological at best. Moreover, while Van Sant regards pity as a *product* of the investigative gaze, my claim is that "pity" is the affect—one might even say the ruse—of that gaze; and the gaze's product is information about the character of the poor that is crucial to the self-definition of those gazing.

12. Todd, for example, writes that in *A Sentimental Journey* "the body is a constant communicator," and "physical sensations reveal one person to another more sincerely than words" (pp. 99–100). On the relation between sensibility and contemporary medical theory see Rousseau, and Mullan, "Hypochondria and Hysteria."

13. See Cash, *Sterne's Comedy*, pp. 25–29; and idem, *Laurence Sterne*, p. 234. In the former book, Cash defends Sterne's sermons from charges of both plagiarism and insincerity, and argues that although "his personal life was sometimes irregular," Sterne was a moral person and a hard-working parson.

14. See *bubble*, *O.E.D.*: "anything fragile, unsubstantial, empty, or worthless; a deceptive show. From 17th c. onwards often applied to delusive commercial or financial schemes. . . . "

15. See Cash, "The Sermon in *Tristram Shandy*," which argues that the sermon reveals "that Sterne had assimilated the most liberal, enlightened tradition of Christian philosophy" (p. 416), as well as being powerfully influenced by Locke. Reading this sermon alongside the others, Cash discusses the concept of "right reason" in Sterne, distinguishing between "the unchangeable obligations of justice and truth" and God's commandments. I do not distinguish between the two kinds of law; for my purposes it is enough to place them together as an intermediary law between the judgment of the heart and the laws of Britain.

16. I have used the word *supplement* in describing the proliferation of laws in Sterne's sermon in order to evoke Derrida's argument about the "dangerous supplement" in Rousseau. The concept of the structure of supplementarity is useful in the case of Sterne's sermon because it allows one to argue that according to its logic, the multiplication of laws meant to supplement the conscience indicates that the conscience itself—a crucial concept in sentimental ideology—is not only flawed (an idea the sermon ex-

plicitly admits) but also derived. It is a product of the laws that continually evoke it rather than an innate, originary, spontaneously emerging faculty. Derrida, pp. 144–57.

17. Like Culture, Nature's supplement in Rousseau, God's law and human laws have the form of the sign, and are regarded by the text as "both humanity's good fortune and the origin of its perversion" (Derrida, p. 147). The written law "perverts" humanity by allowing the conscience to hide behind the letter. But it is required in order to "produce the sense of" the conscience, or self-knowledge, "the mirage of the thing itself."

18. Cash argues that in Sterne "if a man of quiet conscience is really only 'a bubble to himself,' he simply has not *tried* to know the truth of his own moral conduct" ("The Sermon in *Tristram Shandy*," p. 400). I am arguing that self-knowledge is not merely a matter of moral will.

19. Hay, "Property, Authority and the Criminal Law," pp. 18–19.

20. It is no accident that Hume's *Enquiry Concerning the Principles of Morals*, a work that undertakes to justify the utility of morality and to demonstrate that moral sentiments do not arise merely from self-love, is also a lengthy defense of private property. See pp. 192–205, 219.

21. This particular coupling of terms, "my property and my life," may be elucidated by reference to Locke's writings on property in his *Second Treatise*. Locke, the period's major theorist on the relation between property and government, argued that in a state of nature it is lawful to kill a man for robbery, because robbery implies enslavement and possible murder: " . . . [I]t [is] lawful for a man to *kill a thief*, who has not in the least hurt him, nor declared any design upon his life, any farther than, by the use of force, so to get him in his power, as to take away his money, or what he pleases, from him; because using force, where he has no right, to get me into his power, let his pretence be what it will, I have no reason to suppose, that he, who would *take away my liberty*, would not, when he had me in his power, take away every thing else. And therefore it is lawful for me to treat him as one who has *put himself into a state of war* with me, *i.e.* kill him if I can . . . "(pp. 14–15).

22. Hay writes, "the justice of English law was . . . a powerful ideological weapon in the arsenal of conservatives during the French Revolution. Wicked Lord Ferrers, juries and *habeas corpus* were leading themes in anti-Jacobin popular literature. They were usually contrasted with tyrannical French aristocrats, the inquisitorial system of law and *lettres de cachet*" ("Property, Authority and the Criminal Law," p. 37).

23. Cross, p. 86.

24. Cash claims that Sterne's "scattered attacks on Methodism, Romanism, and enthusiasm in general . . . are intended as rebukes of blind unrea-

soned faith, which to Sterne is always pernicious" ("The Sermon in *Tristram Shandy*," p. 408). In this sermon, however, the attack on Catholicism has to do with its extreme legalism—with the way it *departs* from pure faith.

25. See Foucault, to whom this discussion is clearly indebted. According to Foucault, the eighteenth century was characterized by new and widely disseminated techniques that exercised upon the body "a subtle coercion . . . at the level of the mechanism itself—movements, gestures, attitudes, rapidity: an infinitesimal power over the active body" (pp. 136–37). The disciplines function by rendering the body constantly visible; Foucault takes Jeremy Bentham's panopticon as his model for societal mechanisms of surveillance.

26. Smith, *The Theory of Moral Sentiments*, pp. 47–48.

27. David Marshall, p. 170. Marshall's book explores the ways in which theater "represents, creates, and responds to uncertainties about how to constitute, maintain, and represent a stable and authentic self; fears about exposing one's character before the world; and epistemological dilemmas about knowing or being known by other people" (p. 1).

28. David Marshall argues that *The Theory of Moral Sentiments* is obsessed with the gaze. "According to Smith's system," he writes, "we govern our actions and judgments—indeed, we know ourselves—by internalizing the regard of a spectator" (p. 175).

29. Contrasting service to the new, more diffused disciplines of the seventeenth and eighteenth centuries, Foucault describes it as "a constant, total, massive, non-analytical, unlimited relation of domination, established in the form of the individual will of the master, his 'caprice' " (p. 135). I am arguing that in *A Sentimental Journey* service is not as "massive" or "unlimited" a domination as Foucault would have it.

30. Rothblatt, p. 71. Hecht documents the new social mobility of servants, and the efforts to legislate servants' behavior and movement from place to place, through such measures as tracts indoctrinating them with proper principles, and parliamentary bills dealing with the problem of false "characters." The servant class, according to Hecht, was a vital link in the "chain of emulation [that] ran from the apex to the base of the social pyramid" (p. 204).

31. Sedgwick, *Between Men*, p. 70.

32. Ibid., p. 68.

33. In "Narrative Crossings," Seidel reads Yorick's efforts to obtain a passport as an attempt to gain the authority to narrate, or, in his words, "mimetic authorization beyond 'actual' borders." In his notes Seidel quotes Henry James' *Portraits of Places* on crossing into France: "the 'administration' is the first thing that touches you; in a little while you get used to it, but you

feel somehow that, in the process, you have lost the flower of your self-respect" (p. 21). As in Sterne, France is the place where the machinery of government suddenly feels palpable.

34. Shakespeare, *Much Ado About Nothing*, I.iii., ll. 30–35.

35. Citing the mechanical duck invented in 1738 by Jacques de Vaucanson as an exemplary instance, Hugh Kenner claims that that "characterizing achievement" of the eighteenth century was "the concept of counterfeitable man." Vaucanson's duck aroused and exemplified the "novel uncertainties [of people in the eighteenth and nineteenth centuries] about where, if indeed it existed, the boundary between man and simulacrum lay" (pp. 29, 39–40).

36. I am indebted to Seltzer's suggestive discussion of "the relation between . . . disciplinary techniques and the techniques of the novel." Seltzer is primarily concerned with the American realist and naturalist novel.

37. For an account of the relation between lyric poetry and corporeal discipline (spanking), see Sedgwick, "A Poem is Being Written."

38. Seidel, "Narrative Crossings," p. 8.

39. The periodic evocation of his friend "Eugenius" ("wellborn") is a similar act of social affirmation for Yorick.

40. Barrell has argued that the proliferation of professions that resulted from the mercantile and imperial expansion of the eighteenth century generated an epistemological and political problem among poets and gentlemen: how to negotiate for themselves a position from which a random and chaotic collection of individuals and pursuits could seem a coherent society. This became the ideological function of the landed gentleman, who, with an impartiality deriving from his lack of occupation, could best "*describe* those social connections that only he is privileged to *observe*." *English Literature in History*, p. 178.

41. Sterne's own financial position was not bad. By 1759 he had accumulated enough land, through enclosure and the influence of friends, to have reached the status of a small country squire. See Cross, pp. 112–13.

42. Sedgwick, *Between Men*, p. 67.

43. Freud, "Instincts and Their Vicissitudes," p. 91.

44. Sedgwick writes, "The manipulative potential of Yorick's position, even when he exerts and profits by it, is presented to the reader as well as to the other characters as a form of vulnerability and helplessness" (*Between Men*, p. 69). She is arguing that Yorick effaces his manipulations by presenting them as a form of weakness. I want to argue that it is precisely the willed assuming of a position of "vulnerability and helplessness" that allows Yorick to avoid such a position.

45. McKendrick, p. 11.

46. Fielding, *An Enquiry into the Causes*, quoted in McKendrick, p. 24. See McKendrick, pp. 14–29.

47. See, for example, Stout, "Introduction" to Sterne, *A Sentimental Journey*; Cash, *Sterne's Comedy*; Chadwick; Davidson and Davidson; New; Smitten, "Spatial Form as Narrative Technique" and "Gesture and Expression"; and Van Sant.

Chapter 3

1. Smollett, *The Expedition of Humphry Clinker*, p. 286. All further references are to this edition and will be cited parenthetically in the body of the text.

2. Williams, p. 82. Williams is discussing Langhorne's *The Country Justice* (1774–77).

3. Sekora registers the affective flatness of the weddings when he writes that "the triple wedding ceremony does not here have the overtone of universal reconciliation that it has in Shakespeare," and that "much more pale and passive in their virtue than their tutors," the young people "have rarely earned a positive claim upon our attention" (p. 286).

4. See, for example, Copeland; Duncan; and Preston, "Introduction" to Smollett's novel.

5. Hammond and Hammond, p. 17.

6. Chambers and Mingay, p. 77.

7. This is not to say that enclosure is *never* rich figuratively; I am making a claim about this novel alone. Barrell gives what is to my mind an exemplary reading of the late-eighteenth-century agricultural publication *General Views*, in which he demonstrates the effect of current theories of the sublime and the picturesque upon the way these agricultural writers figure the land and its enclosures. See *The Idea of Landscape*, chapter 2.

8. Jameson, p. 79.

9. Hammond and Hammond, p. 73.

10. Snell, p. 139. Snell is summarizing, among other historical studies, Chambers; Chambers and Mingay; and Yelling. Snell argues that most of this work has focused upon the small landowner, primarily because despite considerable methodological problems, land tax assessments have been considered the most valued historical source. He bases his findings upon settlement examinations and literary sources (pp. 140–49).

11. Snell, pp. 168–69.

12. Williams, p. 102.

13. David Davies, *The Case of the Labourers in Husbandry* (Bath: Printed by R. Cruttwell for G. G. and J. Robinson, London, 1795), quoted in Snell,

p. 169. The city version of this transition occurred at approximately the same time, in the gradual abolition of vails—the vestigial remnant of an ancient form of largesse—for servants, and their subsequent dependence upon wages alone. Smollett's servants are always vying for vails: Winifred Jenkins calls Wales *Vails*, confusing the name of her perquisite with the name of her home. On the abolition of vails and the quite heated resistance to it, see Hecht, pp. 158–68. The most influential account of the effects of the extinction of non-monetary perquisites in the period is Thompson, "Patrician Society."

    14. Mingay, pp. 275–76.

    15. Snell, p. 170.

    16. Arbuthnot, pp. 81, 128.

    17. Howlett, pp. 84–85. Howlett is responding to a pamphlet entitled *A Political Enquiry into the Consequences of enclosing Waste Lands, and the Causes of the present High Price of Butcher's Meat, being the Sentiments of Farmers in —— shire.*

    18. Hay, "Poaching and the Game Laws," pp. 203, 245.

    19. Some typical entries in the table of parishes: "To my knowledge, before the enclosure, the poor inhabitants found no difficulty in procuring milk for their children; since, it is with the utmost difficulty they can procure any milk at all. Cows lessened from 110 to 40." "The poor seem the greatest sufferers; they can no longer keep a cow, which before many of them did, and they are therefore now maintained by the parish." "Milk to be had at 1d. per quart before; not to be had now at any rate." "All their cows gone, and much wretchedness." [Young], *General Report*, pp. 150–52.

    20. Young, *An Inquiry into the Propriety*, pp. 42–43.

    21. Zomchick has argued that in the novel's central ideological contradiction, "although Bramble delights in modernization and improvement, he refuses to accept that innovation is often incompatible with social stability and continuity" (p. 178). Zomchick's article deals primarily with the novel's representation of trade, and the concomitant breakdown of class hierarchy, but as he recognizes, the same tension holds true for its representation of agriculture.

    22. Sekora also notes that " . . . [I]n contrast to Paradise Hall or even Grandison Hall, Brambleton Hall is evanescent and abstract" (p. 286).

    23. Sussman, p. 613. Mingay points out that "most . . . landlords contented themselves with a home farm, which in the case of the large owners at least, was little more than a convenient source of produce for the household," while their tenants participated in entrepreneurial agriculture (pp. 168–69).

    24. Zomchick, p. 179.

25. The death of the woman also seems central, however, to an ethos of improvement that is powerfully masculinist. In Bramble's own case, for example, to come into his improvable estate is to come into his *paternal* estate: he sells his mother's estate to clear his father's, and then rids himself of her name in order to take his (p. 305).

26. Freud, "Mourning and Melancholia," pp. 166, 170.

27. Ibid., p. 166.

28. The following quotations come from Abraham and Torok, pp. 5–7.

29. My thanks to Karen Sánchez-Eppler for this sentence, which I have lifted intact from a marginal comment.

30. Smollett, *The Adventures of Roderick Random*, p. 212.

31. Robbins argues that in English fiction ghosts and spirits typically express servants' distrust of the legal order (p. 182).

32. Rothstein writes of the admiral's ghostliness, "That Clinker takes this man to be a spirit suggests the admiral's almost supernatural state, suspended in time as are the ancestral customs and land about him" (*Systems of Order*, p. 141). I am suggesting that his uncanniness comes from his being *fractured* in time—from his representing a tension between that ancestral state and new forms of social organization.

33. Alpers, pp. 11, 13. Smollett quoted this eclogue in a letter to Hume upon his departure abroad. See Knapp, ed., p. 136.

34. Richetti, p. 95.

35. Halpern, p. 75. Smith's characterization of labor as the "most sacred and inviolable" form of property works in a similar way, simultaneously valorizing the rights of working people and implicitly justifying their expropriation. The valorizing impulse finds its version in the novel's enthusiasm about Humphry's various skills. See *The Wealth of Nations*, p. 136.

36. Fabricant, pp. 266–67.

37. Judith Butler, pp. 57–58. As its title suggests, Abraham and Torok's essay is meant partly to counter those interpretations of Freud that see melancholia as a property of mourning in general. As far as *Humphry Clinker* is concerned, I think those two states are in fact separate: as I have argued, in its moments of melancholic disavowal it is setting such a disavowal against mourning.

38. Freud, "Mourning and Melancholia," p. 169.

39. Freud's account of melancholic belligerence must arouse amused recognition in the reader of Smollett: " . . . [T]hey are far from evincing towards those around them the attitude of humility and submission that alone would befit such worthless persons; on the contrary, they give a great deal of trouble, perpetually taking offence and behaving as if they had been treated with great injustice" ("Mourning and Melancholia," pp. 169–70).

40. Abraham and Torok, p. 7.

41. It is this insistence that Richetti admires; he sees it as an unmediated "documentary validity" in the novel's initial representation of Clinker's origins and life as a worker—a documentary quality so profound it seems to him that "a rather too literal and therefore unusable reality has intruded for a moment" (p. 95). John Rule argues that it was quite common for contemporaries to make the connection between work and mortality, although at the same time, it did not register as a serious social concern. See *The Experience of Labour*, chapter 3.

42. Rothstein (in *Systems of Order*) has shown at length how the novel's characters are commented upon through analogical characters who provide a gloss for them. He does not, however, notice the gloss on Clinker provided by Wilson.

43. Robbins, p. 15.

44. Sussman, p. 598.

45. Carson, "Orality, Cruelty, and the Marriage Plot," p. 24. I am grateful to the author for letting me read this manuscript before its publication. See also his excellent "Commodification and the Figure of the Castrato."

46. Williams, p. 30.

47. Ibid., pp. 31–32.

48. Abraham and Torok, p. 6.

49. I owe this trenchant formulation to Sasha Torres.

50. See Sussman on the way "the novel envisions the collapsing distinction between foreign sites of capital accumulation and domestic spaces of consumption" (pp. 598–99).

51. "Introducing a thing or an object—in whole or in part—into the body, retaining it or expelling it, acquiring, keeping, losing—all these are variations of the same fantasy . . . " (Abraham and Torok, p. 4).

52. Rothstein, *Systems of Order*, p. 119.

Chapter 4

1. Burney, *Cecilia*, pp. 1–2. All further references to the novel are from this edition and will be cited parenthetically in the body of the text.

2. A feminist reading of this novel may be tempted to start with the name clause, and the way it scandalously subordinates the husband's name to that of the wife; Epstein, for example, argues that "Burney's precocious theme—that a woman should retain her maiden name upon her marriage—contains the seeds of revolution for a social order that was entering upon a period of chaotic transition at the end of the eighteenth century" (p. 157). It is worth noting in this regard that, as Stone and Fawtier Stone

have argued, this practice was very common in eighteenth-century England (p. 120)—one of the "pious fictions" by which ancient family names were preserved during a demographic crisis "which caused a substantial increase in the probability of family extinction in the direct male line, and of inheritance by someone bearing a different name" (p. 127). They write, "the trouble was that if an heiress should marry the heir to an equally distinguished family, which she often did . . . this solution obviously caused great difficulties, and might be altogether impossible. . . . Full surname and arms change was more easily accepted when a man of distinctly inferior status and income, usually a younger son, either inherited a vast estate including a seat or was left one by a distant relative" (p. 130). I am not suggesting that because this practice was common it is not a feminist issue: just that the transgressive feel to it in *Cecilia* should be read as an index of the Delviles' aristocratic pride rather than a sign of its being an inherently scandalous practice.

3. Castle, p. 269.

4. Gallagher, p. 238.

5. Armstrong, p. 4. Armstrong argues, suggestively, that "Sterne's heroes, like Fielding's Joseph Andrews, clearly declared themselves anomalous when they inverted the model and, as males, experienced life as a sequence of events that elicited sentimental responses" (p. 4). On the domestic woman see also Claudia L. Johnson, chapter 2; and Poovey, *The Proper Lady*.

6. Armstrong, pp. 5, 76–77.

7. See also Marilyn Butler, chapter 1.

8. Claudia L. Johnson, p. 17.

9. As Rule writes, "Adam Smith recognized that the eighteenth century was one by which the separation of labour from capital had become usual . . . " (p. 31).

10. This is a condition akin to the one Gallagher refers to as "debt" or "universal obligation." In her splendid chapter on *Cecilia* in *Nobody's Story*, she argues that Cecilia imagines herself "as the universal debtor," and that debt is "both the condition and the result of morality in the novel" (p. 238).

11. For a useful overview of the historical debates over the nature of the so-called "proto-industrial" period, see Bridget Hill, chapter 2.

12. Berg, p. 315.

13. Ibid., pp. 40, 195.

14. Ibid., p. 40. In Marx's description of manufacture, Berg writes, "workers still ha[ve] some degree of control over the content, speed, intensity and rhythm of their work." In modern industry, that control is taken over by the capitalist, and workers become "mere appendages of the machine" (p. 192).

15. Ibid., pp. 42–43.

16. Ibid., p. 19. Her book is a major contribution to a growing literature on the role of women workers during this period. Another compelling account is Middleton. The foundational texts are Clark and Pinchbeck.

17. See Berg, p. 159; and Rule, pp. 95–96.

18. Andrew, p. 141.   19. Ibid., pp. 141–42.

20. Ibid., p. 142.   21. Rule, p. 106.

22. Thompson, *The Making of the English Working Class*, p. 549.

23. Ibid., pp. 24–25, chapter 4.   24. Tobin, p. 1.

25. Ibid., p. 3.   26. Armstrong, p. 79.

27. Straub, p. 82.

28. Ibid., p. 87. She is quoting from Edgeworth and Lovell Edgeworth, vol. 2, pp. 522, 528.

29. Andrew, pp. 162, 143, 153.

30. On the role of women in evangelical and other charitable societies, see Prochaska.

31. Samuel Johnson, *Rambler* 47, "The Proper Means of regulating sorrow," Tuesday, 28 August 1750 (III, pp. 252–57, quote at 255).

32. As Mullan writes of sensibility in Richardson, it is "poised on the edge of excess" (*Sentiment and Sociability*, p. 218).

33. Ibid., p. 233.

34. Ibid., pp. 208, 221.

35. Ariès, p. 472. See also Stone, chapter 6, on the connections between the growth of "affective individualism" and the increasing separation of the nuclear family from the kin and the larger community; and Thaddeus, who reads Frances Burney's reactions to the deaths of her sister and her husband as illustrative of the shifts in grieving described by Ariès.

36. Johnson, *Rambler* 52: "The contemplation of the calamities of others, a remedy for grief," Saturday, 15 September 1750 (III, pp. 279–84).

37. Smith, *The Wealth of Nations*, p. 11.

38. Ibid., p. 13.

39. Ibid., p. 142.

40. Johnson, *Rambler* 47, "The Proper Means of regulating sorrow," Tuesday, 28 August 1750 (III, pp. 252–58, quote at 257–58).

41. See, for example, *Rambler* 52: "The contemplation of the calamities of others, a remedy for grief," Saturday, 15 September 1750 (III, pp. 279–84).

42. Gregory, pp. 196–97.

43. More, Vol. 4, pp. 5–6.

44. Ibid., p. 24.

45. Doody, "Introduction" to Burney's *Cecilia*, p. xxxiv.

46. In Gallagher's reading, Cecilia's dream is about the complicated po-

sition of the "ethical transcendental subject"—an idealized figure that is both all-encompassing and allied with death (p. 236).

47. Henrietta's status as a poor woman is constituted in part by her inability to mask her feelings. During the course of Cecilia's insanity scene, the narrator describes Henrietta as "unused to disguise or repress her feelings" (pp. 915–16), and as an "unguarded and ardent girl" (p. 915). And when Cecilia awakes out of insanity, her wits intact and the deliriously happy Henrietta by her bedside, some of her first words are "my too kind Henrietta, you must be more tranquil!" and "Ah, sweet Henrietta . . . you must suppress these feelings, or our Doctor here will soon part us" (p. 921).

48. Doody, *Frances Burney*, p. 139. See also Claudia Johnson, who writes that "Although Burney's plots are typically structured around the quest for paternal reconciliation, the yearning for the intimacy of maternal and/or feminine sympathy is a deeper and more potent element in them" (pp. 178–79).

49. Sedgwick, "Queer Performativity," p. 5.

50. Ibid.

51. When Delvile gets sick, Lady Honoria says of his father, " . . . [O]ur great statesman intends to leave us: he can't trust his baby out of his sight, so he is going to nurse him while upon the road himself. Poor pretty dear Mortimer! what a puppet do they make of him! I have a vast inclination to get a pap-boat myself, and make him a present of it"; later she "seized one of the napkins, and protested she would send it to Mortimer for a *slabbering-bib*" (pp. 515–16). Mr. Arnott, who knew Cecilia as a child, enlarges relentlessly on the topic of his childhood, greatly tiring Cecilia: "he talked, indeed, upon no new subject; and upon the old one, of their former sports and amusements, he had already exhausted all that was worth being mentioned; but not yet had he exhausted the pleasure he received from the theme; it seemed always fresh and always enchanting to him; it employed his thoughts, regaled his imagination, and enlivened his discourse. Cecilia in vain tried to change it for another . . . " (p. 30). Gosport, the novel's resident satirist, appears at the masquerade in the costume of a schoolmaster and talks wittily about punishing schoolboys (p. 114), suggesting that little boys might be the novel's primary object of satire.

52. Belfield's description is also evocative of the situation of Fanny Burney's own family. Gallagher has the most penetrating description of the socioeconomic position of the Burneys: "Cultivating talent, polishing performance, making and improving contacts, and collecting and disseminating knowledge were the economic activities of the Burney family, and they were conceived of as contributing to a collective property, a corporate fame. . . . They had no rent rolls, no pedigrees, no real or invented histories

of military or public service; they had only talent and knowledge, copy-rights and such 'symbolic capital' as Dr. Burney's degree from Oxford and (much later) Frances's place at court. . . . [T]he representations of the Bur-neys were the business of their lives" (pp. 216–17). Straub reads Belfield's story as a kind of comment on the contradictions of eighteenth-century female social identity (p. 143).

53. Armstrong suggests that the characteristic political strategy of the novel of this period is to "translate the social contract into a sexual ex-change . . . representing social conflict as personal histories, gothic tales of sensibility, and stories of courtship and marriage" (pp. 38–39). Burney's novel suggests that heroines get damaged when there is a failure to separate the social-economic plot and the courtship plot. Straub argues of *Cecilia* that it has a double-plot structure, one of romantic love, and one of the search for a plan of life suitable for a middle-class woman, and that the two plots "interfere with and frustrate each other . . . because of the specific social conditions of femininity in mid-eighteenth-century culture" (pp. 110–11).

54. Mrs. Belfield is unaware that the poor are supposed to function as conduits for the love of people of quality—that Cecilia and Delvile will route their desires toward one another through their mutual appreciation of each other's charitable efforts to Belfield. It is often the role of the estab-lished working poor to function as mediators in sexual plots, providing refuge, smoothing over the pains of gender trouble, and the like. Having paid the premium for Mrs. Hill to be taken into her cousin's small haber-dasher's shop as a partner (p. 200), Cecilia, "after much deliberation, . . . at length determined to have recourse to Mrs. Hill, to whose services she was entitled, and upon whose fidelity she could rely. . . . She went therefore im-mediately to Mrs. Hill, whom she found already removed into her new habitation in Fetter-lane, and equally busy and happy in the change of scene and of employment" (p. 227). Mrs. Hill's establishment also becomes the rendezvous for Cecilia's clandestine meetings with the "Jew" moneylender (pp. 437, 439).

55. Doody, "Introduction" to Burney's *Cecilia*, p. xxii.

56. Ibid., p. xxiii.   57. Nichols and Wray, p. 1.

58. Ibid., pp. 52, 119.   59. Ibid., p. 125.

60. Andrew, pp. 156–58.   61. Claudia Johnson, p. 165.

62. I read Mr. Hobson's repeated "that's my notion of things" (pp. 409, 449, 878), and his claim that "I've got a fair character in the world, and wherewithal to live by my own liking" (p. 411) as an insistence that he has earned, through sound financial practices, the right to have an interiority.

63. Castle points out that in fact, what Cecilia cannot know is that many characters *are* supporting their characters: "each betrays himself (to the

reader if not always to the heroine) by the oddly lucid form of self-estrangement each has chosen. Costume becomes the somewhat banal sign of the role each character will play in Cecilia's subsequent history" (p. 263). Castle suggestively reads the masquerade as a "fantasy of autonomy . . . the transgressive female aspiration after an unlimited power, the dream of the Heiress itself"; "for Cecilia," she writes, "the Harrels' party is a festival of celebration, in which she is at the center of an effusive and ever-growing throng of sycophants" (p. 270). But in the remainder of the novel, Castle argues, "the retreat is total—and mortifying," a pattern of "masochistic recoil" (p. 276) from this utopian fantasy. See also Epstein, who regards *Cecilia*'s major achievement as the way "its phantasmagoric metaphor of masquerade develops directly out of the surreal quality Burney gives to money and to financial transactions and their repercussions" (p. 159).

64. Ovid, vol. 1, p. 301.
65. Ibid., p. 309.
66. Ibid.

Conclusion

1. Such art forms as landscape painting and georgic poetry worried the problem of rural labor well before the 1780s. See, for example, Barrell, *The Dark Side*, and Landry's account of laboring-class women poets' wrestling with pastoral and georgic conventions.

2. Fielding, *Joseph Andrews*, pp. 21–22. All further references to *Joseph Andrews* are cited parenthetically in the text (*JA*). Focusing on his failure to "perform the Part the Antients assigned to the God *Priapus*," Campbell reads this as a commentary on gender: "a disqualification from phallic office" (p. 646).

3. Robbins, p. 22.

4. Sterne, *A Sentimental Journey*, p. 266. All further page numbers are from this edition and will be cited parenthetically in the text.

5. Doody, "Introduction" to Burney's *The Wanderer*, p. xxxii. All further page numbers are from this edition and will be cited parenthetically in the text. Doody's comment refers, of course to ruling-class writing; women's work was represented with plenty of intensity in the plebeian georgics of such poets as Ann Yearsley, Mary Collier, and Mary Leapor (see Landry).

6. Claudia L. Johnson, p. 165.

7. Doody, *Frances Burney*, p. 323. Doody regards Burney's novel as politically progressive, while Johnson focuses on the conservatism of its gender politics.

8. Doody, *Frances Burney*, pp. 326, 328.

9. Ibid., pp. 332–33.

10. In one scene of *The Female Advocate*, two young gentleman are solicited outside a playhouse for charity, and surprised by the destitute woman's shift into French, they give her an impromptu test on the variety of foreign languages she knows (p. 113). See also the section called "Unfortunate Situation of Females, Fashionably Educated, and Left Without a Fortune" (pp. 25–26). Like Radcliffe, Wollstonecraft complains that "the few trades which are left, are now gradually falling into the hands of the men, and certainly they are not very respectable" (p. 26).

11. Doody, *Frances Burney*; Epstein, chapter 6; Claudia L. Johnson, chapter 7; and Straub.

12. See Tobin, p. 3.

13. Moreover, as Johnson dryly points out, while the novel sharply satirizes the inhumanity of the British class system, "it might by implication seem to countenance the shabby treatment of women who, unlike Ellis/Juliet, do not play the harp and piano, sing, act, or possess the skill of good penmanship, a refinement over which one character makes a big fuss" (p. 169).

14. This attempt, of course, had particular resonance for Burney, whose literary labor occupied a tricky space between labor and female accomplishment.

15. Thompson, *The Making of the English Working Class*, p. 119. According to Thompson, these fantasies originated in a 1794 pamphlet, *Revealed Knowledge of the Prophecies and Times*, written by a retired naval captain named Richard Brothers (pp. 116–17).

16. Austen, *Sense and Sensibility*, pp. 20, 83, 84; and *Mansfield Park*, pp. 431–32.

17. As its mixed-genre status might suggest, *Northanger Abbey* is an interesting and ambiguous swing-novel in that regard. General Tilney insists that even his eldest son Frederick, who will inherit a magnificent estate, have employment. If Austen's later novels argue with equanimity that gentlemen should work, *Northanger Abbey* invites us to read this insistence as a symptom of the General's parsimony and autocratic nature—that is, a symptom of his gothicism.

18. In this sequence, Harleigh and Sir Jaspar function as two faces of the gentleman. Doody argues that Harleigh should be read as a literary descendant of Harley in *The Man of Feeling*, but Sir Jaspar may also be read as a grotesque parody of the man of feeling. For Doody, the man of feeling in these novels creates an impasse for women: "the sensitive male becomes either extremely demanding and childlike, or else obstructive, an exponent of impossible delicacies or asexual proprieties" ("Introduction," p. xxvi). As I suggested before, Harleigh speaks on behalf of gentility, and is a rigid ide-

alized figure of punctilio; as Johnson suggests, he has authority in the novel, "but since he is too 'interested' in Ellis/Juliet, delicacy prohibits him from exerting it on her behalf" (p. 174). His standard of "impossible delicacies" is countered with a figure whose privilege runs rampant in his childlike dotage.

19. Doody, *Frances Burney*, on the "unusual emphasis by a woman author upon male physicality in its grotesque and piteous aspects" (p. 347).

20. For an account of eighteenth-century translations of the Sixth Satire, see Nussbaum, chapter 5.

21. Doody, *Frances Burney*, p. 366.

22. Ibid., p. 364.

23. [Croker], *Quarterly Review*, pp. 125–26.

24. Kelly notes that "the decade of the French Revolution was one of great achievement in polemical prose, of new developments in graphic satire, and of a temporary recrudescence of verse satire" (p. 1). And indeed, this satire was often deployed to attack not only the cult of the self embodied in sentimentalism, but the very idea of a self. See, for example, Marilyn Butler, pp. 97, 102.

Bibliography

Abraham, Nicolas, and Maria Torok. "Introjection—Incorporation: Mourning *or* Melancholia." In Serge Lebovici and Daniel Widlocher, eds., *Psychoanalysis in France*. New York: International Universities Press, 1980.

Alpers, Paul. *The Singer of the Eclogues: A Study of Virgilian Pastoral*. Berkeley and Los Angeles: University of California Press, 1979.

Altick, Richard. *The English Common Reader: A Social History of the Mass Reading Public, 1800–1900*. Chicago: University of Chicago Press, 1957.

Amory, Hugh. "Shamela as Aesopic Satire." *ELH* 38 (June 1971): 239–53.

Andrew, Donna. *Philanthropy and Police: London Charity in the Eighteenth Century*. Princeton, N.J.: Princeton University Press, 1989.

Arbuthnot, John. *An Inquiry into the Connection Between the Present Price of Provisions, and the Size of Farms*. London: T. Cadell, 1773.

Ariès, Philippe. *The Hour of Our Death*. New York: Vintage, 1982.

Armstrong, Nancy. *Desire and Domestic Fiction*. New York: Oxford University Press, 1987.

Austen, Jane. *Mansfield Park*. Oxford: Oxford University Press, 1990.

———. *Sense and Sensibility*. New York: New American Library, 1980.

Bakhtin, Mikhail. *Rabelais and His World*. Trans. Hélène Iswolsky. Bloomington: Indiana University Press, 1984.

Barrell, John. *The Dark Side of the Landscape: The Rural Poor in English Painting, 1730–1840*. Cambridge: Cambridge University Press, 1983.

———. *English Literature in History, 1730–80: An Equal, Wide Survey*. New York: St. Martin's, 1983.

————. *The Idea of Landscape and the Sense of Place, 1730–1840: An Approach to the Poetry of John Clare.* Cambridge: Cambridge University Press, 1972.

Battestin, Martin C. Introduction to Henry Fielding, *Joseph Andrews and Shamela*, pp. ii–xlvii. Boston: Houghton Mifflin, 1961.

Berg, Maxine. *The Age of Manufactures: Industry, Innovation and Work in Britain, 1700–1820.* Totowa, N.J.: Barnes & Noble, 1985.

Bond, Donald F., ed. *The Spectator.* 5 vols. Oxford: Clarendon Press, 1965.

Bourdieu, Pierre. *Distinction: A Social Critique of the Judgement of Taste.* Trans. Richard Nice. Cambridge, Mass.: Harvard University Press, 1984.

Burke, Edmund. "Third Letter on a Regicide Peace." In R. B. McDowell, ed., *The Writings and Speeches of Edmund Burke*, vol. 9. Oxford: Clarendon Press, 1991.

————. "Thoughts and Details on Scarcity." In R. B. McDowell, ed., *The Writings and Speeches of Edmund Burke*, vol. 9. Oxford: Clarendon Press, 1991.

Burney, Fanny. *Cecilia, or Memoirs of an Heiress.* Ed. Peter Sabor and Margaret Anne Doody. Oxford: Oxford University Press, 1988.

————. *The Wanderer; or, Female Difficulties.* Ed. Margaret Anne Doody, Robert L. Mack, and Peter Sabor. Oxford and New York: Oxford University Press, 1991.

Butler, Judith. *Gender Trouble: Feminism and the Subversion of Identity.* New York and London: Routledge, 1990.

Butler, Marilyn. *Jane Austen and the War of Ideas.* Oxford: Clarendon Press, 1975.

Campbell, Jill. " 'The Exact Picture of His Mother': Recognizing Joseph Andrews." *ELH* 55, no. 3 (Fall 1988): 643–64.

Carnochan, W. B. "Satire, Sublimity, and Sentiment: Theory and Practice in Post-Augustan Satire." *PMLA* 85, no. 2 (Mar. 1970): 260–67.

Carson, James P. "Commodification and the Figure of the Castrato in Smollett's *Humphry Clinker*." *The Eighteenth Century* 33, no. 1 (1992): 1–23.

————. "Orality, Cruelty, and the Marriage Plot in Smollett." Manuscript.

Cash, Arthur Hill. *Laurence Sterne: The Early and Middle Years.* London: Methuen, 1975.

————. "The Sermon in *Tristram Shandy*." *ELH* 31 (Dec. 1964): 395–417.

————. *Sterne's Comedy of Moral Sentiments: The Ethical Dimension of the Journey.* Pittsburgh: Duquesne University Press, 1966.

Castle, Terry. *Masquerade and Civilization: The Carnivalesque in Eighteenth-Century English Culture and Fiction.* Stanford, Calif.: Stanford University Press, 1986.

Chadwick, Joseph. "Infinite Jest: Interpretation in Sterne's *A Sentimental Journey*." *Eighteenth-Century Studies* 12 (1978–79): 190–205.

Chambers, J. D. "Enclosure and Labour Supply in the Industrial Revolution." In D. V. Glass and D. E. C. Eversley, eds., *Population in History: Essays in Historical Demography*. Chicago: Aldine, 1965.

Chambers, J. D., and G. E. Mingay. *The Agricultural Revolution, 1750–1880*. London: B. T. Batsford, 1966.

Clark, Alice. *Working Life of Women in the Seventeenth Century*. London: Routledge, 1919; reissued Frank Cass, 1968.

Copeland, Edward. "*Humphry Clinker*: A Comic Pastoral Poem in Prose?" *TSLL* 16 (1974): 493–501.

Cressy, David. *Literacy and the Social Order: Reading and Writing in Tudor and Stuart England*. Cambridge: Cambridge University Press, 1980.

[Croker, John Wilson]. Review of Fanny Burney's *The Wanderer*. *Quarterly Review* (Apr. 1814): 125–26.

Cross, Wilbur. *The Life and Times of Laurence Sterne*. New York: Russell and Russell, 1967.

Dane, Joseph A. *Parody: Critical Concepts Versus Literary Practices, Aristophanes to Sterne*. Norman: University of Oklahoma Press, 1988.

Davidson, Arnold E., and Cathy N. Davidson. "Yorick Contra Hobbes: Comic Synthesis in Sterne's *A Sentimental Journey*." *Centennial Review* 21 (1977): 282–93.

Davis, Lennard. *Factual Fictions: The Origins of the English Novel*. New York: Columbia University Press, 1983.

Defoe, Daniel. *The Compleat English Gentleman*. Ed. Karl D. Bulbring. London: David Nutt, 1890.

Derrida, Jacques. *Of Grammatology*. Trans. Gayatri Chakravorty Spivak. Baltimore, Md.: Johns Hopkins University Press, 1976.

Doody, Margaret Anne. *Frances Burney, The Life in the Works*. New Brunswick, N.J.: Rutgers University Press, 1988.

Duncan, Jeffrey L. "The Rural Ideal in Eighteenth-Century Fiction." *SEL* 8 (1968): 517–35.

Eagleton, Terry. *The Rape of Clarissa: Writing, Sexuality, and Class Struggle in Samuel Richardson*. Minneapolis: University of Minnesota Press, 1982.

Eaves, T. C. Duncan, and Ben D. Kimpel. *Samuel Richardson: A Biography*. Oxford: Clarendon Press, 1971.

Edgeworth, Maria, and Richard Lovell Edgeworth. *Practical Education*. 2 vols. London, 1798; rpt. New York: Garland, 1974.

Epstein, Julia. *The Iron Pen: Frances Burney and the Politics of Women's Writing*. Madison: University of Wisconsin Press, 1989.

Fabricant, Carole. "The Literature of Domestic Tourism and the Public Consumption of Private Property." In Felicity Nussbaum and Laura Brown, eds., *The New Eighteenth Century: Theory, Politics, English Literature*, pp. 254–75. New York: Methuen, 1987.

Felsenstein, Frank. Introduction to Tobias Smollett, *Travels Through France and Italy*. Oxford: Oxford University Press, 1979.

Fielding, Henry. *An Enquiry into the Causes of the Late Increase of Robbers.* Ed. Malvin R. Zirker. Oxford: Clarendon Press, 1988.

———. "An Essay on the Knowledge of the Characters of Men." In Henry Knight Miller, ed., *Miscellanies by Henry Fielding.* Vol. 1. Oxford: Clarendon Press, 1972.

———. *The Grub-Street Opera.* Ed. Edgar V. Roberts. Lincoln: University of Nebraska Press, 1968.

———. *The History of Tom Jones: A Foundling.* Ed. Fredson Bowers. Middletown, Conn.: Wesleyan University Press, 1975.

———. *Joseph Andrews.* Ed. Martin C. Battestin. Oxford: Clarendon Press, 1967.

———. *Joseph Andrews and Shamela.* Ed. Martin C. Battestin. Boston: Houghton Mifflin, 1961.

Foucault, Michel. *Discipline and Punish: The Birth of the Prison.* Trans. Alan Sheridan. New York: Vintage Books, 1979.

Freud, Sigmund. "Instincts and Their Vicissitudes." In Philip Rieff, ed., *General Psychological Theory.* New York: Collier Books, 1963.

———. *Jokes and Their Relation to the Unconscious.* New York: W. W. Norton, 1963.

———. "Mourning and Melancholia." In Philip Rieff, ed., *General Psychological Theory.* New York: Collier Books, 1963.

Gallagher, Catherine. *Nobody's Story: The Vanishing Acts of Women Writers in the Marketplace, 1670–1820.* Berkeley and Los Angeles: University of California Press, 1994.

Gregory, John. *A Father's Legacy to his Daughters.* In *Mrs. Chapone's Letters, Dr. Gregory's Legacy and Lady Pennington's Advice*, pp. 190–240. Boston: Leonard C. Bowles, 1822.

Halpern, Richard. *The Poetics of Primitive Accumulation: English Renaissance Culture and the Genealogy of Capital.* Ithaca, N.Y.: Cornell University Press, 1991.

Hammond, J. L, and Barbara Hammond. *The Village Labourer, 1760–1832.* London: Longmans, Green and Co., 1927.

Hay, Douglas. "Poaching and the Game Laws on Cannock Chace." In Douglas Hay, Peter Linebaugh, John G. Rule, E. P. Thompson, and Cal Winslow, eds., *Albion's Fatal Tree: Crime and Society in Eighteenth-Century England.* New York: Pantheon Books, 1975.

————. "Property, Authority and the Criminal Law." In Douglas Hay, Peter Linebaugh, John G. Rule, E. P. Thompson, and Cal Winslow, eds., *Albion's Fatal Tree: Crime and Society in Eighteenth-Century England.* New York: Pantheon Books, 1975.

Hecht, J. Jean. *The Domestic Servant Class in Eighteenth-Century England.* London: Routledge & Kegan Paul, 1956.

Hill, Bridget. *Women, Work, and Sexual Politics in Eighteenth-Century England.* New York: Basil Blackwell, 1989.

Hill, Christopher. *The Century of Revolution, 1603–1714.* New York: W. W. Norton, 1961.

Himmelfarb, Gertrude. *The Idea of Poverty: England in the Early Industrial Age.* New York: Random House, 1983.

Howlett, J. *Enclosures, a Cause of Improved Agriculture, of Plenty and Cheapness of Provisions, of Population, and of Both Private and National Wealth.* London: W. Richardson, 1787.

Hume, David. *Enquiry Concerning the Principles of Morals.* In David Hume, *Enquiries Concerning Human Understanding and Concerning the Principles of Morals.* Ed. L. A. Selby-Bigge. Oxford: Oxford University Press, 1975.

Hume, Robert D. *Henry Fielding and the London Theatre, 1728–1737.* Oxford: Clarendon Press, 1988.

Hunter, J. Paul. "Some Notes on Readers and the Beginnings of the English Novel." In Alan Charles Kors and Paul J. Korshin, eds., *Anticipations of the Enlightenment in England, France, and Germany,* pp. 259–82. Philadelphia: University of Pennsylvania Press, 1987.

Jameson, Fredric. *The Political Unconscious: Narrative as a Socially Symbolic Act.* Ithaca, N.Y.: Cornell University Press, 1981.

Johnson, Claudia L. *Equivocal Beings: Politics, Gender, and Sentimentality in the 1790s.* Chicago: University of Chicago Press, 1995.

Johnson, Samuel. *The Rambler.* Eds. W. J. Bate and Albrecht B. Strauss. 3 vols. New Haven, Conn.: Yale University Press, 1969.

Kelly, Gary. *The English Jacobin Novel, 1780–1805.* Oxford: Clarendon Press, 1976.

Kenner, Hugh. *The Counterfeiters.* Baltimore, Md.: Johns Hopkins University Press, 1969.

Knapp, Lewis M., ed. *The Letters of Tobias Smollett.* Oxford: Clarendon Press, 1970.

Kraft, Elizabeth. *Character and Consciousness in Eighteenth-Century Comic Fiction.* Athens: University of Georgia Press, 1992.

Landry, Donna. *The Muses of Resistance: Laboring-Class Women's Poetry in Britain, 1739–1776.* Cambridge: Cambridge University Press, 1990.

Liesenfeld, Vincent J. *The Licensing Act of 1737.* Madison: University of Wisconsin Press, 1984.

Locke, John. *Second Treatise of Government*. Ed. C. B. Macpherson. Indianapolis: Hackett Publishing, 1980.

Loftis, John. *Comedy and Society from Congreve to Fielding*. Stanford, Calif.: Stanford University Press, 1959.

Loftis, John, et al. *The Revels History of Drama in English.* Vol. 5: *1660–1750*. Clifford Leech and T. W. Craik, general eds. London: Methuen, 1976.

Malcomson, Robert W. *Life and Labour in England, 1700–1780*. New York: St. Martin's, 1981.

————. *Popular Recreations in English Society, 1700–1850*. Cambridge: Cambridge University Press, 1973.

Markeley, Robert. "Sentimentality as Performance: Shaftesbury, Sterne, and the Theatrics of Virtue." In Felicity Nussbaum and Laura Brown, eds., *The New Eighteenth Century: Theory, Politics, English Literature*. New York: Methuen, 1987.

Marshall, David. *The Figure of Theater: Shaftesbury, Defoe, Adam Smith, and George Eliot*. New York: Columbia University Press, 1986.

Marshall, Dorothy. *The English Poor in the Eighteenth Century: A Study in Social and Administrative History*. London: Routledge, 1926.

Massing, Michael. "Ghetto Blasting." *The New Yorker*, Jan. 16, 1995: 32–37.

Mayhew, Henry. *London Labour and the London Poor*. 4 vols. London: Charles Griffin, 1861–62; rpt., New York: Dover, 1968.

McKendrick, Neil. "The Consumer Revolution of Eighteenth-Century England." In Neil McKendrick, John Brewer, and J. H. Plumb, eds. *The Birth of a Consumer Society: The Commercialization of Eighteenth-Century England*. Bloomington: Indiana University Press, 1982.

McKeon, Michael. *The Origins of the English Novel, 1600–1740*. Baltimore, Md.: Johns Hopkins University Press, 1987.

Middleton, Chris. "Women's Labour and the Transition to Pre-Industrial Capitalism." In Lindsey Charles and Lorna Duffin, eds., *Women and Work in Pre-Industrial England*, pp. 181–206. London: Croom Helm, 1985.

Mingay, G. E. *English Landed Society in the Eighteenth Century*. London/ Toronto: Routledge/University of Toronto Press, 1963.

More, Hannah. *Cheap Repository Tracts: Entertaining, Moral, and Religious*. Vol. 4. New York: American Tract Society, [18–?].

Mullan, John. "Hypochondria and Hysteria: Sensibility and the Physicians." *The Eighteenth Century* 25 (1984): 141–74.

————. *Sentiment and Sociability: The Language of Feeling in the Eighteenth Century*. Oxford: Clarendon Press, 1988.

Neuburg, Victor. *Popular Education in Eighteenth Century England*. London: Woburn Press, 1971.

New, Melvyn. *Laurence Sterne as Satirist: A Reading of "Tristram Shandy"*. Gainesville: University of Florida Press, 1969.

Nichols, R. H. and F. A. Wray. *The History of the Foundling Hospital.* London: Oxford University Press/Humphrey Milford, 1935.

Nussbaum, Felicity. *The Brink of All We Hate: English Satires on Women, 1660–1750.* Lexington: University of Kentucky Press, 1984.

Ong, Walter J. *The Presence of the Word: Some Prolegomena for Cultural and Religious History.* New Haven, Conn.: Yale University Press, 1967.

Orr, Bridget. "Sentimental Lucubrations and Largesse: The Economy of Pity in *The Man of Feeling.*" Manuscript.

Ovid. *Metamorphoses.* Trans. Frank Justus Miller. 2 vols. Cambridge, Mass.: Harvard University Press, 1960.

Paulson, Ronald. *Popular and Polite Art in the Age of Hogarth and Fielding.* Notre Dame, Ind.: University of Notre Dame Press, 1979.

————. *Satire and the Novel in Eighteenth-Century England.* New Haven, Conn.: Yale University Press, 1967.

Pinchbeck, Ivy. *Women Workers and the Industrial Revolution, 1750–1850.* London: Frank Cass, 1977.

Pollitt, Katha. "Devil Women." *The New Yorker,* Feb. 26 & Mar. 4, 1996: 58–64.

Poovey, Mary. "Ideology and *The Mysteries of Udolpho.*" In Gabriela Mora and Karen S. VanHooft, eds., *Theory and Practice of Feminist Literary Criticism.* Ypsilanti, Mich.: Bilingual Press, 1982.

————. *The Proper Lady and the Woman Writer: Ideology as Style in the Works of Mary Wollstonecraft, Mary Shelley, and Jane Austen.* Chicago: University of Chicago Press, 1984.

Pope, Alexander. "Letter to the Publisher." *Dunciad Variorum.* In John Butt, ed., *The Poems of Alexander Pope.* New Haven, Conn.: Yale University Press, 1939.

Prochaska, F. K. *Women and Philanthropy in Nineteenth-Century England.* Oxford: Clarendon Press, 1980.

Radcliffe, Mary Anne. *The Female Advocate; or An Attempt to Recover the Rights of Women from Male Usurpation.* New York/Hildesheim: Georg Olms Verlag, 1980.

Rawson, Claude. *Satire and Sentiment.* Cambridge: Cambridge University Press, 1994.

Reed, Walter. *An Exemplary History of the Novel: The Quixotic Versus the Picaresque.* Chicago: University of Chicago Press, 1981.

Richardson, Samuel. *Pamela; or, Virtue Rewarded.* Ed. T. C. Duncan Eaves and Ben D. Kimpel. Boston: Houghton Mifflin, 1971.

Richetti, John. "Representing an Under Class: Servants and Proletarians in Fielding and Smollett." In Felicity Nussbaum and Laura Brown, eds., *The New Eighteenth Century: Theory, Politics, English Literature,* pp. 84–98. New York: Methuen, 1987.

Rivero, Albert J. *The Plays of Henry Fielding: A Critical Study of his Dramatic Career*. Charlottesville: University Press of Virginia, 1989.

Robbins, Bruce. *The Servant's Hand: English Fiction From Below*. Durham, N.C.: Duke University Press, 1993.

Rothblatt, Sheldon. *Tradition and Change in English Liberal Education*. London: Faber and Faber, 1976.

Rothstein, Eric. "The Framework of *Shamela*." *ELH* 35 (Sept. 1968): 381–402.

———. *Systems of Order and Inquiry in Later Eighteenth-Century Fiction*. Berkeley and Los Angeles: University of California Press, 1975.

Rousseau, G. S. "Nerves, Spirits and Fibres: Towards the Origins of Sensibility." In R. F. Brissenden, ed., *Studies in the Eighteenth Century III: Proceedings of the David Nichol Smith Conference*. Canberra: Australian National University Press, 1975.

Rule, John. *The Experience of Labour in Eighteenth-Century English Industry*. New York: St. Martin's, 1981.

Schwarzbach, F. S. Review of Gertrude Himmelfarb's *The Idea of Poverty*. *Dickens Quarterly* (June 1986): 100–104.

Sedgwick, Eve Kosofsky. *Between Men: English Literature and Male Homosocial Desire*. New York: Columbia University Press, 1985.

———. *Epistemology of the Closet*. Berkeley: University of California Press, 1990.

———. "A Poem is Being Written." *Representations* 17 (Winter 1987): 110–43.

———. "Queer Performativity: Henry James's *The Art of the Novel*." *GLQ* 1, no. 1: 1–16.

Seidel, Michael. "Narrative Crossings: Sterne's *A Sentimental Journey*." *Genre* 18 (Spring 1985): 1–22.

———. *Satiric Inheritance: Rabelais to Sterne*. Princeton, N.J.: Princeton University Press, 1979.

Sekora, John. *Luxury: The Concept in Western Thought, Eden to Smollett*. Baltimore, Md.: Johns Hopkins University Press, 1977.

Seltzer, Mark. *Henry James and the Art of Power*. Ithaca, N.Y.: Cornell University Press, 1984.

Shakespeare, William. *Much Ado About Nothing*. Ed. A. R. Humphreys. New York: Methuen, 1981.

Slack, Paul. *Poverty and Policy in Tudor and Stuart England*. New York: Longman, 1988.

Smith, Adam. *An Inquiry into the Nature and Causes of the Wealth of Nations*. Ed. Edwin Cannan. Chicago: University of Chicago Press, 1976.

———. *The Theory of Moral Sentiments*. Indianapolis: Liberty Classics, 1969.

Smitten, Jeffrey. "Gesture and Expression in Eighteenth Century Fiction: *A Sentimental Journey*." *Modern Language Studies* 9 (Fall 1979): 85–97.

———. "Spatial Form as Narrative Technique in *A Sentimental Journey*." *Journal of Narrative Technique* 5 (1975): 208–18.

Smollett, Tobias. *The Adventures of Roderick Random*. Oxford: Oxford University Press, 1988.

———. *The Expedition of Humphry Clinker*. Eds. Thomas R. Preston and O. M. Brack, Jr. Athens: University of Georgia Press, 1990.

———. *Travels Through France and Italy*. Ed. Frank Felsenstein. Oxford: Oxford University Press, 1979.

Snell, K. D. M. *Annals of the Labouring Poor: Social Change and Agrarian England, 1660–1900*. Cambridge: Cambridge University Press, 1985.

Spufford, Margaret. *Small Books and Pleasant Histories: Popular Fiction and its Readership in Seventeenth-Century England*. Cambridge: Cambridge University Press, 1981.

Stallybrass, Peter, and Allon White. *The Politics and Poetics of Transgression*. Ithaca, N.Y.: Cornell University Press, 1986.

Sterne, Laurence. *The Life and Opinions of Tristram Shandy, Gentleman*. In Melvyn New and Joan New, eds., *The Florida Edition of the Works of Laurence Sterne*. Vols. 1–2. Gainesville: The University Presses of Florida, 1978.

———. *A Sentimental Journey Through France and Italy by Mr. Yorick*. Ed. Gardner D. Stout, Jr. Berkeley and Los Angeles: University of California Press, 1967.

Stone, Lawrence. *The Family, Sex and Marriage in England 1500–1800*. Harmondsworth, Eng.: Penguin Books, 1977.

Stone, Lawrence, and Jeanne C. Fawtier Stone. *An Open Elite? England 1540–1880*. Oxford: Clarendon Press, 1984.

Straub, Kristina. *Divided Fictions: Fanny Burney and Feminine Strategy*. Lexington: University Press of Kentucky, 1987.

Sussman, Charlotte. "Lismahago's Captivity: Transculturation in *Humphry Clinker*." *ELH* 61, no. 3 (Fall 1994): 597–618.

Tave, Stuart. *The Amiable Humorist: A Study in the Comic Theory and Criticism of the Eighteenth and Early Nineteenth Centuries*. Chicago: University of Chicago Press, 1960.

Thaddeus, Janice. "Hoards of Sorrow: Hester Lynch Piozzi, Frances Burney d'Arblay, and Intimate Death." *Eighteenth-Century Life* 14 (Nov. 1990): 108–29.

Thompson, E. P. "Eighteenth-Century English Society: Class Struggle Without Class?" *Social History* 3, no. 2 (May 1978): 133–65.

———. *The Making of the English Working Class*. New York: Vintage Books, 1966.

————. "Patrician Society, Plebian Culture." *Journal of Social History* 7, no. 4 (Summer 1974): 382–405.

Tobin, Beth Fowkes. *Superintending the Poor: Charitable Ladies and Paternal Landlords in British Fiction, 1770–1860*. New Haven, Conn.: Yale University Press, 1993.

Todd, Janet. *Sensibility: An Introduction*. New York: Methuen, 1986.

Van Sant, Ann Jessie. *Eighteenth-Century Sensibility and the Novel: The Senses in Social Context*. Cambridge: Cambridge University Press, 1993.

Watt, Ian. *The Rise of the Novel*. Berkeley: University of California Press, 1957.

————. "*Shamela*." In Ronald Paulson, ed., *Fielding: A Collection of Critical Essays*, pp. 45–51. Englewood Cliffs, N.J.: Prentice-Hall, 1962.

Williams, Raymond. *The Country and the City*. New York: Oxford University Press, 1973.

Wollstonecraft, Mary. *Thoughts on the Education of Daughters*. In Janet Todd and Marilyn Butler, eds., *The Works of Mary Wollstonecraft*, vol. 4. New York: New York University Press, 1989.

Wrigley, E. A., and R. S. Schofield. *The Population History of England, 1541–1871*. New York: Arnold, 1981.

Yelling, J. A. *Common Field and Enclosure in England, 1450–1850*. London: Macmillan, 1977.

[Young, Arthur]. *General Report on Enclosures*. London: B. McMillan, 1808.

Young, Arthur. *An Inquiry into the Propriety of Applying Wastes to the Better Maintenance and Support of the Poor*. Bury St. Edmunds, 1801.

Zomchick, John M. "Social Class, Character, and Narrative Strategy in *Humphry Clinker*." *Eighteenth-Century Life* 10, no. 3 (Oct. 1986): 172–85.

Index

In this index an "f" after a number indicates a separate reference on the next page, and an "ff" indicates separate references on the next two pages. A continuous discussion over two or more pages is indicated by a span of page numbers, e.g., "21–22." *Passim* is used for a cluster of references in close but not consecutive sequence.

Library of Congress Cataloging-in-Publication Data

Frank, Judith, 1958–

Common ground : eighteenth-century English
satiric fiction and the poor / Judith Frank.

    p.   cm.

Includes bibliographical references and index.

ISBN 0–8047–2908–5 (alk. paper)

1. English fiction—18th century—History and criticism.   2. Poor in literature.   3. Literature and society—England—History—18th century.   4. England—Social conditions—18th century.   5. Satire,
English—History and criticism.   6. Social classes in
literature.   7. Poverty in literature.   I. Title.

PR858.P66F73   1997

823'.6099206942—dc21   97–7071

                                              CIP